MW01122288

The feminisation of public relations

Greg Smith

The feminisation of public relations

Why males avoid the profession

VDM Verlag Dr. Müller

Impressum/Imprint (nur für Deutschland/ only for Germany)

Bibliografische Information der Deutschen Nationalbibliothek: Die Deutsche Nationalbibliothek verzeichnet diese Publikation in der Deutschen Nationalbibliografie; detaillierte bibliografische Daten sind im Internet über http://dnb.d-nb.de abrufbar.

Alle in diesem Buch genannten Marken und Produktnamen unterliegen warenzeichen-, marken- oder patentrechtlichem Schutz bzw. sind Warenzeichen oder eingetragene Warenzeichen der jeweiligen Inhaber. Die Wiedergabe von Marken, Produktnamen, Gebrauchsnamen, Handelsnamen, Warenbezeichnungen u.s.w. in diesem Werk berechtigt auch ohne besondere Kennzeichnung nicht zu der Annahme, dass solche Namen im Sinne der Warenzeichen- und Markenschutzgesetzgebung als frei zu betrachten wären und daher von jedermann benutzt werden dürften.

Coverbild: www.purestockx.com

Verlag: VDM Verlag Dr. Müller Aktiengesellschaft & Co. KG
Dudweiler Landstr. 99, 66123 Saarbrücken, Deutschland
Telefon +49 681 9100-698, Telefax +49 681 9100-988, Email: info@vdm-verlag.de
Zugl.: Rockhampton, Central Queensland University, 2006

Herstellung in Deutschland:
Schaltungsdienst Lange o.H.G., Berlin
Books on Demand GmbH, Norderstedt
Reha GmbH, Saarbrücken
Amazon Distribution GmbH, Leipzig
ISBN: 978-3-639-16475-6

Imprint (only for USA, GB)

Bibliographic information published by the Deutsche Nationalbibliothek: The Deutsche Nationalbibliothek lists this publication in the Deutsche Nationalbibliografie; detailed bibliographic data are available in the Internet at http://dnb.d-nb.de .

Any brand names and product names mentioned in this book are subject to trademark, brand or patent protection and are trademarks or registered trademarks of their respective holders. The use of brand names, product names, common names, trade names, product descriptions etc. even without a particular marking in this works is in no way to be construed to mean that such names may be regarded as unrestricted in respect of trademark and brand protection legislation and could thus be used by anyone.

Cover image: www.purestockx.com

Publisher:
VDM Verlag Dr. Müller Aktiengesellschaft & Co. KG
Dudweiler Landstr. 99, 66123 Saarbrücken, Germany
Phone +49 681 9100-698, Fax +49 681 9100-988, Email: info@vdm-publishing.com

Printed in the U.S.A.
Printed in the U.K. by (see last page)
ISBN: 978-3-639-16475-6

The predominance
of women
in public relations

Central Queensland University
Thesis for Degree of Doctor of Philosophy
Greg Smith
Faculty of Arts and Humanities

Principal Supervisor: Professor Alan Knight
Associate Supervisor: Kate Ames

"We need balance"
(Dan Edelman, 2000)

Abstract

As (almost) everyone in the Australian (and international) public relations industry knows, there are more women than men. On average, the numbers in Australia favour women by slightly more than three to one. According to Australian Bureau of Statistics, these figures, make PR one of the most female-intensive industries in Australia. This growing imbalance may have long-term effects which have yet to be identified. This thesis, however, seeks to consider the reasons for this situation.

The research aims to:

1. Examine the reasons for the growth in numbers of women and numerical decline of men within public relations in Perth, Western Australia, by considering the development of public relations and how it has impacted on the profession.

2. Examine future trends within the profession for both women and men and what an imbalance may mean.

In government, PR practitioners are 71 per cent of the profession, while in private practice (both nationally and in WA) it is 74 per cent. In WA charities the figure is 75 per cent. At the universities the enrolment varies between 72 and 87 per cent. This study examines the reason for the imbalance and whether an imbalance is good. Whether the industry (professional bodies, educators, students and practitioners) is concerned is up to it.

This work provides the first study of the gender composition of the industry in Australia. As such, it should be a valuable tool in a number of areas. Like many initial studies, it raises just as many questions as answers, and it provides pathways for future study. It should lead to a wider examination of further issues.

Contents

Acknowledgments

My wife, Jeanette. For setting me on the path to study and then putting up with countless hours at the keyboard. Vroom. Let's go for a ride.

To my Dad, who encouraged me for almost the entire journey, but did not live to see the final product.

My supervisors, Alan Knight and Kate Ames.

Vince Hughes, who supplied constant valuable advice.

Paul 'Alfonse' Ellercamp, one of the 'good things', whose industry knowledge was invaluable, particularly in the survey phase.

Rebecca Folmar, Gina Noble and Fiona McCurdy, who were on the same path, and provided their work.

To the professionals and students who participated in the study; in particular, those who provided their time in focus groups and interviews. Without you there would be nothing.

1   Introduction

In his introduction to the book, *The Gender Challenge to Media*, Nathaniel Clory (2001, p.6) wrote quite passionately about an "awakening". Clory was taken aback by a "seemingly worldwide conspiracy that devalued women". In a roundabout way, Clory came to realise that what the media says may affect thousands of people, including those who want to study PR. The definition of media also extends to the Internet; both business and personal sites and forums. My work will not delve into conspiracy theories, nor ponder on how to change the world. It analyses why the communications (public relations) industry is increasingly attracting higher proportions of women (or conversely, why there are so few men).

This thesis does not target academia as its primary readership. As Eaton (2001, p.177) points out: "Much of the scholarship in the discipline ends up as journal articles that are read by some professors and fewer students." My supervisor, Prof. Alan Knight, said: "At the end of the day someone will take this home one weekend, read it, and then it will end up gathering dust on a shelf." I would hope it has some impact. For that reason, the work is aimed at practitioners in the "field". In that regard, the writing style sometimes uses first person and second person accounts to explain my findings. It has been influenced by my use, in part, of a mixed methodology, which is discussed in chapter 3.

For the most part, most of the resource material – literature, survey and focus groups – is sociological. It should also be noted that while this thesis does not serve to give feminists a voice, it briefly considers the way in which a male-managed industry presides over an ever-growing female workforce – an interesting combination. While my study focuses on the reasons for the predominance of women in PR, conversely it would probably be just as apt to focus on why there are so few men. However, taking that path proved to be difficult, as there are so few men entering the profession. Rush and Grubb-Swetnam's (1996) call to communication students to become aware of the absences in their lives and profession is apt. They suggested we ask ourselves: "What is missing here? Why is this picture incomplete or distorted?" (np). The answer is simple: men are missing. They are missing, however, only in non-management levels. That situation certainly may change in the future.

Background to the research

> If we're called in by a client to influence behavior, our input should come from a group of people balanced by gender (Harold Burson, founder and chairman of Burson-Marsteller, in Hampson, as cited by Folmar, 2005).

Primarily, this thesis is about the feminisation of public relations. Conversely, it could be about the dearth (or is that death?) of males in the industry. 'Feminisation' of the industry means that women have numerically become the dominant force. It does not intend to specifically include women at any particular level: just all women in the industry. The title arose because of the number of women doing communications courses. How could it not, when I was severely outnumbered?

The project has its origins as a result of my 22-year professional career in the media and public relations (PR) professions. While studying for my Masters Degree in Perth, I was surprised by the high number of women undertaking communication courses at Edith Cowan University. This sparked initial interest. Unconsciously, I had observed and analysed the trend of what appeared to be increasing numbers of women in the media. There is also growing professional anecdotal evidence of this trend. To date there has been no attempt to explain the growing drift of women (and decline of men) into public relations – a profession that is male-managed.

The issue of women in public relations, or the 'feminisation of public relations' was first raised in 1989 when, according to Grunig, Toth and Hon (2001), the *Public Relations Journal* published one of the first articles to note the growing prevalence of female practitioners. They were probably referring to an article by Karlene Lukovitz (1989) *Women practitioners, how far, how fast?*, which recorded that women had grown from 27 per cent of the United States industry in 1970, to 56.6 per cent in 1987. Lukovitz also noted a salaries gap between men and women "as a result of past discrimination and the recent heavy influx of young women into the lower-salaried entry-levels of the profession" and raised concerns that this could flow on to "a decrease in status and salaries for the profession as a whole" (1989, p. 14). It is interesting to note that, in the same volume of *Public Relations Journal*, Philip Lesly also published an article suggesting public relations was "losing stature and respect" (1989, p. 40), although he attributed the status loss to increasingly technical practice, rather than to gender reasons. Lukovitz quoted the then president of the Public Relations Society of America (PRSA), John Paluszek, as saying he was not aware of any problems relating to women in public relations, and there was no need for an industry-wide examination of women's issues. However, Paluszek later acted on the many replies his comments drew, and established a Task Force on Women in PR, which later became the Committee on Work, Life and Gender Issues.

Grunig, Toth and Hon (2001) wrote one of the main texts on females in public relations. The book, *Women in public relations: how gender influences practice*, deals mainly with status, salary, equity, gender, gender bias and sexual discrimination. The book's aim, as the authors note, is: "to make an issue out of sex discrimination in our field" (Grunig, Toth and Hon, 2001, p. 30). That's appropriate, as it was written by three women for women, addressing important issues of imbalance. On the other hand, this study is more concerned with the reasons why there are so many women (and, perhaps more apt, why so few men) in PR. The issues Grunig et al. raised certainly have a role to play in some areas of this study, but the book really deals with women's role/s in PR, at a time when little was being done to address the imbalances and issues that women faced within the industry. One could argue that with the predominance of women now entering PR, it is time for a study on male issues, and this thesis may become the catalyst for that future work.

There is one thing on which all communications scholars agree: women outnumber men, insofar as comprising the bulk of the PR workforce. As mentioned, this situation does not apply to management within PR. This is an important distinction, showing the difference between management and technician roles in PR, with technician roles being best described as those roles which do not contribute in any significant form to the higher-level planning roles, such as budgeting and key strategy.

Writing in the *PR Reporter*, DeRosa and Wilcox (1989) questioned the influx of women into public relations. They attempted to discover why women were entering the field in increasing numbers. Their survey of the public relations field showed almost 80 per cent of the respondents were female. A similar trend was seen in colleges and universities. DeRosa and Wilcox found that in 1970, about 75 per cent of the students majoring in PR were men. By 1980, women were predominant at 67 per cent. The research was quantitative, and did not consider the views of PR professionals, who have the wisdom of years of industry observation. Similarly, Toth and Aldoory (2000, np) reported in a year 2000 gender study of the US industry (the most recent study) that "the current demographic in the profession is 70 per cent women and 30 per cent men. This reflects a steady increase of women entering public relations over the past 20 years". The study's figures are strikingly similar to the current male/female participation in the Australian PR

9

industry and at university. Grunig et al. (2001, np) also recognised the paradigm shift in the US, when in "1989, public relations shifted from a male to female majority".

In Singapore, female preferences for 'soft' subjects like the social sciences in lieu of technical courses like engineering also determine the kinds of occupations they are likely to undertake. A study on the social progress of Singapore women by the Singapore Ministry of Manpower suggests that female tertiary students tend to concentrate in non-technical subjects. "In 1997, 75% of the female undergraduates in local universities were in the Arts and Social Sciences, Business and Accountancy and Sciences courses compared with 38% of the males" (Singapore Manpower Research and Statistics Department 2000).

The mention of "soft" subjects applies particularly to PR. In the course of this study, several interview and survey subjects made mention of PR fitting this description.

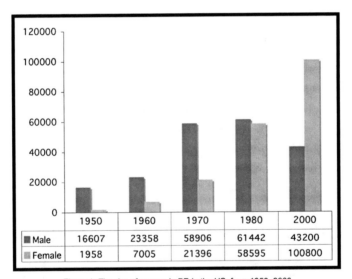

	1950	1960	1970	1980	2000
Male	16607	23358	58906	61442	43200
Female	1958	7005	21396	58595	100800

Figure 1: The rise of women in PR in the US, from 1950–2000
(US Dept of Labor, 1980, and Toth 2001).

The Public Relations Society of America's 2000 world conference, which drew more than 3500 public relations professionals, students, vendors, and trade journalists, addressed the issue. Industry heavyweights Harold Burson and Dan Edelman expressed concern during the conference that "the vast majority of people entering the PR field are women" (Miller 2002).

At the time, Jack O'Dwyer's Newsletter noted that women comprised 70 per cent of Burson-Marsteller's staff. Edelman briefly answered a question about the predominance of women entering PR by stating: "We need balance." Edelman (pictured) was not alone. Burson, continued: "Unless more men are attracted to public relations, it runs the risk of being regarded as a 'woman's job' ... "we'll lose a lot of good men" (Burson, as cited by Folmar, 2005). These sentiments were echoed in the PRSA's Year 2000 gender report. "One male participant said: 'I think the glass ceiling will naturally go away and the bigger question is what are they left with? An entire female-dominating industry. Then there will be some other kind of ceiling" (Toth, 2000).

My study will attempt to examine the reasons for the growing predominance of women in public relations (and conversely, the diminishing number of men), which is reflected in Australian university enrolments (particularly in Perth) and overseas, and in the workplace (both government and private enterprise). It will do this by a rigorous analysis through comprehensive on-line and paper surveys, focus groups and interviews.

My study has its origins in my 22-year professional career in the media and in public relations. The high number of women undertaking communications courses at Edith Cowan University sparked my initial interest. However, to date in Australia there has been no attempt to explain the growing drift of women (and decline of men) into the public relations profession. Some related research has been done by American academics, most notably Brenda Wrigley, Elizabeth Toth, Linda Aldoory, Larissa Grunig, Carolyn Cline and Linda Hon. However, there are only eight major published texts on the subject. These mostly concentrate on the inequalities regarding salary and responsibility in decision-making. This also was the major content of the now unobtainable 1986 *Velvet Ghetto* report. There are few journal articles that deal directly with the subject. Consequently, a need for current, original research is required.

My study is well positioned by reference to Larissa Grunig, who, in a 1998 interview with *Salon* magazine said: "public relations is NOT female-dominated. It is female-intensive" (Brown 1998). By this, she meant that while numerically females dominate the industry, they do not control it through the management function. There is an important differentiation to be made here.

This study is only concerned with the fact that females are taking to the profession in increasing numbers; hence the emphasis is on the "female-intensive" nature of the profession. The predominance of males in management could easily be the subject of another study. In fact; the point was raised in an e-mail and subsequent phone conversation I had with a female practitioner at one of the WA mining companies. She was puzzled as to why female PR practitioners in the mining industry never reached management level. In part, some of the reasons for that are addressed further in my study in interviews with two senior male professionals.

Research objectives

The objective was to examine:

• The numerical growth of women, and decline of men, in the public relations profession in Perth, Western Australia.

The research objective is addressed by presenting a picture of the past, and the current state of public relations practice, primarily in Perth, but drawing on material from Australia and overseas; notably the US and, to a lesser extent, the UK. Essentially, I argue that the industry is in danger of becoming "over-feminised", and that this trend is not healthy for the profession – a stance taken by several scholars and professionals.

There are clear boundaries (limitations) associated with this research, mostly imposed by the limited availability of prior related material. In fact, with the exception of some US statistical information and material used in the literature review, most information contained in this thesis is original. This is the first time any research into gender in PR has been conducted in Australia. The only data the National and State PR organisations had (at the time this study commenced) was for the current year (2004-05). There is also a limitation associated with the number of PR professionals (63) and students (295) surveyed. This was the maximum number possible, due to privacy limitations imposed by the PRIA, companies and government departments, which made it difficult to access the entire sub-group. With regard to universities, many students seemed unwilling to participate, particularly in focus groups and interviews.

My history as a PR practitioner and student over 10 years has brought me to this point, where I have seen and questioned the puzzle of a female-intensive industry. By combining my personal and professional experience within a framework developed by my academic training, I have formulated my principal research question to be:

Why has there been a rapid and continuing growth of women (and decline of men) in public relations?

The question needs to be addressed, as it may have long-term implications for the industry; particularly as to how PR is practiced and taught. When discussing the topic as a likely study, most, if not all professional and academics were interested in the outcome – and this proved to be the case throughout the study. The significance of such a trend may not be apparent now. However, if such trends are identified early, industry bodies and universities may at least be aware of the change and be prepared for any eventualities which may arise.

Summary of Learning Outcomes

This section presents the synthesis of my action research and learning.

Different lessons are learned depending on the perspective of the learner (figure 2).

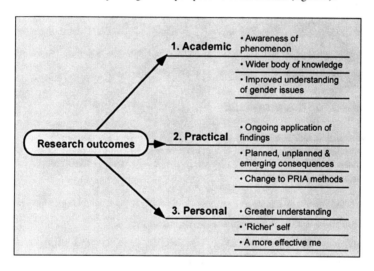

Figure 2: Summary of research learning outcomes.

From an **academic perspective**, the learning outcomes indicate that at present the reasons for the phenomenon of an increasing female PR workforce are difficult to capture. While it is shown that awareness is high, there is little impetus to addressing the situation. It will be also demonstrated that the research contributes to knowledge and raises the issue at a national and international level for the first time in a detailed study.

Throughout this thesis, it will be shown that:

❏ The enquiry was carried out systematically,

❏ The values used to distinguish the claim to knowledge are clearly shown and justified.

❏ The assertions are clearly warranted; and evidence is presented throughout of an enquiring and critical approach to a work-related problem.

From a **practical perspective** I believe there can now be more research undertaken in this field, with the material and findings being of use to the profession, if it so chooses. Certainly the practical nature of the project is reflected in changes the Public Relations Institute of Australia has indicated it will make with regard to changing the way it records membership data.

From a personal perspective, I have endeavoured, for the past five years, to align academic and work-related pursuits. I have no doubts this research thesis has added to this quest by providing me with a more balanced view of work, career and family.

Justification for the research

> Look around any public relations department or college classroom and
> you're likely to find a majority of women. For reasons still unknown,
> women have flocked to public relations, and the trend is likely to continue
> (Childers-Hon, 2003).

Having been fascinated by the high numbers of women in communications courses at university, I fulfilled a primary prerequisite, according to Merriam, 1998, for undertaking such a study, and that is the premise of "questioning something that perplexes and challenges the mind". Certainly, the introductory quote for this section from American PR academic Linda Childers-Hon posed the question as recently as two years ago.

On commencing readings for the project, it soon became obvious that little work had been done academically on the gender composition of the industry, either by scholars or professional bodies. That such a gap should exist is, in itself, cause for concern. Those scholars who have delved into the field have all made similar comments.

"Historical studies of women in public relations . . . have been rare," notes Gower (2001). Others, like Rea (2002) echo these sentiments, citing "little sustained and formal interest in gender equity matters in our professional organisations or in the agendas of industry or academic conferences . . . not because gender discrimination is not an issue for the Australian industry, but rather that it has not been addressed." One of the most recent articles on the topic appeared in the March 2005 issue of *Public Relations Review*. "Future professionals' perceptions of work, life, and gender issues in public relations", written by Bey-Ling Sha and Elizabeth Toth, once again focused on salary and management issues only. The other most recent reference was from 2003 – an article which simply revisited the 1986 *Velvet Ghetto* report. The lack of subject-specific research applies to student perceptions of gender issues within PR. There has been only one US survey (Farmer, B and Waugh 1999). There has only been one Australian survey of students, which indicates that original research is severely lacking. As of August 2005 I became aware of work being done by Griffith University Honours student Fiona McCurdy, who was "looking at the work completed by Grunig, Toth and Hon, as well as Farmer and Waugh in the US. McCurdy wanted to ascertain whether the problems they found in regards to females in PR [both in the university system and the professional community] occur in the 'South East Queensland context'.

McCurdy, 2005, surveyed 169 third-year PR students at four south-east Queensland Universities (Bond Griffith, Queensland University of Technology and the University of Queensland) and local practitioners. This was 66 per cent of all enrolled students. It was found that 141 (83.43%) were female and 28 (16.56%) were male. The results collated from the practitioners survey could not be called conclusive, as only 12 were surveyed. However, they returned almost equal findings as the student survey, with 83.33 per cent of participants being female and 16.66 per cent of participants being male.

The issue of women in PR, or the feminisation of PR, was identified in 1989, when the (US) *Public Relations Journal* published an article about female practitioners. The then president of the Public Relations Society of America (PRSA) was quoted as saying he was not aware of any problems relating to women in PR. However, he acted on the many replies his comments drew, and established a Task Force on women in PR, which is now called the Committee on Work, Life and Gender Issues.

Grunig et al's. 2001 book, *Women in public relations: how gender influences practice*, is probably the main text on female issues in public relations. "It is the only significant and comprehensive research on gender in public relations . . . their findings provide a useful comparative starting point for Australian investigations" (Rea, 2002, np). However, it deals mainly with status, salary, equity, gender, gender bias and sexual discrimination. Primarily, Grunig et al. aimed to: "[make] an issue out of sex discrimination in our field," (p. 30). That is understandable, as it was written by three women, for women, addressing important issues of imbalance. As a text it has received criticism, particularly with regard to its definitions of gender and sex, which form a large part of this thesis. "They equate the term gender with biology, and the term 'sex' with characteristics that have been associated with men and women, such as assertiveness and submissiveness. They later seem to contradict themselves by arguing that gender is socially constructed," (Scrimger 2001).

However, this study is more concerned with why there are so many women (and, perhaps more apt, why so few men) in PR. The issues raised by Grunig et al. certainly have a role to play in some areas of this study, but the book really deals with women's role/s in PR, at a time little was being done to address the imbalances and issues that women faced within the industry. One could argue that with the predominance of women now entering PR, it is time for a study on male issues. This thesis may become the catalyst for that future work. One of the leading US PR academics, Denis Wilcox, certainly believes now is the time to undertake research in this area.

In e-mail correspondence of 19 April 2005 between myself and Prof. Wilcox, who is head of PR at the University of San Jose, Wilcox said:

> There have been many articles about gender differences in public relations but most of it has been about differences in the workplace (salary, title, years of experience, etc.). I can't recall any recent replication of a study that explores the perceptions of current public relations majors (male and female) about gender differences in the public relations field.

This research will provide an excellent starting point for continued research into gender issues in the PR "industry" (that is, tertiary institutions, private and government sectors). It should also provide an insight into future industry trends.

Methodology

Primarily, my research uses a mixed method drawing on phenomenalism and positivism, undertaken primarily in the context of an action research approach, which McNiff, Lomax and Whitehead (2003) defined as "practitioner-based [and] conducted by any practitioners who regard themselves as researchers" (p. 12).

I felt that an action research study (Reason 2001) was best suited to my situation and offered the best opportunity to address my research question. One reason for this was that because of my experience in PR I was sensitive to the topic under study, which is a distinct advantage in eliciting information and understanding the subtlety of individuals within the industry (Fernandez, Lehman and Underwood, 2002). The emphasis of an action research study is that researchers are actively involved with the situation or phenomenon being studied; ensuring that any knowledge developed in the investigation process is directly relevant to the issues (Robson, 2002). Dick (1993) also suggests that it is reasonable that there can be choices between action research and other paradigms, and, within action research, a choice of approaches. "When practitioners use action research it has the potential to increase the amount they learn consciously from their experience. The action research cycle can also be regarded as a learning cycle, with the educator Schön (1983, 1987, as cited in Dick, 1993) arguing strongly that systematic reflection is an effective way for practitioners to learn". The reflection was carried out at all stages of the process. However, it occurred mostly during the research and interview phases, when interaction with subjects was a constant occurrence. Reflection involved several processes. Overall, it could also be described as personal evaluation. It included obtaining feedback on methodology, subject matter, and project structure from (local) industry associates, notably Dr Vince Hughes. Primarily, the technique involved a constant referral back to material and obtaining industry feedback. On a wider scale this involved the use of regular e-mail and web-site updates to 63 practitioners who participated in the initial surveys. At all times, participants were encouraged to provide feedback.

The mixed methodology research approach is part phenomenalistic, in that it has "taken place in natural 'everyday' settings. The leaning towards phenomenalism is reflected in my roles as an observer of the phenomenon being studied (the increase of women in PR) and that I have clearly chosen what was being observed (student and practitioner numbers) as the subject. There is also an element of positivism, in that initial consistencies in patterns of female employment and university enrolment were noted through the use of quantitative data. There are also elements of positivism, in that it was "preceded by research questions, as in positivistic research," Allison, et al. (1996). However, I have not ventured far down that track, as it is now generally accepted that positivist research criteria are not always appropriate in achieving social research outcomes (Klein and Myers, 1999).

The methodologies used, therefore are a mix of qualitative and quantitative, with the emphasis heavily on qualitative (focus groups and interviews), using a combination of:

- Historical (retrospective) – university enrolment data,

- Descriptive – surveys, case studies and trend studies,

- Phenomenological (qualitative) – focus groups and interviews, with myself as observer).

It has been suggested that qualitative research methods, specifically action research, can begin by being free from predetermined theories, with the theory developed in conjunction with or after the findings. I agree with this approach, as it facilitates enhanced creativity (so much a part of PR) and discovery of new insights (Dick, 1997; Jacob, 1988). Previously, qualitative approaches to research, including case studies, have been criticised for a lack of rigour and validity, especially in relation to the validation of data and conclusions (Benbasat and Zmud 1999; Lee, 1994; Sarantakos, 1993). However, such criticisms are waning, mainly because contemporary researchers now accept that since all research methods are never completely flawless, no single method, quantitative or qualitative, is better or worse than the other (Balnaves and Caputi, 2001).

The learning journey

I have endeavoured, for the past several years, to align academic and work-related pursuits. I have no doubts that this research thesis, through the action research process, has added to this quest. Figure 3 (below) represents the various stages of what can best be described as my learning journey over the past five years. The academic process began as far back as 1984, when I enrolled in a Bachelor of Arts at the University of NSW. Due to work and family commitments, I never completed it. It wasn't until 2001, after returning from Army service in East Timor that I enrolled in a graduate certificate of communications. From there, the learning process developed to this stage.

Figure 3 (below) represents the various stages of what can best be described as my learning journey over (primarily) the past 22 years. It began in 1973 when I started work as a newspaper copy boy, then cadet journalist. The immediate 10 years certainly taught me many of the skills I have employed in this thesis (discipline, research, working to deadline, writing and editing) However, I do not consider the true academic journey began until 1984. Though interrupted by a young family, I have finally arrived at my destination.

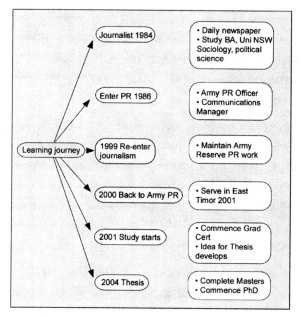

Figure 3: My learning journey.

A definite process occurred. From the initial realisation that there was a phenomenon came the question of what I wanted to achieve and development of the question (Figure 4). This in turn led to the three stages of research (Figure 5).

Figure 4: Process for developing the central question.

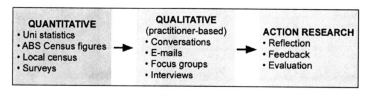

Figure 5: The second part of the learning journey and the process involved.

The initial quantitative approach was highly structured and led me to develop a qualitative (unstructured) approach involving interviews, e-mails, phone conversations, focus groups and ad-hoc conversations. The qualitative phase was unstructured insofar as free thought in interviews and focus groups was encouraged. The process itself was highly structured, particularly with regard to selecting subjects. For example, I approached mostly male PR practitioners and students, as I believe their opinions on gender imbalance affected them more than females, simply because they are the ones who are in short supply. In effect there have been two learning journeys: one in developing my question, and the second in developing the methodologies.

Initial data was obtained by undertaking a census of the population (the Perth PR industry). The population was initially stratified into two industry groups (university students/academics and practitioners). The university students were further stratified into second- and third-year students. First-year students were not selected, as it was considered they had not decided on PR as a Major. These groups were surveyed using non-probability quota sampling, which are of "considerable value in the early exploratory research ... before launching a major study" (Broom and Dozier, 1990).

Survey techniques used included: a census, interviews, questionnaires and observation (focus groups). Media used included the use of the World Wide Web, e-mail, PDF surveys, paper surveys, telephone and in-person interviews and focus groups for all key groups identified, including academics, students and industry professionals.

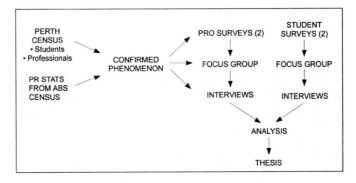

Figure 6: Investigative process of information-gathering.

In order to help gauge the views of professionals, and to compare those with students, two surveys were conducted among this group. The methodology for surveying PR Professionals is discussed in Section 3. The first survey was sent in August 2005. It contained a total of 26 questions. These were broken into two visibly indistinguishable sections. The first 14 questions were a combination of three categorical questions (gender and education), with the remainder mostly ordinal. They covered various aspects of PR work and general career aspirations. The second set of 12 questions was mostly ordinal and more gender-specific. The second part of the first survey, consisting of 12 questions, was structured to obtain basic information on practitioners' views, with a view to providing information for interviews and focus groups. In effect, this is a pilot study, as no research of this nature has been done before.

With most of the second set of questions, a definite response was deemed necessary. This is why many of the questions do not offer a neutral choice (for example, "don't know" or "neither"). This was meant to prevent respondents from being "fence-sitters". However, in line with the "rich" nature of the research, there was an option for an open-ended response in all but two of the questions, giving practitioners a chance to express themselves. Generally, most respondents did not avail themselves of this opportunity.

Following the first professional survey, I deemed it necessary to conduct an on-line supplementary survey in order to cross-analyse results with themes developed in the student surveys – (a) areas of interest and (b) motivation to work in PR. These questions were not originally included in the first survey. They were:

What aspects of PR interest you most?

Name the types of industry that interest you most

Reasons for working in PR vary. What was the main factor that motivated you to choose a PR career?

If you had the chance to start your working life again, would you choose PR?

The quantitative analysis of the main survey was done through SPSS and Excel, with the qualitative aspects through a Mac-based program, HyperResearch. All responses were edited and imported as plain text files into the program, where a series of common themes, or concepts were developed through observation. Each respondent's answers were read again, and coding was applied, according to the recurring themes in answers. Once all responses were coded, the program was activated to produce a series of reports, which enabled the themes/concepts to be grouped for further analysis. The method I chose was to analyse each answer in the first group (questions 1–14), then each question in the second group, but also expand the process to include analysis of the main recurring themes, of which 30 were identified.

As no survey has been done of Australian PR students' attitudes toward their careers, and because mass communications students represent a female majority, it is important to know more about gender perceptions in the classroom, as these views may continue to influence students after they enter the workforce. While it would have sufficed to only survey professionals, the future of the industry lies with today's students.

The first student survey was conducted in the second semester of 2005 (July–September) among students majoring in public relations at two WA universities offering a sequence or a degree in public relations. The four institutions participating were Edith Cowan University [ECU] (Perth), Curtin University (Perth), Murdoch (Perth) and Notre Dame (Fremantle).

The PR programs at the four universities are comprehensive, with all institutions offering PR Majors and specialist Degrees in PR. However, Edith Cowan, Curtin and Murdoch's programs are the most comprehensive. ECU's courses are part of the School of Creative Industries, and Curtin's and Murdoch's are part of the School of Business. PR at Murdoch and Notre Dame is offered as units as part of business, communications or marketing degrees, although some students do major in PR. Although this study was exploratory, using only Perth students, the results with regard to the predominance (statistically) of women in PR confirm my findings in surveys of private practice, both nationally and in Perth: that women outnumber men by more than three to one.

The student questionnaires were administered in public relations lectures and tutorials at the four selected universities, with the cooperation of faculty staff, over a period of four weeks, from 27 July to 30 August. A purposive sample produced 105 usable questionnaires. There were 34 unusable returns from Murdoch, due to students studying non-PR Majors.

The focus groups were largely aimed towards eliciting response from students, as I believed they would be more forthcoming with their opinions in a group situation. Professionals indicated that they were reluctant (in general) to participate in focus groups. In fact, of the 63 professionals who took part in the survey, only six indicated they could participate in a focus group, which was held in December 2005. For this reason, most professionals were interviewed. Organising focus groups was the most difficult aspect of this study, largely because it depended on voluntary participation of (mostly) students. Originally intended to start in the first few weeks of the second semester of 2005, it became increasingly difficult to get at least four to five students from any university in the one place at the same time. Consequently (after dozens of e-mails) only one focus group could be arranged in semester 2 (at ECU on 19 October). The focus group was held at a university for practical reasons, allowing students to gather in a familiar location, and one they are used to accessing.

All focus groups were videotaped. I acted as moderator. Ethics approval was gained in the survey phase, by students and professionals earlier indicating on their return of their intention to participate. They were informed before the session that the focus group would be videotaped, that their involvement was voluntary and that no person (or venue) would be identified. Course coordinators were advised of the focus groups and, in some cases, attended. Interviews were stored on my personal computer at home and later transcribed. Files were converted to QuickTime movies and are included on disc at Annex S. As with the interviews, all focus group data was entered and coded in HyperResearch, Transcripts were analysed line-by-line and word-by-word to conceptualise the data in code. A coding paradigm emerged from the data that included core categories such as 'career choice', 'expressed Gender Role Stereotypes,' 'Career Plans,' and 'Family Influences'.

Being highly exploratory, the main purpose of these activities was to understand current thinking towards the phenomenon, to expand on people's reasons for undertaking PR and to see if this differed between males and females. In reality it produced many streams of thought, with opinions overall finding a high degree of common ground.

Students were mostly left to discuss various aspects and results of the survey, with an emphasis on the reasons for studying PR, and what attracted them to it. In reality this proved to be difficult. All groups took a while to "warm up". In interviews, professionals were, as one would expect, more expansive, and delved into their industry experience to prove the first insight into what makes PR practitioners "tick".

All focus groups and interviews were transcribed into MS Word, edited, then imported into HyperResearch for analysis of common themes/concepts. This technique is known as content analysis, which is defined as "any technique for making inferences by systematically and objectively identifying special characteristics of messages (Simpson, 2005). From these interviews, data was imported into Excel for graphing.

Interviews were conducted at a location of the subject's choosing. This was either their workplace or a coffee shop. The relaxed setting was to help contribute to subjects providing as much information as possible. Subjects were asked whether the interview could be recorded, and informed that their identities would remain anonymous. Questions were worded to allow participants to determine what they would talk about within broad parameters. I used informal and familiar language, so that the interview appeared more as a friendly conversation than a formal interview. This is consistent with qualitative methodology. If the initial general questions did not elicit a full elaboration, I used additional (ad-libbed) questions. For instance, under the general question: what has PR at university been like for you as a guy? I could also ask: what percentage of the class is male? Or: do you socialise with female students? I was the only interviewer. This ensured consistency of questioning.

This industry focus group took place in the boardroom of Scarboro Surf Life Saving Club on Monday 5 December, 2005, from 5.30pm to 6.45pm. Participants were informed the session would be videotaped and voice-recorded. Identities would be anonymous. Originally six practitioners indicated they would attend. However, one had to withdraw for family reasons, and the other (a male) got the days mixed up. Four were senior female practitioners. HF is currently undertaking a PhD, lectures at university and has managed the communications section of WA Government Departments; RW is a media relations specialist for a government agency; HL has worked for several government departments and was working in an international promotions role at the time; HM has several years' PR experience and is working for a quasi-government research/charitable organisation with a staff of 300. (A copy of the session – in .MOV and MP3 format – is included at Annex P on CD).

In both the focus groups and interviews, certain themes or concepts emerged. These were analysed for the number of times they were mentioned, but also for what people said about them. The transcripts were analysed two ways – quantitatively by counting the number of keywords and phrases, and qualitatively through the transcribing and editing process.

Following the first survey, interviews and focus groups, it was decided that more information was required on the thought processes and characteristics of students, to more fully consider if there are common personality characteristics among those who choose to study a PR career. In mid-March 2006, a second survey, also on second- and third-year students, was conducted, using items from the Bern Sex Role Inventory. This measures personality traits. I used it as a measure of gender-type personality traits, and not as a general measure of "masculinity" and/or "femininity". These personality traits are most strongly associated with gender-stereotypes of men and women, and therefore well suited to the limited role I assigned it – measuring personality traits clusters of male and female PR students. The survey consisted of 12 questions (Annex E) and was distributed in lectures at the two major Perth universities which teach PR – Edith Cowan and Curtin. It was also made available on the Internet (via Web Monkey) to the 55 students who indicated their willingness to continue participation in my study. Of these, 30 responded.

Definitions

I would like to make three important definitions for the purpose of this Study.

1. Gender. I have settled on Aalito and Mills' (2002) definition of the term gender, being:

> Sex is a biological classification of humans into women and men, whereas
> gender is a cultured knowledge that differentiates them. Thus, feminine
> and masculine genders consist of values and ideals that originate from
> culture.
> (p. 4)

I have used this definition because it considers that [Western] culture shapes our values and ideals. In the context of PR, a profession that shapes images and messages, this is particularly relevant. It is also in keeping with Kimmel (2004) who said:

> Sex refers to our biological apparatus; gender refers to those meanings
> that are attached to those differences within a culture. Sex is male and
> female; gender is what it means to be a man or women. Or cultural and
> attitudinal characteristics distinctive to the sexes. (p. 3)

2. Imbalance. As noted in Hopkins, 2004 the Department of Employment, Education and Training (1990) suggested that equity in a university student population should be interpreted as meaning that the balance of the student population should reflect the composition of society as a whole. As this Study shows, the proportion of female to male PR students in Australia (and Perth) is more than 7:1. This clearly does not reflect the balance of society.

3. **The PR industry**. For the purposes of this study the "industry" is defined as any people practising PR at a either a scholarly or professional level. Specifically, this includes PR students (second-, third- and fourth-year), academics that teach PR, people who work as PR practitioners in any of the following areas: government, in-house, consultancies and non-profit organisations. I further narrowed down the definition of people working in PR to include only those who were directly involved in writing, editing, strategic planning. The term "industry" does not apply to people working for PR departments in "peripheral" areas such as video production and graphic design. The latter were excluded from my own Census, university statistics and interviews.

25

Delimitations of scope and key assumptions

There are clear boundaries associated with this research, mostly brought about by the limited availability of previous material. In fact, with the exception of some US statistical information and material used in the literature review, the overwhelming amount of information in this thesis is original. This is the first time detailed research into gender in the PR industry has been conducted in Australia. The National and State PR organisations had no membership data. As original research, there is nothing with which to compare it to, so it must be considered a benchmark study of the industry.

While I recognise that the ratio of women to men in the industry is quite different from women to men in industry management, I am primarily interested for the purpose of this Study in why people take up PR as a profession. For this reasons I am focusing on a broad approach.

Summary

The introduction outlines background to the thesis (that is, why it was undertaken). The thesis examines a topic that has not been directly studied and may have long-term implications for the profession, both in practice and at university.

It includes a brief history of the limited research undertaken on the subject. It demonstrates a gap in research, which itself provides a primary justification for the thesis, and provides a brief explanation of how it was undertaken, outlines the research questions, justification and methodology and limitations of the thesis.

Primarily, the thesis seeks to explain why there has been a steady increase in the number of women entering PR and why this male-managed industry is failing to attract males. This research was undertaken after continual observation of the phenomenon, and based on my experience within communications (journalism and PR) and at university, both as a student and tutor.

To achieve its objectives, the thesis takes a mixed methodology approach, which includes predominantly a qualitative, action-based style of research to examine the PR industry in Perth, Australia and internationally.

The research involved a census and surveys of the Perth PR industry (students and professionals), with 53 practitioners and almost 200 students participating. The questionnaires included a wide range of questions in a variety of formats, including multiple choice, Likert-style and open-ended. Surveys were followed by two focus groups and interviews with students and professionals.

Definitions of key terms and delimitations were also outlined.

2 Research issues (literature review)

Introduction

The initial research (gathering of literature) for this project proved to be quite difficult because of the scarcity of material available. PR scholars have mostly approached the subject from purely feminist issues (that is, pay, gender, inequality, management). However, there is a great deal of statistical evidence, general as it is, to show that women undoubtedly outnumber men within public relations, both academically (student enrolments) and professionally. Most of the material relating directly to PR is US-centric, simply because there is virtually no literature on the Australian industry, and little on the industry in Europe. In fact, the PRIA does not keep membership statistics, though I was assured in 2005 by the then national president that this would change, as a result of my enquiries.

Other disciplines

Because my study is attempting to discover why women are entering PR in ever-increasing numbers, the simple reliance on PR literature and statistics can not present a full picture. Other works found relevant to my study included references to the ways in which society has changed and the different ways women and men approach the "traditional" PR functions of creativity, written English and verbal presentation. Sociological and psychological literature also proved invaluable. A brief comparison is also made with the highly male-dominated Information Technology (IT) sector in Western Australia.

Immediate discipline – PR literature

Early signs of interest regarding women in PR began in the late 1970s, when Gower (2001) began the process of "rediscovering" women in (US) public relations by examining the *Public Relations Journal* for the presence of women from 1945 to 1972. Women, Gower found, had always been working in the profession, contrary to popular belief that it was a male-only industry – the preserve of former journalists, who in turn, tended to be mostly male.

Edward L. Bernays, who is widely held responsible for defining the modern function of public relations as 'an advisor to management', had a female business partner. Many historians failed to credit Bernays' wife, Doris E. Feleischman, with any of the credit for their shared accomplishments in public relations. She interviewed clients and wrote news releases, edited the company's newsletter and wrote and edited books and magazine articles, among other duties. (Wilcox, Ault and Agee, 1998, pp 90-91)

An important trend in hiring of women in public relations is that it had happened much more dramatically than the entry of women into all occupations. Reskin and Roos (1990) listed public relations as one of the occupations in the 1970s to show a "disproportionate" increase in female workers, "during a decade in which their advancement into most male occupations was modest at best" (p. 6). One of the biggest factors in the sudden rise of women into the (US) PR workforce was the advent of affirmative action in the 1970s. Legislation forced companies to hire a certain percentage of women. "Employers may have found it useful to place women in visible positions" (Donato, 1990, p. 129).

Recognition of the growing numbers of women in (US) public relations probably came to prominence in the mid-1980s and resulted in the benchmark 1986 report, *The Velvet Ghetto* (now unobtainable). This report, commissioned by the International Association of Business Communicators, concentrated on gender issues, touching on the issues of women's "over-population" of the profession. Two years later, the report's authors said that "women working in business communication shows an increase that is wildly out of proportion – 44.56 per cent of the US workforce is female, but the proportion in business communication is over 70.56 per cent" (Cline et al., 1986). This thesis, however, has been recently debunked, with (Hutton, 2005) saying it consists "almost entirely of anecdotal evidence and very small-scale studies that lacked statistical validity. It included no comprehensive or statistically significant studies capable of providing a benchmark or presenting a scientific argument." Hall (2005) quotes Hutton: "The academics … have known full well that the gender 'research' has been nothing but propaganda and a disinformation campaign – political correctness run amok."

Controversial though it may be, Hutton continued:

The majority of [American public relations professors] know almost nothing about business. Therefore, they don't even understand what Business Week was talking about when it coined the term 'Velvet Ghetto' about 25 years ago. 'Velvet' did not refer to women being mistreated, but referred to the fact that women were being treated so well in PR; often given preferential treatment as the beneficiaries of affirmative action.

Some early statistical evidence showed how women once were by far the minority; the earliest of these being membership of the Public Relations Society of America (PRSA) from 1949 to 1952. Of the new members admitted in that time, only 3.8 per cent were women. Gower's study of the *Public Relations Journal* showed that from 1958 to 1961, PR was still a male-orientated profession: "The lack of a female presence fitted with the ideal or feminine myth promulgated by the mass media in the 1950s of the married woman happily at home with her children" (Gower, 2001, p. 18).

Women continued to enter public relations, accounting for 25 per cent of its practitioners by 1960. The US Census showed an increase in women in public relations and publicity writing of 263.6 percent from 1950 to 1960. "Public relations student societies started on college campuses in 1968, and women accounted for 34 per cent of the membership in those societies" (Gower, 2001, p. 20).

In the United Kingdom the situation is virtually identical. A study commissioned by the Chartered Institute of Public Relations (CIPR) and undertaken by the Centre for Economics and Business Research Ltd shows "Public relations is a female-dominated profession with almost two thirds of workers being women compared to only 46 per cent for the workforce at large" (CIPR 2005).

According to Zawawi (2000), the first Australian PR business was set up by Asher Joel and George Freeman just after the Second World War. Joel was a former journalist who joined the navy and ended up serving on (US) General Douglas MacArthur's PR staff (of 35). Freeman was a fundraiser. Joel was also instrumental in setting up the PRIA.

> The establishment of the first public relations degree courses in the 1960s (Mitchell College, Bathurst, and the Queensland Institute of Technology, Brisbane) not only allowed businesses to employ trained junior staff but helped open the profession to women. In the early 1970s only around 10 per cent of public relations practitioners were women. It is estimated the ratio of men to women hit the 50/50 mark some time in the early 1980s. In 1997 a survey of Queensland members of the PRIA showed two-thirds were women (Zawawi, 2000).

There appeared to be an absence of research between 1989 and 1993, according to Grunig, Toth and Hon (2001, p. 45). "In 1989, when the *Public Relations Journal* published an article about female practitioners". The then president of the PRSA was quoted as saying he was not aware of any problems relating to women in PR. However, he acted on the many replies his comments drew, and established a Task Force on women in PR, which was called the Committee on Work, Life and Gender Issues. Grunig et al.'s 2001 book,

Women in public relations: how gender influences practice, is arguably the main text on female issues in public relations. However, like all texts in this field, it deals mainly with status, salary, equity, gender, gender bias and sexual discrimination: not reasons for the high numbers of women. The issues raised by Grunig et al. certainly have a role to play in some areas of this study, but the book really deals with women's role/s in PR, at a time when little was being done to address the imbalances and issues that women faced within the industry.

One of the central issues raised by Grunig et al. (and others) is the effect of the feminisation of the PR industry. "If women become the majority in public relations, the practice will be typecast as 'women's work'. It will lose what clout it now has as a management function and become a second-class occupation. In the process, gains made over 50 years to build and sustain the value of public relations will disappear" (Bates, 1983, as cited in Grunig, 2001).

Downturns in wages in industries that become female-dominated professions is also raised by Kimmel (2004). This is often cited as a fear among PR practitioners: that an imbalance will lead to a 'cheapening' of the profession. This is a theory put forward by many academics across a wide range of disciplines. Kimmel (2004) cites the changes that have occurred to the clerical profession. Interestingly, the changes to this occupation are similar to what has happened in PR.

> Clerical work was once considered a highly-skilled occupation in which a virtually all-male labour force was paid reasonably well. In both Britain and the US the gender distribution began to change and by the middle of the century most clerical workers were female. As a result, clerical work was revaluated as less demanding of skill and less valuable to the organisation; thus workers' wages fell. As sociologist Cohen notes, this is a result, not a cause, of the changing gender composition of the workforce (Kimmel, 2004, p. 190).

The question is: will this have the same effect on PR?

Kimmel also points to veterinary medicine, which in the 1960s only had about a five per cent female workforce. Today it is closer to 70 per cent. "In the 1970s, when males dominated the profession, the wages of vets and medical practitioners were roughly equal. Today the average wage for a vet is $70–80,000, while a physician earns double that" (Kimmel, 2004, p. 190).

31

The opposite happened in computer programming. In the 1940s women were hired as key punch operators (in effect, early computer programming). "It required skills in abstract logic, maths and electrical circuitry. But once 'programming' was recognised as 'intellectually-demanding' it became attractive to men, who began to enter the industry and drove up wages" (Mimmel, 2004, p. 191).

Dorer (2005) calls this process "re-coding". According to Dorer, discussion in Germany about the "re-coding" of PR (from a male to female profession) started at the beginning of the 1990s. The profession in Germany and Austria, however, still has balance, but is changing. In Austria in 1993 there was a 36 per cent female representation. In 2003 it had reached almost 48 per cent. "What these figures show is that ... PR is gradually turning into a predominantly female profession in German-speaking countries – a 20-year lag on US developments notwithstanding" (Dorer, 2005, p. 186). The "re-coding" of an industry can work both ways. Female typists became male typesetters, while male secretaries became female. For example, when I think of journalism, it was only recently (probably up to 10 years ago) that women sports reporters were not considered "serious" journalists by their peers. It was only a little after that time that barriers such as female reporters being allowed into rugby teams' dressing rooms were removed.

While the movement of women into a profession is widely believed to herald a decline in wages and a "de-skilling" of an occupation, Game and Pringle (1983) hold a contradictory view, in that "the reverse is frequently the case – work is de-skilled and then women move in" (p. 18). If this is the case in PR, could it be that the work of the profession has become "trite" and "devalued" due to a variety of factors, including low scores necessary to enter university and the large numbers allowed to study the subject. This then removes the prestige and value of the subject and, in turn, the profession.

In Australia, this problem was highlighted by Pockcock and Alexander (1999). From an analysis of the 1995 Australian Workplace Industrial Relations Survey, it was found that wages fell in professions dominated by women.

> Women in industries that were close to 100 per cent female-dominated
> earned 32 per cent less per hour than women with otherwise identical
> characteristics in industries that were close to 100 per cent male-
> dominated, [with] the penalty for women being in a highly feminised
> occupation, compared to one that is male-dominated, was 15 per cent
> (Pockcock, et al. 1999, p. 75).

In a US context, Donato (1990) notes that while PR paid women 60 per cent more than the median female wage in the 1970s, that figure had dropped to 37 per cent in 1980. That it dipped markedly is further evidence that when a profession is feminised, wages drop.

Most recently, Grunig (2001) quotes from a 1993 PRSA monograph, *Ten Challenges to PR during the Next Decade*, in which Challenge Six addressed the problem of the shrinking number of males in the profession.

> Much more needs to be done . . . to encourage more men into the field . . .
> Public Relations is stultified when it reflects a limited slice of a diverse
> population. Steps should be taken to identify the factors responsible for ...
> the declining numbers of males entering the field (Grunig, 2001).

In the Australian context, there are indications that the feminisation of PR does not make it an attractive career option. McCurdy (2005) found that:

> 80 per cent of female practitioners indicated the belief that public relations
> is viewed as a female industry, with the one female interviewee indicating
> that the only young male she knew who worked in public relations left
> because he was told it was a 'girls job'. One of the male interviewees even
> admitted that he does not tell people he works in public relations because
> of the negative responses he receives as a direct result of the industry
> being perceived as a female majority. (McCurdy, 2005, p. 93)

Sha (2001) concluded that feminisation would make public relations more ethical, "not merely in appearance, but in practice" (p. 45). Others, like Larissa Grunig (2001), Dozier (1988) and Rakow (1989) argued the prevalence of women would introduce characteristics such as collaboration, sensitivity towards audiences and better two-way communication. Several theories on reasons why women enter PR have been put forward. They do not reveal much detail, but are included to demonstrate current thinking:

• "Primarily to write and be creative" (Creedon, as cited in Aldoory, 2001).

• Women's interest in more creative pursuits are examples of socialisation (Cline, as cited in Aldoory, 2001).

In summary, there can be no doubt the PR literature on this specific topic is scarce, as Noble, 2004 points out. In her Masters thesis on the same subject, Noble draws on material which focused on the advertising industry. However, I found the findings to be of limited value to this thesis, as these two statements demonstrate.

"Most advertising students at two major universities chose advertising as a major because they found the field of study interesting" (Fullerton and Umphrey, as cited in Noble, 2004, p. 5) ... and

"Students majoring in advertising were drawn to the field because it seemed interesting and challenging" (Schweitzer, as cited in Noble, 2004, p. 5).

Having interest in a subject is, of course, a valid reason, but does not explain why females and males choose the subject.

Socialisation

Socialisation: "The process by which culture is learned" *(Oregon State University)*.

Gendered socialisation: "The process by which children acquire the knowledge and internalise the values of socially-determined sex roles *(McGraw Hill Higher Education)*.

The issue of socialisation is not covered in any depth by PR researchers with regard to its being a factor in determining career choices. Even the basic question of what type of person practises PR has never been answered. For the purposes of this study, the term socialisation is taken to mean the learning of a society's customs, attitudes and values. Henslin, as cited in Wikipaedia, 2006, contends that "an important part of socialisation is the learning of culturally-defined gender roles". Gender socialisation refers to the learning of behaviour and attitudes considered appropriate for a given sex. The central question that arises is therefore: is the nature of PR shaped by the way our society perceives it? Are certain types of people drawn to PR because of what they have learned about PR and the way they learn it? Learning, of course, comes from a variety of sources – family, peers, work colleagues and the media. All of these will have an effect on the way our society views PR. The subject certainly raises more questions than it answers.

Deaux (1976) looked at how variations in our environment can lead to differences in behaviour. With the PR "environment" changing markedly with regard to gender composition, does this in turn lead to a change in how people in the industry (and those entering it) view it? The core of Deaux's study recognises that "in nearly every area of social behaviour, differences between men and women have been observed" (1976, p. 3). The "environment" is an area that Barnett and Rivers looked at in their 2004 book, *Same Difference: How Gender Myths are Hurting Our Relationships, Our Children and Our*

Jobs. Ohlott (2005) noted that "unlike many proponents of currently popular gender theories, Barnett and Rivers suggest we are each a product of many interacting forces, including our genes, our personalities, our environments and chance." This is a theme I follow in more detail further on.

In considering whether gender may play a part in people selecting PR as a career, we should look (from a socialisation perspective) at whether there are differences between males and females. Deaux cites a 1974 study *(Psychology of Sex Differences)* of more than 2000 cases by Macoby and Jacklin, who found solid evidence for only four behavioural differences (aggression, spatial, verbal and maths), only one of which is directly pertinent to PR, based on the premise that it (verbal skills) appears constantly in the literature. Once again, women were found to be superior to men in verbal ability, while men excel in maths. "In both instances, these differences are not observed in early childhood but show divergence after adolescence" (Deaux, 1976). Macoby and Jacklin (1974) also found men and boys to be constantly more aggressive. However, on their own they do provide a reason why more women than men women enter PR. Noble (2004) cites fours studies that indicate gender influences subject selection at university: "These studies suggest women choose majors consistent with traditional roles, such as teaching, rather than technology-related careers, such as computer programming and engineering" (p. 6).

At this point in time I think it necessary here (rather than in the literature review) to mention the more recent (2005) research by Noble into US students' reasons for studying PR. Noble surveyed 159 PR students at one university. While this certainly limits that study, as only one university was sampled, the work is highly relevant. It is one of only a few pieces of literature that started to appear (all about the same time) a year into my study. Noble sought not so much to focus on gender, but to more broadly understand why students enter PR, their misconceptions, and ways of developing methods to correct those misconceptions. Once again, Noble reinforces the frustration I (and one of two others found): "A review of literature reveals virtually no research related to the specific reasons why public relations students select the major" (Noble, 2004, p. 5).

While surveys have been undertaken to determine whether students select a course major in line with traditional gender roles, the findings are consistently contradictory. Noble (2005) pointed to research by Eide (1994) which said students did not choose courses that were in line with gender roles, and that of Dawson-Threat and Huba (1996) who refuted this.

35

Because there is almost no research on why more women than men study PR, it helps to look at other careers where research has been done. The gender balance in the sciences and maths is the opposite to PR, in that they are male-dominated. By looking at how researchers have approached the socialisation of maths and science, we may better understand the situation in PR. In 2005, Harvard University psychologist Elizabeth Spelke debated the notion of how great a part socialisation plays in why males or females take up careers in the sciences and maths. In a 2005 debate with colleague Steven Pinker, Spelke made mention of the Macoby and Jacklin research, saying nothing much had changed. Taking the "nurture" stance, Spelke is adamant that the "gap" is caused by social factors. "There are no differences in overall intrinsic aptitude for science and mathematics between women and men," she says (Pinker, 2005). So if differences in intrinsic attitudes don't cause a gender imbalance, what does? According to Spelke, gender stereotypes influence the ways in which males and females are perceived. Spelke believes:

> Knowledge of a person's gender will influence our assessment of factors
> such as productivity and experience, and that's going to produce a pattern
> of discrimination, even in people with the best intentions. Biased
> perceptions earlier in life may well deter some female students from even
> attempting a career in science or mathematics (Spelke, 2005).

When analysing why more women than men choose a certain career, there should also be consideration of what Spelke termed the *snowball effect*, which is when we "imagine ourselves in careers where there are other people like us. If the first two effects perpetuate a situation where there are few female scientists and mathematicians, young girls will be less likely to see math and science as a possible life" (Pinker, 2005). Others have also adopted this mantra.

> The key lies in the perceptions of the qualities and work values of
> different occupations. I stress the word 'perceptions' because I do suspect
> that these are stereotyped views, which are not necessarily based on
> realization. (Cumming, 1997, p. 9)

Using this rationale, it follows that biased perceptions (of potential male students) may deter them from attempting a career in PR. Similarly, if there are few male PR professionals, the idea is perpetuated that PR is a female profession, and males will not see it as a viable career choice. This is supported by many of the comments from both males and females in this thesis's interviews, focus groups and survey responses. Cumming (1997) and Couch and Sigler (2001) found that perceptions about occupations continue to be a determining factor in students' choice of occupation. In reference to the continued perception that "occupations are associated with a particular sex, one answer lies in the representation of professions in the media." Certain occupations are portrayed in a stereotyped way. "Professions such as lawyers, government officials, physicians, etc, continue to be masculine-oriented." Similarly, Gottfredson, as cited in Glick, Wilk and Perrault (1995), found that "people perceive occupations similarly, no matter what their sex, social class, educational level, ethnic group, area of residence, occupational preferences or employment, age, type of school attended, political persuasion, and traditionality [sic] of beliefs". This suggests that people organise their images of occupations in a highly stereotyped, socially-learned manner – a point I will explore, and argue for, later. This is particularly apt with regard to PR – an industry that bases much of its success on portraying a certain perception of a client. This notion is also supported by Anne Parry, IPR Midlands group chair and deputy MD of Quantum PR in Birmingham, who said in a 2004 interview with *icBirmingham* (a UK-based web business site): "The root cause of the problem is perhaps the perception of PR, which is still not being taken seriously enough and is often viewed as a bit girlie in certain quarters" (np).

In her Honours thesis, McCurdy (2005) highlighted the role that perception of the industry plays in attracting people, and of how the community perceives an industry, in this case, PR.

> It could be assumed that although public relations students and
> practitioners do not state a direct belief that a female majority has caused a
> threat to the overall status of the public relations industry, the negative
> viewing of the industry in the general community may dictate that a
> female majority has posed a threat rather than contribution. In order to
> help change the negative view of the industry currently held by the
> general community, public relations has to be redefined and definable.
> Once people can understand the functions undertaken by practitioners they
> may then understand the value of the industry not only towards the
> business community but also the general community. Secondly, public
> relations has to "get out there". In other words, advertising should be
> conducted in order to educate (McCurdy, 2005, p. 94).

Research shows that perceptions about certain occupations develop well before university. Levy et. al., (2000) cite research by Huston, 1983; Ruble and Martin, 1998, which shows "preschoolers and primary school children demonstrate substantial knowledge of gender-typed occupations". Specifically, girls choose significantly more feminine occupations (for example, teaching, nursing), while boys chose significantly more masculine occupations (for example, police officer, truck driving). "Thus, it appears that young children hold strong gender-typed perceptions of adult occupations and presumably use these standards when contemplating future work choices" (Levy, Sadovsky and Troseth, 2000).

37

The fact that women are better in spoken (and written) English is a point continually raised by many of the subjects surveyed and interviewed in my study. On university entrance tests, for example, "verbal aptitude test scores for women are consistently higher than those for men" (Deaux, 1976, p. 7). The fact that these differences develop in adolescence indicates that social conditioning comes into play (that is, we are a result of our social surrounds). If that is the case, it stands to reason that an individual's and, in turn, a society's opinions of PR (indeed, any career) can be shaped progressively through time.

Kimmel (2004) says the reason why girls outpace boys in English is "not the result of 'reverse discrimination' but because boys bump up against the norms of masculinity (of what we regard as masculine or feminine). Boys regard English as a feminine subject. Kimmel pointed to research in Australia by Wayne Martino and colleagues, who found that boys are uninterested in English because of what it might say about their masculine pose.

> 'Reading is lame, sitting down looking at words is pathetic,' commented
> one boy. 'Most boys that like English are faggots', commented another.
> Boys tend to hate English for the same reasons that girls love it. In English
> they observe, there are no hard and fast rules, but rather one expresses
> one's opinion about the topic and everyone's opinion is equally valued.
> 'The answer can be a variety of things; you're never really wrong,' said
> one boy. 'It's not like maths or science, where there is one set answer for
> everything,' another noted (Kimmel, 2004, p. 170).

Compare this to the response of some of this Study's subjects, and the answers are remarkably similar. Male students simply feel 'out of their comfort zone' with English. As one male student said to me in an interview:

> To be honest, one thing that has turned me off PR is that it seems
> ambiguous compared to marketing and advertising. It's hard to measure
> PR, and you don't know if the work you are doing is working or not.

There are conflicting views on whether or not gender differences are part of our biology, or just a result of 'socialisation'. That we are a result of our social conditioning is made clear by Deaux (1976, p. 6), who argues that "if a difference between men and women is found consistently across a variety of societies, then we can have more faith in a biological component [being responsible for behaviour and attitudes]." For example, not every society on earth is aggressive, so aggression can not be a result of biology. Therefore, humans' traits must be a result of social processes. On the other hand, Moir and Jessell (1996) argue that "the differences between the sexes are biological, not sociological" (pp 5-17). They say that aggression is a result of our biological makeup. "We do not teach our children to be aggressive – indeed, we try to vainly un-teach it. This is a male feature and one which can not be explained by social conditioning" (p. 7).

From a socialisation perspective, Deaux (1976) says "young boys are given more physical stimulation, while young girls are given more vocal stimulation" (p. 7). The fact that most parents expect boys should not be feminine and girls should not be masculine would indicate that sociologically males would not be attracted to a career that appears feminine.

I found illuminating the study cited in Moir and Jessell (1996) of an Israeli kibbutz which tried to eliminate stereotyping (clothing, hairstyles, toys, behaviour). Despite the efforts, boys still went on to study physics and engineering. The girls went on to study sociology and became teachers. Moir and Jessel saw that as proof that "the minds of men and women are different, and that ultimately boys and men live in a world of things and space; girls and women in a world of people and relationships" (1996, p. 154). In exploring the lack of women within IT in Australia, Walters (2006) said: "Women approach design of technology in a different way from men."

The question of whether gender (and differences) plays a part in determining someone's entry into PR may, for the moment, remain elusive. Tavris (1992) notes that this type of research "can not explain, for instance, why if women are better than men in verbal ability, so few women are auctioneers or diplomats, or why, if women have the advantage of making rapid judgments, so few women are air-traffic controllers or umpires" (p. 54).

Grunig, Toth and Hon (2001) argue that public relations is an industry founded on feminine values, such as honesty, justice, and sensitivity, which will enhance the symmetrical communication patterns of public relations. Furthermore, the two-way symmetrical model of public relations requires resolving conflict and building relationships, which are intrinsically feminist values. "Feminist theorizing about public relations proposes that the profession is inherently feminine in nature because of its purposes, practices, and attributes" (Childers-Hon, 1995). Only four (industry) areas (of 11 put forward) were significantly more male- than female-oriented, and those specialties entail areas of expertise that have traditionally been male – technology, finance, sports, and industry. These findings support comments found in previous interviews with PR practitioners regarding gender segregation in the field. According to Aldoory (2001), the proportion of practitioners not only favours women, but younger women. This is supported by figures from PRSA and IABC surveys.

Much discussion in the mid-80s to 1990s was on the feminisation of PR. Fears were held that this trend would lead to a drop in status and salaries. Sha (as cited in Aldoory, 2001) concluded that feminisation would make public relations more ethical, "not merely in appearance, but in practice". Others, like Larissa Grunig and Dozier (1992) and Rakow (1989) said the prevalence of women would introduce characteristics such as collaboration, sensitivity towards audiences and better two-way communication. Certainly PR has become more open and two-way. But perhaps this may be just a result of media fragmentation and the development of the Internet, which encourages PR practice to be more "in tune" with its target audiences.

There are other less-scholarly views. Richard Brandt, editor-in-chief of *Upside*, said: "I have this uneasy feeling that the reason there are so many women in PR is that it's a form of journalism that's less respected and therefore easier for them to get ahead" (Brown, 1998). Perhaps wanting to protect himself from the avalanche that would follow that statement, Brandt continued: "But I have also seen the profession increase its role, its influence and its importance very dramatically over the last couple of decades. And at the same time that's when a lot of women have gotten into it."

Hutton (2005) dealt with the issues of the often-raised issue of salary discrimination in PR. In doing so, he touched on what was assumed to be the early research on gender issues and finds the methodology to be wanting. For example, he debunked the findings of the 1986 *Velvet Ghetto* report in a number of areas, mostly in salary, finding little discrimination (this is covered in the conclusions to Chapter Seven). Hutton also found that gender discrimination work presented through the PRSA was also flawed, with "the claim of pervasive discrimination was based on the opinions of a single, non-randomly selected, four-woman focus group, whose views were directly contradicted by a single, 11-man focus group. In other words, "the authors of the monograph completely dismissed the comments of the 11 men, while extrapolating the comments of four women to the entire US PR profession" (Hutton, 2005).

One interesting aspect to the study is reverse discrimination – a byproduct of the changing nature of PR. The issue was raised by two senior male practitioners and one student and warrants discussion, as it may become a growing problem of a reshaped profession. In such a small study it is enough to be flagged as a warning in any future discussion on the gender composition of the industry. The fact that a senior government (male) PR officer alleges bias in employment against males, and there is discrimination against a male PR student is cause for concern.

With regard to the impact on individual males, a British study by Cross and Bagilhole (2002) reports on a small-scale, qualitative study of 10 men who have crossed into what are generally defined as 'women's jobs'. In doing so, one of the impacts on them has been that they have experienced challenges to their masculine identity from various sources and in a variety of ways. This aspect briefly reared itself in the case of the second-year male PR student. However, I believe, as do most in the profession, that this aspect is of concern at this point in time. It may, however, remain an influencing factor on students, who are still, by and large, conditioned by society to believe in what constitutes men's and women's work. This perception, fuelled by the media, is enough to guarantee the continued increasing entry of females into PR.

While this study does not (and should not) attempt to dwell on the issue of discrimination in PR, it should outline an associated phenomenon which could be taking place in tandem with the rise in the number of women in PR. Discrimination against males (reverse discrimination) is something that came to my attention in October-November 2005. Firstly I received an unsolicited e-mail from a male PR student at the Canberra Institute of Technology. The student (Bill – not his real name), who had almost completed his studies, was one of two males in a class with 28 women. In Bill's own words:

> I have actually been faced with a lot of issues that relate to my gender in
> this industry. I am judged by people outside the industry as strange, being
> a male studying PR. By teachers, I have been ignored or had ideas put
> down. General thoughts that I have shared with the rest of the class, have
> been put down and stated as sexist, purely because they come from my
> mouth. My theories and skills have been questioned due to my gender.
> The list goes on, but overall I have come across quite a few boundaries
> placed up against me due to my gender. I have even had my sexuality
> (questioned) several times because I am studying a female-dominated
> industry *(Student 2005)*.

As a result of this contact, Bill was 'dismissed' by the PR firm he sent the e-mails from, and failed his professional placement: something I felt was outrageously unfair. The last message I had from him was on 6 December:

> A package was sent to them (the consultancy) from the internship boss
> with a letter of complaint for me making contact with you. So it all ended
> in disaster, but I have no regrets on making the contact. She has just
> proved that I really do have something to be concerned about as I go into
> the industry.

The issue became apparent again a month later, after I interviewed a leading Perth (male) PR practitioner, who mentioned a colleague who had misgivings about the way the industry might be heading, due to the gender imbalance. I obtained the colleague's thoughts on the issue. While in some parts they are quite scathing about the way he perceives many females operate in PR (he labels the current crop of female practitioners 'Grimbos' [that is, no sense of humour, hence grim] and with a take on the word bimbo), there were pertinent points about concerns for males in the industry. Agree or not, the practitioner has more than 20 years experience with major corporations and government departments.

> I believe it is unstoppable (female predominance) now, and difficulties for
> males in PR will continue to grow as many key marketing and HR
> executives are now female and make up the panels one fronts for both jobs
> and also when you pitch for a PR account. You can tell you're dead in the
> water as soon as you walk through the door. It is especially prevalent in
> my field, tourism and hospitality, where, for example, most hotel GMs
> now see PR exclusively as a young/blonde/female role. I've been in PR
> for more than 20 years … (and) the past five years has been the most
> difficult because, I firmly believe, of this growing gender bias, which of
> course one can never prove (practitioner, 2005).

Wilcox et al. (1998) also points to this 'reverse discrimination'. "Some men have complained about 'reverse discrimination' because some companies are seeking women. A 70-30 ratio [of women to men] in fields that virtually demand a university education is exceptionally high." I mention it principally because it resulted (un-announced) directly from this study. Obviously, there is room for specialised research in this topic.

Wilcox, et al., (1998) was one of the few scholars to mention reasons for the predominance of women in PR. However, Wilcox's brief reference is a succinct précis of what many of this study's subjects, both male and female, believe.

> Public relations attracts well-educated women for several reasons. The
> availability of its jobs is better than in the mass media; salaries and career
> advancement opportunities are relatively good, and the work is widely
> regarded as glamorous. Women bring to PR an instinct for building
> personal relationships and a sensitivity towards social problems. (pp 90-
> 91)

Some of these points are raised further in my study by professionals and students: particularly the issue of glamour being an incentive to pursue PR as a career, and the general notion that women "have the instinct" for PR.

I make mention of what is (apart from Noble, 2004) the first detailed attempt to define the phenomenon. In 2005, The University of North Carolina's Janie Folmar presented her Masters thesis, titled, *Why are more women than men attracted to the field of public relations? Analyzing students' reasons for studying PR*. As I was halfway through my research it came as a godsend, though I felt slightly "beaten to the punch". Folmar was most cooperative and provided the thesis. Like Noble, and others, she also was stymied by the lack of research, and proceeded down the gender path as a way of trying to obtain some answers. "The conceptual framework supporting this study revolves around gender" (Folmar, 2005). She concluded:

> Specifically, women's reasons for being attracted to public relations
> included: it is a profession for which they feel well-suited, allowing
> opportunities for relationship-building, interpersonal communication, and
> creativity; and it is a broad, portable career path that allows opportunities
> for advancement, as well as flexibility for family demands. (Folmar, 2005)

These finding are similar to the views expressed by Wilcox et. al., 1998.

Societal change

> The so-called traditional system of dads who go out to work every
> morning, leaving mum to stay at home with the children, a fulltime
> housewife and mother, was an invention of the 1950s, and part of a larger
> ideological effort to facilitate the re-entry of American men back into the
> workforce and domestic life after World War II, and to legitimate the
> return of women from the workplace and back into the home (Kimmel,
> 2004).

History shows we are a male-dominated culture (patriarchy). Stereotypes have been, and continue to be passed through the generations. Women served Australia's industrial society well up to the Second World War, when they increasingly took on hard labour (farming, manufacturing) traditionally the preserve of their menfolk, who were fighting overseas. Now, with the expansion of technology we have changed our needs again, although our work values are still, to a large extent, locked into a bygone era. "Success in dealing with continuing accelerating change will be our ability to make decisions and to modify our values, beliefs and attitudes" (Chater et al., 1995).

Widespread change became apparent in the 1970s, with the advent of the feminist movement. This led to the entry of more women into the workforce. In the US, "more than 50% of American women [joined] the work force by 1980, while the largest increase of working women due to the women's movement was, not surprisingly, white, middle-class, well-educated females" (Reciniello 1999). What was once a phenomenon of women entering the workforce is now commonplace.

Wooten (1997) points to the following factors which have contributed to the ever-increasing numbers of women entering the workforce:

The advances of the women's movement,

The enactment of laws prohibiting sex discrimination,

Increases in female enrolment in higher education and professional schools,

The steady increase in women's labor force participation, and

Reductions in gender stereotyping in both education and employment.

Figures from the Australian Bureau of Statistics (ABS) clearly show women's participation rates advancing over men's during the 1990s. "In Western Australia, since 1984–85, the number of women employed has almost doubled, increasing by 94.2 per cent to reach 445,381 in 2004–05" (Australian Bureau of Statistics 2006). According to the ABS, factors that have contributed to the State's labour force growth over the past two decades include:

A doubling in the number of women employed (from about 229,000 in 1984–85 to 445,000 in 2004–05),

More than half of women in WA are now participating in the labour force (58% in 2004–05 compared to 48% in 1984–85).

Year	Female workforce participation (000s)	Female growth rate (as % of workforce)	Male growth rate (as % of workforce)
95-96	3.59	3.4	1.5
96-97	3.63	1.2	0.9
97-98	3.69	1.4	0.9
98-99	3.77	2.3	1
99-00	3.89	3	0.4
00-01	4.03	3.1	1.3
01-02	4.06	1.3	1.5
02-03	4.2	3.3	1.1
03-04	4.25	1.2	1.5

Table 1: Female participation (fulltime and part-time) as a percentage of the Australian workforce, 1995–96 to 2003–04. Source: ABS, April 2005.

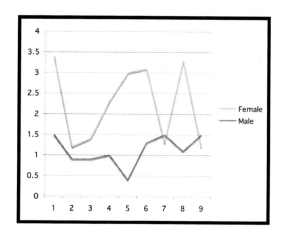

Figure 7: Comparison of female and female employment (fulltime and part-time) growth rates from 1995–96 to 2003–2004. Source: ABS, April 2005.

Added to this change in workforce participation rates, is the fact we are now living and working in what everyone regards as the "Information Age". We (in Australia) have passed from being an industrial society to a technology society, characterised by the exchange of information. Previously, males dominated the workforce because their contributions were seen as more valuable than females. However, the changes brought about by the information age can be seen as favourable to women, as "the needs of the information age are inconsistent with the structures, bureaucracies and rules of the industrial era" (Chater and Gaster, 1995).

Chater and Gaster (1995) noted that the way business is done today is markedly different from previous eras. The most notable impact of change is the increased emphasis on ethical practice. This includes attention to the environment and the proper treatment of staff. The emphasis on these values can be seen to be more compatible with the way women work, presenting an ideal opportunity for women to take the lead in these areas. It is interesting to note the traditional "male-dominated" industries of finance and technology, previously referred to by Hon, are not attracting females. The nature of the work and traditional values associated with these industries works against them. Reciniello (1999) refers to a 1995 study of the information technology industry conducted by accounting firm Deloitte and Touche in explaining why women are held back in certain industries. Three myths held by men were identified as major contributors to the women's lack of advancement in that industry:

- women lack technical competence compared to men;

- women lack the toughness to compete, and

- women will not work the long hours required (*A Woman's Place*).

Taking the opposite views of some these results may yield a partial explanation (or at least provide theories) why women succeed in PR: (a) women can be technically-competent in a industry (PR) which does not favour numerical skills; (b) women do not need to be as "financially tough" to compete in PR.

In Western Australia, the IT industry has a shortage of personnel which, according to O'Neill and Walker, 2001, "mirrors the declining trend in the representation of women in the IT industry". O'Neill and Walker cite several reasons why women are not attracted to the industry, including long hours and the masculine image of IT ("a lads' network"). As with PR, in IT "there certainly is no physical barrier to females being able to undertake any aspect of the work" (O'Neill and Walker, 2001). Interestingly, women have made strong inroads in PR within the IT industry. "It's the only area, actually, where the plaudits go more often to women than men" (Brown, 1998).

> While the industrial society was created by men for men, the information
> society needs people, both male and female, who are well educated and
> technically trained. This has created a unique opportunity for women, as
> all levels of business are now potentially open to us. (Chater and Gaster,
> 1995, p. 8)

Added to this is the way business must now respond rapidly to changing economic conditions.

It may be that the predominance of women in PR is simply a response to the traditional ways we have viewed different occupations, such as engineering (male), nursing (female), economics (male) and social work (female). According to Aires (1997):

> A division of labor in contemporary society allocates different work and responsibilities to men and women. Overall, men are allocated roles with greater power and status. Likewise, women are believed to be communal and emotionally expressive because they are assigned to domestic roles and occupations that require these traits. (p. 92)

Traditional hierarchical structures, with their inflexible rules and procedures, are not suited to the new era in which flexibility and creativity are valued. Many of the attributes necessary to PR professionals are outlined by Chater and Gaster (1995) who state:

> We are moving from industrialisation, where the patriarchal model worked brilliantly, to an era where our survival and progress will depend on not our ability to set rules, control production lines, establish bureaucracies, assert status and focus on the bottom line, but on our ability to communicate, negotiate, work with emotions, create solutions to ever-changing problems and opportunities, respond to change, think globally and strategically and work with and value people . . . The playing field is moving in the direction of feminine values, so what the 'game' now needs are the skills that women can bring to it. (p. 10)

Other scholars also agree with this 'worldview'. In her book, *Gender Games* (1998), Australian PR practitioner Candy Tymson took a broader look at gender differences in management. However, as a PR practitioner, her views are interesting as they could be seen to have a PR "bias". Basically, she says there are two styles of management:

1. Information (or status) management, which is male-centric and focuses on goals, and

2. Relationship management, which is female-centric and focuses on the process.

On reading the summary of Tymson's outlook (table 2) one can not feel (on the surface) that the increase in the number of women entering PR is a result of "natural" forces, with the characteristics of females more suited to the way in which modern PR is practised.

GENDER DIFFERENCES	
MALE	FEMALE
Information-focused	Relationship-focused
Report-speaking	Rapport-speaking
Goal-driven	Process-orientated
Single-task	Multi-task
Succinct language	Storytelling approach
Works towards a destination	On a journey
Needs answers	Asks the right questions
Talks about things in workplace (politics, sport, etc)	Talks about how they feel about things
Seizes opportunity to do business in social setting	Reluctant to raise business socially
Focus on latest development	Focus on "how you are going"
Large groups	Small groups

Table 2: Summary of Tymson's views on male/female gender differences.

With regard to language, Tymson has drawn on the work of Deborah Tannen, author of 15 books, including the 1990 best-seller, *You Just Don't Understand*. Tannen, a professor of linguistics, maintains the two sexes do not understand each other because they have distinctly different conversational styles, brought about by the way they grow up. According to Tannen, girls' groups are structured around pairs of friends who share secrets, grow up to become women, strive to make connections in their conversations, to be supportive and focus on details. The way boys play produces men who develop a competitive, confrontational style, are reluctant to talk about their problems and prefer abstractions. The result is that women talk in the above-mentioned "rapport-speaking" style, whereas men are more comfortable speaking in public ("report-speaking"). However, these traits have been shown to disappear in a short space of time. Wheeland and Verdi (1992), as cited in Aires (1997) showed that during a four-day group communication exercise that men were initially more task-orientated, while women focused on being friendly and offering support. "This gender difference disappeared in the later sessions ... over time in groups, men and women engaged equally in both forms of talk" (Aires, p. 95).

While women would certainly seem to be more "naturally" more suitable to PR roles than men, that should not discount males from the practice altogether. "We have argued for the hiring and promotion of both women and men in our field, because we understand that few if any of today's organizational environments are composed solely of men" (Grunig, L, 2001).

The changing nature of how we accept women in the (PR) workforce, in part, is perhaps recognition of our society's changing values. Women are seen to be equal to men in occupations which require little physical effort. It shows how we should highly value the entire range of communication skills, both personal and technical.

Noble (2005) was probably the first in the US to look at "why public relations students select the major". Also stymied by lack of research, Noble conducted research at her university and gleaned some important information from the literature on gender differences and how they influence selection of (university) courses. The findings from Noble's study that are relevant to my Study, and are compared in Chapter 5, include:

- Women (73.8 per cent) were more likely to agree they selected public relations as a major because of the creative aspects than did men.
- Slightly more women (55.6 per cent) than men (51.5 per cent) agreed they chose public relations because of the business aspects.
- Women (71 per cent) were more likely to disagree that public relations courses are easier than the average college course than men (53 per cent), while more men thought public relations is an easy major (31.4 per cent) compared to women (18 per cent).
- More than 60 per cent of public relations majors (64 per cent) said English was their favourite or second favourite subject in high school.
- The news media's mention of public relations and influence from friends were both more prominent than college advisers in students' decision to study PR.
- Sports public relations (29.4 per cent) and entertainment public relations (23.8 per cent) were the most popular choices for public relations careers.

While they may appear unrelated to the study, the final two points (above) are relevant because (1) the news media, as I will outline further on, heavily shapes our perception of PR, and (2) the type of PR students want to practice is also explored in more detail. It is also shown how their perception changes once they start practising.

Citing studies by Niles 1997, Walsh and Srsic 1995, Jepsen 1992, Blakemore 1984, Noble said: "These studies suggest women choose majors consistent with traditional roles, such as teaching, rather than technology-related careers, such as computer programming and engineering" (p. 6). This view correlates to that held by Moir and Jessel (1996) who contend that "we should not be surprised that men and women gravitate to sex-specific jobs. We always have, as a species, divided labour" (p. 158).

Dawson-Threat and Huba, 1996, as cited in Noble, 2005, reported that while less than half of all students in a survey identified themselves with traditional sex roles, more than half of these students selected a major considered traditional for their gender. Eide, 1994, as cited in Noble, 2005, refuted these studies, reporting that in the 1980s, women were migrating toward high-skills majors, which led to higher paying jobs. A later study disagreed with Eide's findings, suggesting that during the 1990s into the 2000s, women were not shifting to higher paying career fields and majors at the same pace they were in the 1980s, and were still selecting more traditional career fields (Turner, 1999, as cited in Noble, 2005). These studies demonstrate conflicting evidence regarding gender career selection based on traditional gender roles, and demonstrate the continuing evolution of gender career choice.

Femininity and masculinity (male/female values/traits)

While the changing nature of society would go a small part of the way to explaining women's rise to prominence in public relations, in order to further understand why there is a gender imbalance in PR, a study of the way males and females approach work (and life) would seem necessary.

MALE AND FEMALE VALUES	
MALE	FEMALE
Power	Harmony
Money	Service
Freedom	Loyalty
Status	Enjoyment
Profit	Friendship
Control	Commitment
Success	Family
Wealth	Love
Security	Receptivity
Achievement	Responsibility
Task focus	Caring and nurturing
Independence	Relationships

Table 3: Comparison of male and female values (Chater and Gaster, 1995)

The tables, above and below, of our traditional views, offer guidelines on why men still hold senior positions in management, in a culture that values competition, success and linear thinking. It is interesting here to compare what has happened in the industry, with what was predicted. *Business Week* in 1978 reported that PR was a quasi-management function in which women could be catapulted, but that it was "a fast track to a short career" (Donato 1990). Of course, the reality has proved somewhat different. Traits described as common in 1995 (Table 4) are similar to those described recently.

| COMMONLY-PERCEIVED TRAITS OF MEN AND WOMEN ||
Men	Women
Logical	Intuitive
Strong	Weak, timid
Unemotional	Emotional
Aggressive	Gentle, caring
Assertive	Submissive
Decisive	Indecisive
Leaders	Followers
Independent	Dependent
Scientific	Humanistic
Rational	Irrational
Competitive	Cooperative
Objective	Sensitive

Table 4: The way we perceive the most common traits of men and women
(Chater and Gaster. 1995).

In a web article for the Maynard Institute of Journalism, Farmer (2003) highlighted an interview with MNET television's manager of human resources, Mark Morales, who pointed to some of the feminine traits of women, who have transformed the culture at Channel 13. According to Morales:

> If you look at management in America, it's always fraught with macho overtones. But I think women have a higher level of emotional intelligence. They look at resources, they use people's strengths, and involve people in problem solving. I don't see these women so much making decisions as gathering information and making choices based on their explorations.

MNET's station manager Paula Kerger agreed that women often make *better listeners.* "Women tend to try to *broker compromise*," she says. "Sometimes men are just in it to win" (Farmer, 2003).

These narratives tally with commonly-held beliefs about women in general, which are borne out further on in this study in surveys, focus groups and interviews. Other traits that women possess include being able to "make greater eye contact" (Exline, as cited in Deaux, 1976, p. 61). Other beliefs could be that women respond more positively to being touched, or that when in groups, women do not all try to win, but try to achieve the best outcome for all. This was a theme that was touched on in the professional focus group.

Alvesson and Billing (2002) suggest a possible path in gender research involves exploring cultural forms of masculinity and femininity. A central task is to study the way behaviour, work area, feelings, attitudes, priorities and so on, in a particular culture, society, class, organisation or profession, etc., are regarded as masculine or feminine. For me this prompts the questions: is PR masculine or feminine in the context of our society? The answers, as provided by this study's subjects indicate it is feminine. This ties in with Alvesson and Billing (2002), who point to the rise in the number of 'soft' industries (ecology and psychotherapy), saying: "In certain respects the transformation of industry can be described in terms of de-masculinisation." Further in my study, one of WA's most prominent PR practitioners and academics also points to the type of "soft, lifestyle PR" increasingly being practised. Today we use buzzwords such as 'corporate culture' and 'networking', which send signals about the importance of feelings, community, and social relations (all integral and associated with PR). These are attributes, according to Blomqvist, as cited in Alvesson (2002), which are more in accord with femininity.

Taking this a step further to indicate how our culture in turn shapes the notion of feminine or masculine, and in turn shape the way industries (in this case, PR) are perceived, Alvesson and Billing (2002), cite studies by Hines (1992) which suggest that femininity and masculinity refer to four distinct elements in gender construction. Two of these are relevant to PR:

• The gender aura or image of the activity (that is, the ideas that people in the surroundings of the activity have about the work).

• The values and ideas that dominate the activity (p. 13).

If that is the case, it can be said that (a) the gender aura/image of PR is inherently feminine, as evidenced by surveys and comments in this study, and (b) that the dominant values and ideas in PR involve those feminine traits and values highlighted in tables three and four. According to Hines (1992), "the construction of women becomes stronger and more clear cut ... in a particular women-dominated activity [that is, PR]. For example . . . if the activity is regarded as feminine."

Alvesson and Billing (2002) studied the Swedish public service and found, as I will show in Australian (and also US and UK) PR, that "there seems to be an idea it is natural for women to work in the public sector". This finding is not unlike the general consensus of this Study's respondents, that PR is "naturally" women's work. Soderston (1996, as cited in Alvesson) said that because the Swedish public service had grown this way, many people conclude that women can only be employed there. Could this be the case in Australian PR: where PR has evolved (for whatever reasons) into a feminine industry and men simply do not see the doors open? This view is backed by comments in this study's surveys and interviews such as:

- Gender does influence entry into PR because males think PR is women's work. (F student)

- Yes, gender does influence [entry into PR], because it is now pretty well established as a female-dominated profession. (F professional)

- As the numbers of females grow in the industry they tend to influence others to pursue the profession. (M professional)

Stereotyping

> Think of the occupation of accountancy. What image comes to mind?
> Most probably you formed an image of a person, perhaps a prototypical
> accountant or someone you know who holds the job. (Glick, Wilk and
> Perreault 1995, p.570)

Whether or not the above findings have anything to do with how men and women's workplace roles have developed, males and females are still stereotyped. This takes place at an early age. Kimmell (2004) cites the examples of sex segregation occurring in the workplace at a young age, with girls working as babysitters and boys earning pocket money mowing lawns.

Sex segregation is a term coined by sociologist Barbara Reskin (as cited in Kimmel, 2004) which refers to "men's and women's concentration in different occupations, industries, jobs and levels in workplace hierarchies" (p. 188). A year 2000 report by the Singapore Government similarly noted: "the tendency for men and women to be in different occupations" (*Occupation segregation: a gender perspective,* 2000). Different occupations are seen as more appropriate for one gender or the other. "Sex segregation in the workplace is so pervasive that it appears to be the natural order of things – the simple expression of women's and men's natural predispositions" (Reskin, as cited in Kimmel, 2004). You would be forgiven for thinking that if that is the case, people in western societies would be working in different occupations with an equal mix of male and female in each occupation. But that is not the case. There are wild fluctuations, even between cities in the same country. Kimmel (2004) says: "In New York there are only 25 women fire-fighters (.03%) out of 11,500. But in Minneapolis, 17 per cent are women. In the US, dentistry is a male-dominated profession, but in Europe most dentists are female."

According to a report commissioned by the UK Equal Opportunities Commission: "Individuals typically prefer those occupations in which they see their own gender represented" (Miller et al., 2003). In our society, men traditionally have entered the sciences, engineering, accountancy and suchlike. Women have traditionally taken up careers in sales, clerical, nursing, and public relations (Chater and Gaster, 1995). This is backed by Brown (1998) who said: "Communications, marketing and PR are still stereotyped as "female," and therefore less important, tasks." Chater and Gaster (1995) observe that "we may never reach an equal distribution of women and men throughout all occupations, simply because of the genetic imbalance that dictates males and females have different brain patterns". They used the term "genderlects" to show different behavioural patterns between the sexes. Genderlects could best be described as systems of traditional and widely-accepted values influencing the different ways males and females act, or that masculine and feminine styles of communication are best viewed as two distinct cultural dialects and not inferior or superior ways of speaking.

The key differences are outlined in table 5.

Male genderlect patterns	Female genderlect patterns
Status	Intimacy
Independence	Connection
Hierarchy	Minimising differences
Giving instructions and orders	Consensus; giving suggestions
Arguing and interrupting	Harmony; negotiating conflicts
Elaborate systems of rules	Encouraging participation
Winners and losers	Cooperation
Protection	Helping
Silence	A talking/listening process
Responds to problems with solutions and advice	Responds with empathy and understanding

Table 5: The key differences between male and female communication patterns.

Because we recognise a man or a woman, we also form initial opinions about how he or she will act and/or talk. These are stereotypical beliefs we hold, based on the way we have been "socialised". We've come so far, yet have we in the way we pigeon-hole people? My views are backed by several studies. "Gender stereotypes have changed little in the past 20 years" (Aires, 1997, p.92). "People organize their images of occupations in a highly stereotyped, socially-learned manner" (Glick, Wilk and Perreault, 1995, p. 565).

Table 5 (above) displays the commonly-held perceptions we hold about the sexes. But these are simply preconceptions, based on our social conditioning. Aires cites experiments by Wood and Karten (1986); Pugh and Wahrman (1983 and 1995) and Wagner and Ford (1986) which indicated that women can exhibit male genderlect behaviour when preconceived norms are altered. As Aires summarises: "It is time to rethink our understanding of gender to move away from the notion that men and women have two contrasting styles of interaction that are acquired during socialisation – a notion that is promoted by Tannen and in the popular press" (p. 97).

Kimmel (2004) believes that individuals become "gendered" during the course of their lives. "We learn the 'appropriate' behaviours and traits that are associated with hegemonic masculinity and femininity, and then we each, individually, negotiate our own path in a way that feels right to us. In a sense we each 'cut our own deal' with the dominant definitions of masculinity and femininity" (p. 16). This *genderisation* is a result of the mores and/or rules imposed by whatever society a person develop in. Kimmel (2004) believes this, and points to studies by legendary anthropologist Margaret Mead, who was clear that sex differences were 'not something deeply biological', but rather were learned. Mead studied three different cultures in New Guinea: the Arapesh, the Mundagmor and the Tchambuli.

- Tribe 1: All members of the Arapesh appeared gentle, passive and emotionally warm. Males and females were equally happy, trustful and confident. Individualism was relatively absent. Men and women shared child-rearing; both were maternal, and both discouraged aggressiveness among boys and girls.
- Tribe 2: The Mundagmor, a tribe of head-hunters and cannibals, viewed women and men as similar, but expected both sexes to be equally aggressive and violent. The women hated to be child-rearers.
- Tribe 3: The Tchambuli women and men were extremely different. One sex was primarily nurturers and gossipy consumers who dressed up and went shopping. They wore lots of jewellery and were described as 'charming and graceful'. **They were the men.** The women were dominant, energetic, economic providers. They fished, held positions of power, controlled commerce and culture and initiated sexual relations.

"The point is that each culture believed they were that way because of their biological sex, which determined their personality. Mead showed how we can be moulded by our society. Unfortunately, she did not explain why women or men turn out to be different or the same" (Kimmel, 2004, p. 54).

There is a perception that women are nurturers. "When women say: 'I like people,' they are really saying that they are natural nurturers and like to encourage people. There seems to be a widespread belief that women work well with clients" (Cline, 1999, p. 266). This is supported by Kolb (1997) who states: "Women view things in terms of relationships, and this fact affects significant aspects of their social lives. They are oriented towards nurturance and affiliation, and make meaning through interconnection"

(p. 139). Similarly, Gidon Freeman, editor of Britain's *PR Week* believes: "PR is all about developing relationships and bringing influence to bear, which historically women have always mastered better than men." (The gender readership split of *PR Week* in 2004 was 65:35 in favour of women).

Those views would be disputed, however, by a female practitioner who took part in a focus group, who said (somewhat tongue-in-cheek): "I don't think (at work) I've ever nurtured anyone." However, this notion of women being nurturers is outdated, and has its roots in the way Western society has been structured (men at work, women at home), and the fact that mothers, rather than fathers, nurture their children. This, however, is changing, and there is evidence to show that (given the opportunity) men can be as nurturing as women. (Barnett 2004, p.7) certainly believes this, stating:

> There is no evidence of an innate 'maternal instinct' that leads all women
> to be good nurturers. Fathers who are primary caretakers are just as
> nurturant [sic] toward their children. When confronted with the need to
> care for their children, men exhibit the same capacity as women, and
> indeed are indistinguishable in their care-taking from mothers. Fathers
> appear to have the capacity to nurture, although in many situations it is not
> evident because it is not called upon.

There have been several studies that seek to explain gender stereotyping in certain occupations. Rozier et al. (2001) looked at the specific factors influencing career decisions of male students to choose the female-dominant profession of physical therapy, finding that "occupations may be segregated by gender if the particular attributes of the job are viewed as masculine or feminine and if the majority of workers are male or female. Men may be discouraged from selecting a female-dominant profession because of perceptions that the attributes of the job are feminine." As shown later, from this study's interviews and surveys, the perception of the PR industry (and, in the case of students) is that the attributes need to perform PR are seen as being feminine. Rozier et al. (2001) also found that factors such as the belief that female-dominant careers have less social desirability and prestige than male careers also discourage men from pursuing gender-atypical careers.

Brain function

> I've been torn for years between my politics and what science is telling us.
> I believe that women actually perceive the world differently from men. –
> US neuro-psychiatrist Louann Brizendine, as cited in Midgley, (2006).

The subject of brain function is also a relevant topic in discussing male and female differences. It is linked to socialisation, in that are males and females different because of their brains (nature) or of the way their brains are conditioned (nurture)? Brain function is a controversial area, and certainly one that I am not professionally equipped to deal with, other than to weigh current trends. The sheer weight of research on brain function and its relationship to gender is enough to warrant a look at its role (if any) in determining why more women than men enter PR.

In a highly-relevant book on communication, Wahlstrom (1990) is clear in her reasons for including it in an analysis of the topic: "Any examination of women and communication can not proceed without considering the human communicator at the most basic level." Janet Emig (1980, as cited in Wahlstrom, 1990) suggests that "to understand communication processes at all we must know their neuro-psychological underpinnings." According to Moir and Jessel (1996) "the nature and cause of brain differences are now known beyond speculation, beyond prejudice and beyond reasonable doubt" (p. 11).

While brain research data is abundant, it often results in emotional debate, which "reflects the emotional values that come to the fore so readily when issues of nature versus nurture emerge, as they do in analysing intellectual capability" (Wahlstrom, 1990, p.23).

Early research showed there are differences in men's and women's thought processes, characterised by differences in the way the brain operates. Much research has been undertaken highlighting the differences in construction between the male and female brains and how they operate. Psychologist Herbert Landsell (as cited in Chater and Gaster, 1995) found male brains have specific locations for language and spatial skills, while women have the mechanisms for these skills in both hemispheres of the brain. In simple terms, they said: "a typical male brain is more specialised, and a typical female brain is more diffuse". Generally, in creative terms, it means men and women do things and think about things differently.

WOMEN	MEN
Develop language skills earlier. Communicate more fluently.	Process visual and spatial information better
Express and release emotion more easily than men	Greater capacity for mathematical reasoning
Can focus on multiple tasks	Focus more easily on single task

Table 6: Summary of the different thought patterns in men and women (Chater et al.,1995).

The key characteristics of left and right hemispheres are summarised in table 7. From it, the general pattern shows the creative skills, so often presumed to be apparent in women, and traditionally associated with public relations, belong in the right hemisphere, which is where most women's thought processes take place. This, of course, is a generalisation, as some other process necessary in PR (notably, tact, analysis, language and verbal) are located in the left hemisphere. And if women are predominantly "right-brained", how is they are using the brain's left-hand verbal and language functions to do so well in PR?

LEFT	RIGHT
Sequencing	Random
Logic	Intuition
Tact	Creativity, imagination
Words, numbers	Rhythm, music
Black and white	Colour
Small picture	Big picture
Detail, parts	Whole
Reality-based	Fantasy-oriented
Time	Space
Analysis	Synthesis
Thinking	Feelings, emotions
Language, reading	Shapes, patterns
Verbal	Non-verbal
Symbols	Concrete
Listening	Visualisation

Table 7: Key characteristics of the brain's left and right hemispheres.

Unfortunately, for Chater and Tymson, and Moir and Jessel, the method of splitting up the brain's tasks into left and right may be somewhat simplistic. Take the notion of creativity – commonly regarded as a prerequisite for success in PR. *Science Daily*, in reporting on schizophrenia, quotes Vanderbilt University psychologist and researcher Brad Folley, who says: "In the scientific community, the popular idea that creativity exists in the right side of the brain is thought to be ridiculous, because you need both hemispheres of your brain to make novel associations and to perform other creative tasks" (Moran, 2005). Research in the past 20 years has established the fact that areas of the two cerebral hemispheres in humans are specialised for different functions. Wahlstrom 1990, p. 22) cites 11 studies that reach this conclusion. From a series of 13 studies, these are summarised (and simplified), according to Witelson, as cited in Wahlstrom (p. 23) in figure 8 (below).

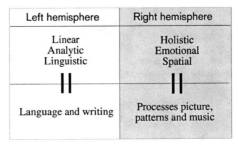

Figure 8: Brain functions.

The major problem with studying brain function as it relates to gender is that traditional ways of viewing what is female and what is male have literally been reversed. In the 70 and 80s we were told the right hemisphere was female, and the left male. According to research in the late 80s and 90s, those positions are reversed. "After centuries of being accused of being devious, intuitive, roundabout and anything but linear in their thought processes, women are suddenly being told that is it, in fact, men who are capable of 'simultaneous integration' and that women are sequential reasoners" (Wahlstrom, 1990, p. 28). Kimmel (2004) also follows this train of thought: "Scientists can't seem to agree on which side of the brain dominates for which sex. They keep changing their minds about which hemisphere is superior, and then, of course, assigning that superior one to men" (p. 33).

Recent research by American neuro-psychiatrist Louann Brizendine, outlined in a review (Midgley, 2006) of her book, *The Female Brain,* points to the fact that men and women simply perceive the world differently because of brain differences. Women, she says, have 11 per cent more neurons in the area of the brain devoted to emotion and memory. "Women tend to use both hemispheres for language tasks, which may be why girls learn to talk earlier than boys" (Midgley 2006) – once again another skill crucial to practicing PR successfully. "Steve Jones, a geneticist and author of *Y: The Descent of Men*, has said that there is absolutely no consensus about this science" (Midgley, 2006).

Despite the shortcoming of this type of science, most researchers agree that women:

- Have "superior linguistic performance related to verbal fluency" (Witelson, 1976, as cited in Wahlstrom, 1990; Moir and Jessel, 1996).

- Have earlier maturation of speech organs (Darley and Witz, as cited in Wahlstrom, p. 29; Moir and Jessel, 1996)

- Are more verbally fluent than males (Gari and Scheinfeld, 1968, as cited in Wahlstrom, 1990; Moir and Jessel, 1996)

- Make fewer grammatical mistakes (Schucard, et al., 1981, as cited in Wahlstrom; Moir and Jessel, 1996)

- Produce more complex and longer sentences (Bennett, Seashore and Wesman, 1959, as cited in Wahlstrom, 1990; Moir and Jessel, 1996).

Wahlstrom (1990) says there are too many hypotheses with differing methodologies, leading to a myriad of results, and also doubts what influence the research would have, but for different reasons. She suggests:

> With such a growing store of frequently inconclusive or contradictory data available it is hard to decide what specific conclusions we can draw regarding gender, brain function and communication. Yet we must consider the issue. We need to encourage more research in order to determine, first, if differences in cognitive functioning exist and, if so, whether or not they are sex differences or differences that are caused by cultural forces. If no sex differences exist in the cognitive 'functionings' of males and females, then in some ways we can carry on pretty much as we have, except that we will have to engage in publicising data that indicate no difference.

Kimmel (2004) highlighted what is probably the most comprehensive study on the subject ever undertaken. Janet Hyde, a psychologist at the University of Wisconsin, reviewed 165 studies of verbal ability that included information about more than 1.4 million people and included writing, vocabulary and reading comprehension. She found no gender differences in verbal ability. She found there is a far greater range of differences among males and among females than there is between males and females. "Many investigators seem determined to discover that men and women 'really' are different. It seems that if sex differences do not exist, then they have to be invented" (Kimmel, 2004).

Gender differences

Grunig, Toth and Hon (2001) imply that there are feminine attributes that make women particularly suited to carry out public relations work. These are listed as "co-operation, respect, caring, nurturance, interconnection, justice, equity, honesty, sensitivity, perceptiveness, intuition, altruism, fairness, morality and commitment". However, they do not delve into the reasons why, but rather concentrate (as most scholars have done) on the discrimination against the appointment of women to senior levels and opposition to the promotion of feminine values when public relations strategy is decided.

Kimmell (2004, p. 15) supports this in a wider context. "In the past 30 years, feminist scholars properly focused most of their attention on women – on what Catherine Stimpson has called the 'omissions, distortions and trivialisations' of women's experiences."

The behavioural sciences provide more insight into the attributes that may point towards women being better at PR than men. Reciniello (1999) refers to "the school of object relations (Fairbairn, 1952; Winnicott, 1965; Klein de Riviere, 1964) [which] also contributed to the psychoanalytic theory of women by enlarging traditional drive theory to encompass a primary drive to create relationships."

In an unpublished thesis, Rea (2002) came closer than Grunig et al. (2000) in trying to analyse the link between gender types and an ability to perform PR. However, it was a fleeting insight into the issue.

> When we think about women, are we really thinking about gender, which we consider biological, or a constellation of socially-determined sex roles, which encompass stereotypical qualities associated with either femininity or masculinity? We all know that not all people biologically classified as "women" act alike. People of either gender may have feminine characteristics. We value the qualities associated with femininity, but of course not all women exhibit female characteristics or are feminine. Not all men act 'masculine'. Men who remain antagonistic to women and to women getting ahead will find themselves increasingly marginalised over time. The modern public relations industry will reflect the enormous changes in gender relations and roles sweeping though society. Therefore, the industry will be best placed to understand and represent the interests of clients and of society.

What is apparent, though, is that in trying to analyse why there are more females than males in PR, one can not ignore sexuality as an issue. There are several theories which provide clues as to why women find PR a 'niche' field.

Noted American PR scholar James Grunig (1992) suggests women are more effective in PR because theirs is a worldview – one that suits the engagement of all publics and leads to balanced, two-way communication. This is backed by research by Smith, as cited in L. Grunig (2001) who found:

> Public relations is a highly intuitive business. The ability to recognise what sort of behaviour brings about what kind of response is a talent inborn in little girls and developed to a higher degree of sensitivity by the time they are through their teens. It's an invaluable asset in public relations. (np)

The common thread that runs through the PR literature is that 'social' factors are a prime motivation. Becker et al. (2003) found "some 63 per cent of the [US] female bachelor's degree recipients said a desire to work with people was a very important reason for their decision to study journalism". Only 41.9 per cent of men nominated this as a reason. While that is not the only motivation, Becker et al. found it to be highly important. Of the women, 29.2 per cent sought a public relations agency job; of the men, only 20.2 per cent sought such a job.

Chater and Gaster (1995) observe that the way business is done today is markedly different from previous eras. The most notable impact of change is the increased emphasis on ethical practice. This includes attention to the environment and the proper treatment of staff. The emphasis on these values can be seen to be more compatible with the way women work, presenting an ideal opportunity for women to take the lead in these areas.

Most people tend to agree that men and women DO think differently. It is just why they think differently that they can not agree on. Is it biology or culture that determines gender differences? There are two schools of thought: biological determinism and differential socialisation, more commonly known as nature and nurture. Men and women could be different because they are naturally that way (nature), or are they different because they've been taught to be (nurtured).

Kimmel (2004) asks: "is biology destiny; or is it that human beings are more flexible and thus subject to change? The answer is an unequivocal maybe. Or, perhaps more accurately, yes and no. Few people would suggest there are no differences between males and females. There are sex differences (anatomical, hormonal, chemical and physical differences). But there are also shades of maleness and female-ness in those areas" (p. 2)

Clearly, despite the hundeds of studies that have been conducted on the subject, there is still no agreement. In fact, many studies on gender differences may not have even been studies, but merely ideas and hypotheses that have taken on lives of their own. However, there is strong belief among students and professionals that gender differences do exist. Whether these are simply a result of conditioning, it is hard to know; particularly considering the wildly differing academic viewpoints that exist. There are those who say gender differences are a result of our cultures, and those who say (as recently as 2005) that the difference is due to biological reasons (Shute, 2005).

According to Alvesson and Billing (2002) "biological differences are not regarded by many as the ultimate determination of the way men and women act". Some feminists believe we should neither exaggerate nor deny the importance of biological differences (Cockburn, 1991). Bearing and nursing children, according to some researchers, does give a women a certain orientation that is quite distinct from men's (Choworow 1978, Hartsock 1987, as cited in Alvesson and Billing, 2002). Others claim that gender can be explained almost exclusively by reference to social processes, irrespective of biological or gender differences. What may look like gender-specific inclinations (that is, in PR) can be better explained in terms of the positions of external social conditions in which men and women find themselves (that is, the rapid increase of women into the workforce, and the appearance of tertiary courses for PR). However, this is a forum to display current thinking among today's professionals and students.

The views expressed by high-profile practitioners are important, as ultimately they do have a considerable influence on the composition of the profession in terms of who is being hired, the type of PR being practised, etc. First, consider the views of several high-profile US female executives.

Muio (1998, p. 17) quotes Sharon Patrick, the president of Martha Stewart Living, who says the differences are all about men 'hunting' and women 'gathering':

> I believe that 'gathering' is at the crux of how women view and use power differently from men . . . Men have tended to demonstrate a 'go-for-the-kill' mentality. They try to get as much as possible through pressure, intimidation, and the sheer desire to defeat at any cost whoever is sitting across the table from them. Women have tended to prefer searching for common interests, solving problems, and collaborating to find win-win outcomes.

Patrick's views were shared in the same article by several other leading female executives. The views give some insight into what leading female executives think about the way power is used differently by male and females and why there are gender differences, but from a corporate viewpoint.

Janice Gjertsen, of Digital City (New York) said:

> Men are oriented toward power, toward making fast decisions in a black-or-white mode. Women are more skilled at relationships. They see shades of gray and explore issues from different angles. It's instinctual. Men come to the negotiating table in full battle armour. What's interesting is that the kinds of companies we admire today are also those that depend increasingly on female attributes. We are in the relationship era: Its all about getting close to customers, striking up joint ventures, partnering with suppliers. Warriors don't make good CEOs in companies based on relationships. The new CEO is a seeder, feeder, and weeder – and those are women's roles.

Harriet Rubin, Founder and Editor at Large Doubleday/Currency, said:

> Women need to become more like men than men are. We need to become hyperaggressive and hyperdetermined - because business is about intense daring and a reckless abandon to succeed. Of course, men have those qualities. It has to do with their once being boys. While girls learn to be good, boys play at being great. And men build their companies the way they used to build their forts - as clubs of exclusion.

Kathryn Gould, General Partner, Foundation Capital:

> Let's be honest: The culture of any management team, even if there are
> women on it, is still a male culture. It all comes down to football. Most
> women haven't played team sports. They don't understand how men feel
> when they're part of a team – the sense of camaraderie, the joy of victory.
> I haven't met many women who are conditioned to touch people's hearts
> as leaders – which is quite different from touching their hearts as
> nurturers.

Sara Levinson, President, NFL Properties Inc:

> My emphasis on group communication, on soliciting their ideas and
> opinions, is a major characteristic of my management style. They also say
> it's why they think I'm a good leader. Is this a distinctly 'female' trait?
> The members of my team - all of them male - seem to think so.

[Barry] Leggeter (2005) highlighted the gender imbalance issues facing the industry,
though did not pursue it far. Responding to articles in *PR Week* on 2 and 12 September
2005, Leggeter, the principal of Bite PR (UK, US and Sweden) expressed concern at the
phenomenon.

> It's the way that our business sells public relations at the
> college/university level that I think needs our attention. Why is it that PR,
> apparently, appeals to less male undergraduates than female? I'm not
> trying to reverse anything. I'm simply concerned with dominance. What I
> am questioning is do we have the right balance in our business? I believe
> this is an issue we should look at thoughtfully and thoroughly. Let's
> simply find out what is happening here – whether it is a recruitment issue
> or a reality that the balance of our account teams has apparently
> irreversibly changed.

In the company's blog site, Leggeter gave the issue further 'airing' and the issue was taken
up be several writers, who agreed with his views. The following response of one particular
female student summed up the feeling of many in my study.

> I was actually curious about the gender in the PR department earlier this
> semester because there is only one to three males at most in my PR
> classes. I think Public Relations is just not that appealing to males as it is
> to females. I also think there maybe a lack of knowledge of exactly what
> you can do with a major in Public Relations. I know a few guys that want
> jobs in areas that a communication or public relations major would be
> ideal. But instead they choose marketing because they think PR is more
> for females. It is natural for women to be better at PR-type task, and
> women are also better at understanding the public than males. Multi-
> tasking and being sensitive to people's needs might not sound that
> enjoyable to [men].

Are these views, which are supported by many of the comments found in both my professional and student surveys, valid? Or have we all simply been duped by faulty research? Barnett and Rivers (2004) cite a study conducted in that year by researchers at Purdue University, which could not find support for the idea that women and men have different 'communication cultures'. The results were based on three studies that used questionnaires and interviews with 738 people – 417 women and 321 men. "Both men and women view the provision of support as a central element of close personal relationships; both value the supportive communication skills of their friends, lovers, and family members; both make similar judgments about what counts as sensitive, helpful support; and both respond quite similarly to various support efforts." Barnett and Rivers describe a range of what they call 'bandwagon concepts', as dangerous. Among these are:

Women are inherently more caring and more 'relational' than men.

For girls, self-esteem plummets in early adolescence.

Boys have a mathematics gene, or at least a biological tendency to excel in maths, that girls do not possess.

> "While the industrial society was created by men for men, the information
> society needs people, both male and female, who are well educated and
> technically trained. This has created a unique opportunity for women, as
> all levels of business are now potentially open to us." (p. 8)

It is also widely recognised that women are better at relationship-building. After all, public relations is about the relationship between an organisation and its publics. Grunig (2001) cites studies by Reif, Newstrom and Monzka (1978) and Knowles and Moore (1970) that demonstrate women have a greater concern for relationships. "The two-way symmetrical model of public relations requires resolving conflict and building relationships, which are intrinsically feminist values" (Grunig, Toth and Hon, 2000). Many of the attributes necessary for PR professionals are outlined by Chater and Gaster (1995), who state:

> We are moving from industrialisation, where the patriarchal model
> worked brilliantly, to an era where our survival and progress will not
> depend on not our ability to set rules, control production lines, establish
> bureaucracies, assert status and focus on the bottom line, but rather on our
> ability to communicate, negotiate, work with emotions, create solutions to
> ever-changing problems and opportunities, respond to change, think
> globally and strategically and work with and value people . . . The playing
> field is moving in the direction of feminine values, so what the 'game'
> now needs are the skills that women can bring to it. (p. 10)

Cline, as cited in Newsom, et al. (2000), alludes to the problem being not only just the large numbers of women entering the profession, but to the innate skills females bring to PR being responsible for the industry's low standing.

> The major problem facing public relations' move into top management today may be not only the large percentage of women in the field, but the dominance of the profession by the intuitive. An intuitive worker seeks the furthest reaches of the possible and the imaginative, and is comparatively uninterested in the sensory reports of things as they are. This conflicts with the methodology of a sensate worker, who prefers an established way of doing things, relying upon skills already learned, working steadily, and focusing on now. The sensate type of worker accounts for 70 to 75 per cent of the American population.

Gender issues, however, are a complex matter. Not all women (or men) act alike. People of either gender may have feminine characteristics, and vice-versa. While most females have certain feminine characteristics, not all women are feminine. Similarly, not all men act masculine.

The literature also provides some statistical clues, fragmented as they are, regarding the rise in the number of women within PR.

US Department of Labor statistics for public relations in 1960 showed 25 per cent of the PR workforce were women. This increased to 51 per cent in 1983, 65.7 per cent in 2000. At the same time, membership of the PRSA went from 10 per cent women members in 1968 to 15 per cent (1975), 54 per cent in 1990 and 60 per cent in 2000 (Figure 3). By early 2002, 69 per cent of the practitioners surveyed were female (Andsager and Hust, 2004). Female participation in America's other peak communications body, the IABC, is 76 per cent (Willams, 2002).

The Occupational Employment Statistics Survey (US Department of Labor 2004) reports "employment of public relations specialists … is expected to grow faster than the average for all occupations through 2012" (OES Survey, May 2004). Similarly, the United States Department of Labor Bureau of Labor Statistics' *Career Guide to Industries* reports that "public relations jobs are projected to increase by at least 19 per cent through 2012, compared to a 16 per cent growth rate average in all other industries".

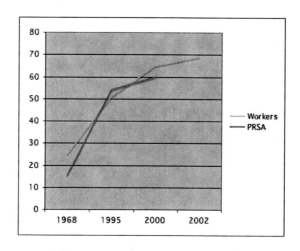

Figure 9: Rise of American women in PR from 1960–2000.
Sources: US Dept. of Labor and PRSA. Gap in years due to lack of statistics.

Year	Total	Male	Female	% Female
1950	18,565	16,607	1958	10.5
1960	30,363	23,358	7005	23.1
1970	80,302	58,906	21,396	26.6
1980	120,037	61,442	58,595	48.8
2000	129,000	49,000	80,000	62
2002	136,000	38,000	65,000	63.1
2003	129,000	43,000	85,000	63.4
2004	133,000	52,000	81,000	66.4

Table 8: There has been a steady increase in number of women entering PR
from 1950–2004 (Source: US Dept of Labor).

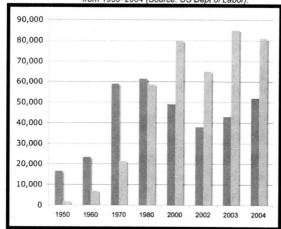

Figure 10: In the US, there has been a steady increase in women entering PR,
and a leveling of male entry. Source: US Dept of Labor.

The increasing number of women in PR [in the US], is demonstrated in Table 8 and Figure 10 (above) from the Department of Labor (Martin, 1993; US Dept. of Labor, 2005) showing women's representation increasing markedly, from 10.5 per cent in 1950 to 66.44 per cent in 2004.

The trend is mirrored at US universities.

"Since 1977 the majority of students enrolled in (US) journalism and mass communication programs have been female. In the early 1980s, national enrolment patterns stabilised at about 60 per cent female to 40 per cent male, and a similar ratio has also become the norm for graduates of mass communication programs" (Peterson, as cited in Creedon, 1989, p. 14).

In a follow-up report on the *Velvet Ghetto*, Cline (1986) reported that "female (US) communications students outnumbered men by more than 8 to 1 [and that] communication may soon be 80 per cent female". The prophecy may be proved correct, as Cline (1999) reported that at the University of Texas in 1985 the figure was close to 90 per cent female.

> Fact. For more than a decade, women have made up the majority of students enrolled in American schools of journalism and mass communication. Fact: these female graduates are finding employment and due to this influx of women, mass communication is becoming a female-intensive occupational category" (Creedon 1989, p. 16).

Beasly (1999) also considers the impact of journalism within communications. In 1985 the University of Maryland College of Journalism released preliminary findings of a study that called attention to the 'new majority' in schools of journalism and mass communication. This referred to the growing influx of young women, who had changed the balance of journalism school enrolment from predominantly male to predominantly female in less than a decade. At that time journalism enrolment was about 60 per cent female.

"In 1977, when [US] journalism enrolment nationally reached a record 64,000, the proportion of women students reached more than 50 per cent, but little notice was taken. Today, two-thirds of all graduates (64.1 per cent) are women" (Beasley, 1999). Journalism enrolments at Perth universities also show more females than males study the subject. At Curtin University, the institution with the largest number of students in Mass Communication, the breakdown for journalism from 2001–05 shows a constant predominance of women. Statistics for 2005 fell for both male and female, but this can be explained by a general national downturn in applications for university places across all subjects.

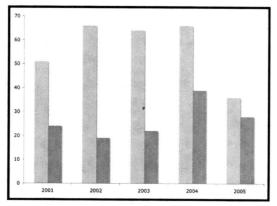

Figure 11: Journalism enrolments at Curtin University. Source: Curtin University.

Interestingly, this has not manifested itself within the Perth media industry, where the ratio is 57 per cent male (256) to 43 per cent female (195). Ten news organisations were surveyed in April 2006. Some within the industry expressed surprise at the figure. However, that is probably because we tend to be influenced by what we see, and to a lesser extent, hear. Most newsreaders and weather presenters tend to be female; particularly in Perth radio.

	Female	Male
Channel 9	12	4
Channel 10	12	9
Community newspapers	29	24
Radio 6PR	3	4
Channel 7	8	12
ABC Radio and TV	20	18
Nova FM	3	0
92.9/94.5 FM	1	0
Sunday Times	22	37
West Australian	85	148
TOTAL	195	256

Table 9: Perth news media employment (journalists only).
These include chiefs of staff and news editors. Source: direct from each organisation.

"[In Europe] the share of women [journalists] has stagnated at around one third, [while] the growing field of public relations continues to attract increasing numbers of women" (Dorer, 2005, p. 185). In Australia, the situation is little different. There is certainly no dominance if either gender within the major media outlets in Perth. In a census (6 April

2006) of all but one Perth news organisations (Community Newspaper Group, ABC radio and TV, three commercial TV channels and four radio newsrooms) there were 72 males and 73 female journalists. However, the balance is slightly tipped by the large number of males employed at *The West Australian*. The drift of women from journalism into PR may be because that women in journalism simply find entrenched male attitudes and behaviour (that is, chauvinistic, hard-drinking, prying, etc.) still too prevalent and 'overbearing', so they choose a more values-orientated and 'family-friendly' industry such as PR. The notion of the family-friendliness of PR has been raised in several interviews conducted, and noted in surveys, during this study. As mentioned elsewhere, female practitioners regard PR as a flexible occupation in which the hours and location, to a large degree, can be moulded to suit the demands of working mothers. For [most] males, this would probably not be a consideration. On the other hand, the entry of women into communications courses may simply be a result of more women studying. That's certainly the view of Sydney academic Matthew Byrne, of the University of Technology, who said in a phone interview with me:

> In New South Wales we have an extremely high UAI (Universities
> Admissions Index) score to enter communications courses – PR and
> journalism. It's 96 per cent, and we attract the top four per cent of the
> State's students, who happen to be women. So you look at the HSC
> (Higher School certificate) and there is a female dominance at the top.

This move of women into PR may be explained by several other factors affecting the general workforce, as outlined by Wootten (1997), including "the advances of the women's movement, the enactment of laws prohibiting sex discrimination, increases in female enrolment in higher education and professional schools, the steady increase in women's labor force participation, and reductions in gender stereotyping in both education and employment". One of the biggest factors in the sudden rise of women into the (US) PR workforce was the advent of affirmative action in the 1970s. Legislation forced companies to hire a certain percentage of women. "Employers may have found it useful to place women in visible positions" (Donato, 1990, p. 135).

Certainly PR in Australia, the US and UK has 'ridden the expansive wave' of jobs creation, sucking up eager graduates. "The [US] Bureau of Labor Statistics tagged public relations as one of the three fastest-growing industries in the United States (No. 1 is computer and data processing services, and No. 2 is health services)" (Brown, 1998). How could PR not fail to attract women, who benefited not just by an expanding labour force, but by new workforce rules? US Department of Labor statistics show between 1975 and

1995 women's employment in areas of professional specialty, which PR is part of, grew by 53 per cent (9,800 to 18,100) – the highest growth rate of 12 general employment categories. Generally, it can be said that "in the past 15 years, women entered the workforce in ever-increasing numbers" (Wootton, 1997).

Donato (1990) is another of the few academics to have broached the reason/s for women entering PR, points to several reasons for the rise of women in the profession. These included:

• Some [employers] saw women as a better financial **'bargain'**. Women were (and probably still are) disproportionately represented as technicians, while men were in management positions. Women stayed in those roles longer than men. The wage gap was maintained. "Women earned less, therefore were a better bargain" (np). However, Donato does not explain why this happened. Certainly the fact that women remained in technician roles longer than men may be connected to their careers being interrupted to have families. I found anecdotal evidence of this in surveys and focus groups. Or was/is it simply a case of men seeking to maintain their positions of power?

• Women were recognised as a new and important **'public'**. As far back as the 1940s it was recognised women could help shape opinion. "The expansion of women's consumer roles [buyers] made them advertising [and presumably PR] targets" (np).

• The (presumed) **nature of women** being 'nice' and being suited to 'emotional work'. This type of PR may be prevalent in industries that dump waste, or have unsafe or controversial products. "People [presumably management] believe women have better interpersonal skills" (np). Once again, this is influenced by the way we are 'socialised' and conditioned to accept traditional notions about gender.

• Financially, PR generally offered better **opportunities** than journalism, which had a (US) female population of 60 per cent in the 1980s, and which continues to be a career path for many practitioners. In fact PR offered rewards which were/are "competitive with other accessible occupations, and is better paid than the average female job" (np).

The pay situation is similar in Europe. Dorer (2005) asserts that pay is one factor which attracts more females than males. "PR offered 'varied opportunities', 'attractive pay levels' and "promotion' – as reasons for attracting females" (p. 187). However, those factors would be equally as appealing to males and surely would not be valid reasons for the growth of females into PR in Austria and Germany. Certainly, if the pay of PR people was so good in those countries, men would have deserted journalism. One suspects that the pay may not have been as good, as Dorer (2005) believes.

The most comprehensive [US] survey of communications students is the Annual Survey of Journalism and Mass Communication Enrolments, which has operated at the Henry W. Grady College of Journalism and Mass Communication at the University of Georgia since September 1997. While not wishing to draw too much on US research, it is necessary, owing to the lack of material in Australia. The parallels between American practice and ours are strikingly similar; probably because a high percentage of university course content is American.

Becker et al. (2004) summarised the findings of the 2003–04 study, which surveyed 463 journalism and mass communication programs (194,500 students) thus:

• Women were more than twice as likely as men to have majored in public relations.

• Female students were about twice as likely as male students to have had an internship in public relations.

• Female graduates on graduation are more likely to have sought work in public relations.

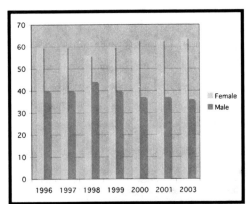

Figure 12: Percentage of women and men enrolled in undergraduate communication courses at all US universities 1996–2003 (Becker, et al.).

While that survey is comprehensive, it is the only survey of PR students. With the industry now being fuelled almost exclusively by students, now is the time to undertake research in that area. As Noble (2004) points out: "A review of literature reveals virtually no research related to the specific reasons why public relations students select the major."

The US statistics show women clearly outnumber men, with male enrolments slowly declining from 44 per cent since 1998. These statistics cover the entire US, and there are bound to be discrepancies, as is the case at the University of San Jose. In e-mail correspondence of 19 April 2005 between myself and Prof. Dennis Wilcox, head of PR at the University of San Jose, Wilcox said: "In many of our classrooms now, it's almost like teaching in a women's college. About 80 per cent of our PR majors are women."

The statistics are strikingly similar in the UK. Hall (2005) refers to an article on the *Icbirmingham* (2004) website, which states: "According to latest membership figures released by the [now Chartered] Institute of Public Relations, women now outnumber men by 60:40 – a massive swing since 1987, when figures highlighted the opposite at 20:80."

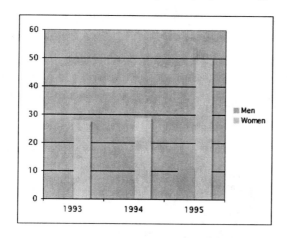

Figure 13: The rise of female enrolments in PR courses at US universities from 1993–95.

In Australia, for example, the Royal Melbourne Institute of Technology (RMIT) public relations undergraduate degree course's trend has been similar. In 1993, a total of 28 women and six men graduated. In 1994, 29 women and seven men graduated. In 1995, 50 women and 11 men graduated.

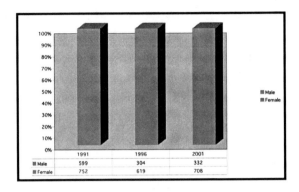

Figure 14: Rapid increase of female graduates at RMIT, 1993–95.

Australian Bureau of Statistics workforce figures taken over three censuses in 1991, 1996 and 2001 for PR in Western Australia show women clearly dominating the field. A breakdown for Perth is not available. However, as there are few PR professionals operating out of the metropolitan area in WA (due to the few major regional towns), it can safely be stated the figures are an accurate reflection of the numbers employed in the profession in Perth.

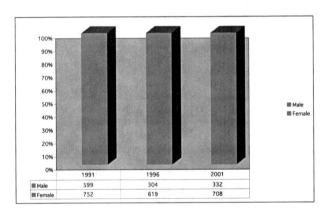

Figure 15: Australian Bureau of Statistics Census figures for public relations practitioners in Western Australia. Source: ABS 2005.

NB: The above graph is perhaps not an ideal representation, as the 1991 Census figures do not accurately reflect the industry participation rates, as PR practitioners were grouped with marketing and advertising.

From the most recent two Censuses (1996 and 2001) the trend in Western Australia (and Australia) shows women as predominant, occupying 68 per cent of the workforce in 1996 and 67 per cent in 2001. Nationally the percentage of women in PR was 60 per cent in 1996, rising to 67 per cent in 2002.

	Female practitioners		Male practitioners	
	WA	Aust.	WA	Aust.
1996	619	7240	304	3613
2001	708	8117	332	3936

Table 10: ABS Census figures for PR Officers (national and WA) 1996 and 2001.

From ABS figures (Table 10 and Figure 15, above) it can be seen that the growth in PR practitioners from 1996 to 2001 has favoured women, both nationally and in WA. In WA (read Perth) the number of women employed in PR increased by 89, while the number of males employed in PR rose by 28. Nationally the trend showed women increasing their majority, with 877 women joining the ranks, compared to 323 men. More current statistics are presented as part of the methodology (Chapter 3).

The ABS figures do not indicate as marked a difference in male and female participation rates in PR as does my 2005 survey, which shows industry participation rates at 74 per cent for women. The main factor for this discrepancy could simply be the continued increase in the number of female graduates. The ABS survey also depends on people's honesty when listing their occupation. PR has traditionally been an occupation in which people say "oh, I'm in PR" (which, for them, could cover many different areas, including hostessing and function management.

More work opportunities for women

The needs of today's information age have created more opportunities for women. Manual work within western society has decreased and been replaced by a knowledge-based economy based on the use of computers and other technology. "Mental tasks have replaced mechanical ones. Work is what goes on inside people's heads at desks, on airplanes, in meetings, at lunch. It is how they communicate with clients, what they write in memos, what they say at meetings" (Naisbitt and Aburdene, as cited in Chater, 1995). This new way of working, particularly when applied to public relations, is ideally suited to women, who not only can exercise their penchant for language, creativity and communication, but also adapt to the new environment simply because they haven't learnt the old work ways (physical labour). Because women can handle multi-tasking better than men, they would also be better suited and attracted to public relations because of the growing demand for practitioners to be multi-skilled (web design, publications, writing, strategic planning).

In a article for *Salon* magazine, (Brown, 1998) had a "stab" at the reasons why women enter PR.

> Public relations jobs currently pay significantly more than, say, a newspaper job. Public relations also entices young careerists with its management potential and the opportunity to learn business skills, plus it's a flexible career that can be used as an entryway to any industry, from entertainment to high-tech.

It may be interesting to pause and consider Brown's comments. She compares PR to journalism in terms of pay. However, because the two fields overlap in many of the skills needed (writing, news-gathering, interviewing) and the fact that journalism initially was the main source of PR practitioners (until the advent of university courses) that a comparison between the two might also extend to creativity. This factor was mentioned by several respondents in my surveys and in interviews and is covered in more depth later on. Most participants, however, regarded PR as the more "creative" of the two professions. Hamilton (1999) said: "the general consensus is that journalism killed their (journalists') natural creativity".

With all the advantages they have (on paper at least) it would seem women are ideally placed to break through the 'glass ceiling'. However, that still seems a way off. With communication such a powerful tool, and one that women use better than men, experts are fearful of the future. "These natural advantages have not so far benefited women in the business world" (Chater and Gaster, 1995). Just as Tymson laments the fact that women are not perceived to be serious contenders for the boardroom, Chater and Gaster (1995) also point to our social structures which work against women. "Women, especially in business have been forced to change in the direction of conforming to the male picture of the world." However, this has created opportunities in information-based fields such as PR. The changes brought about by the information age can be seen as favourable to women, as "the needs of the information age are inconsistent with the structures, bureaucracies and rules of the industrial era" (Chater and Gaster, 1995).

Conclusion

Chapter Two was concerned with the research issues, as derived from a comprehensive review of the available literature. The review included research from the immediate (PR) discipline and, because of its subject nature (gender imbalance), extended into the social sciences (gender studies), touching on psychology, brain differences (thought patterns). It also compared PR to other industries with a gender imbalance. There was a detailed presentation of statistics on PR employment from the Australian Bureau of Statistics, which was found to correlate with my own census of the Perth PR population. These figures also closely matched enrolment figures for the four Perth universities – all showing a steady increase in the number of women studying and entering PR.

The literature review showed:

- An overall lack of study into the issue.
- Though some figures date to the 1960s, the issue was "formally" identified in the 1970s, but only came to prominence in the 1980s, but with most studies focusing on salary and management inequalities for women in PR.
- The first UK study into the phenomenon was undertaken in 2005.
- The main cause of the rise of women in PR in Australia is attributed to the introduction of PR degrees in the 1960s.
- In Australia, figures show there was a 50/50 gender split in PR in the 1980s. By 1997 this had risen to 70/30 in favour of females.
- There is an issue of PR becoming typecast as "women's work" and a second-class" occupation. This has been labelled "recoding", and it has happened in several industries throughout the past 50 years (IT, clerical and veterinary science). Some academics believe this has already occurred in PR and will lead to a "cheapening" of the profession.
- Socialisation plays an important part in the way we perceive PR.
- Perceptions of occupations play a vital part in whether males of females enter them. PR's problems are that it is perceived as being "girlie, flaky, fuzzy and/or soft".
- Women are better than men at the base skills that are vital in PR (the ability to listen, form lasting relationships, speak and write English.

3 Methodology

> Phenomena are really out there, and we discover their nature by through
> finding appropriate measures. Metaphors are re-phrasing of what is there,
> and metaphors are never completely right or wrong. The investigator must
> cover many possibilities and alternative interpretations, casting a wide net,
> quickly identifying and abandoning those measures that show nothing,
> and moving lightly to avoid being buried in the data. (Faulkner, Maanen
> and Dabbs, 1984, p. 60)

Introduction

In order to show why more women than men are entering the PR profession it was necessary to use a variety of methods to prove and explain the phenomenon. I have used two methods in the research, making this a mixed methodology approach – being a combination of quantitative and qualitative research.

Primarily, the form of research is phenomenological, in that it has "taken place in natural 'everyday' settings and (was) not preceded by research questions, as in positivistic research" (Allison et al., 1996). The leaning towards phenomenalism is also reflected by observation of the phenomenon being studied (the increase of women in PR) and that there is a clear choice on what was being observed (student and practitioner numbers). However, there is also an element of positivism, in that initial consistencies in patterns of female employment and university enrolment were noted through the use of quantitative data (e-mail and phone surveys). The methodologies used, therefore, are a mix of qualitative and quantitative, with the emphasis heavily on qualitative (focus groups and interviews).

Overall, however, the research could be categorised, according to a definition offered by McNiff, et al. (2003) as 'action-based', as it is being conducted by a "practitioner [who regards himself] as a researcher, and it is qualitative, concerned with human experience" (p. 14). The qualitative nature of this research project fits neatly with all of the above, and the following processes, as "qualitative research is concerned with individuals' own accounts of their attitudes, motivations and behaviour ... [and] offers rightly descriptive reports of individuals' perceptions, attitudes, beliefs, views and feelings" (Hakim, 1987).

Hughes (2005) used this method in his DBA thesis, noting that "while academics have consistent views regarding research rigour and relevance, they had developed varying philosophies and approaches to achieve those outcomes" (p. 7). It became clear to me that research students do not have to rely solely on the traditional positivist approach or isolate themselves from their natural environment to conduct credible research. In fact, they can achieve rigorous, relevant, timely and realistic studies by identifying emerging phenomena within their own profession. This interaction between student-academic, student-employee and industry is effective because not only does it provide access to rich data sources, "it also allows for the observation of complex organisational environments where many important variables are at play" (Fernandez, Lehman and Underwood, 2002, as cited by Hughes, 2005). Action research also has both a personal and social aim. My personal aim was to further improve my ability to undertake higher-level research. The social (or professional) aim of this research was to provide the base for future research on a topic I find fascinating and one which may have wide implications for the industry.

The techniques used are a combination of:

Historical information (university course enrolment data)

Descriptive information (surveys, case studies and trend studies)

"Rich" information (focus groups and interviews, with myself as observer)

The initial survey methodology was, in effect, a census of the 'population', defined as the Perth PR industry, which comprises six key groups, as outlined in Chapter One. The purpose was to examine whether the phenomenon existed. Additionally, another census was taken of a similar industry 'population', the media. The purpose of this second census was to compare the way in which the two populations differed in their composition, and to prove the research problem did exist (that is, whether women did actually form the numerically-dominant group within public relations, primarily in Perth). Additionally, as part of the initial data collection, I have included statistics, fragmented as they are, from various US publications to highlight the increase in the number of women entering PR during the past 20 years. These statistics are incorporated into the literature review, as they appeared only in passing in general literature and did not form any separate studies in their own right.

Justification for the paradigm and methodology

The approach taken follows Oliver's (2004) outline of paradigms; this being one of naturalistic enquiry, in which qualitative and naturalistic approaches (literature review, focus groups, interviews) form the predominant part of the research process, with a view to bringing about a rich understanding of people's experience in specific settings (in this case, the PR work and academic environment). Paton (1990) as cited in Merriam (1998) argues that "the logic and power of purposeful sampling lies in selecting information-rich cases for study in depth".

The primary population is defined as the Perth PR industry.

The population sampling frames consisted of three sub groups:

- Students
- Practitioners, private business and consultants, government PR, non-profit PR, private PR)
- Academics (minor).

The four universities could not provide staff details. These were taken from the Internet, and reflect numbers that teach in the generic "communications" discipline. Academics were therefore not surveyed, but some were included in the interviews. The number of PR-specific academics in Perth is likely to be no more than 12-15 fulltime staff, which would have little effect on the gender composition of the primary population, nor on the result of survey information. In fact, academics do not comprise a core component of the population (the industry, which I define as those working in, or about to work in the commercial sector). However, academics' opinions were considered to have great value in the qualitative research phase; particularly as they would have been able to observe the traits and trends of the student population. For that reason they were included in interviews.

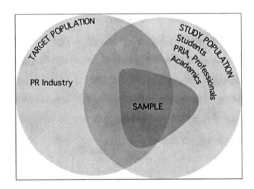

Figure 16: Target population and sub-groups.

A census of the entire population was conducted to gather the initial statistics on how many males and females comprise the industry in Perth. The definition of a census is "the collection of information from all members of a population" (Broom and Dozier, 1990). This was considered the best method because the population is small, and "not every public is so large that sampling is necessary" (Broom and Dozier, 1990). I conducted the census by phoning every PR consultancy listed in the Perth metropolitan phone book, and every government Department PR division. I phoned all 62 PR practices listed in the 2005 Perth Yellow Pages. About 15 of the businesses listed had closed, giving a total of 47 practices contacted.

A phone census of all 30 WA (Perth-based) Government Departments with PR professionals was undertaken, with a 100 per cent return. Respondents were asked to provide the number of fulltime male/female workers involved directly in the PR function.

The four Perth universities offering PR Degrees or PR majors (Edith Cowan, Curtin, Notre Dame and Murdoch) were asked to provide student enrolment statistics, with male/female breakdown, in communications courses (and PR where possible) for as many years as possible. All four responded.

All companies, government agencies, charities and universities provided figures. By conducting a census, exact information about the entire population could be obtained, rather than relying on estimates about the population based on a sample. The census was conducted between 21 February and 18 March, 2005.

The PRIA State and national bodies were contacted by e-mail and asked to supply membership figures (male/female) for as many years as possible. Unfortunately, neither body could provide statistics other than for the current financial year (2004–05).

A purposive sample was obtained by sending e-mails to all 126 accredited practitioners listed on the PRIA's national website (the PRIA only lists members who consent to public listing).

The population was initially stratified into two industry groups (university students and practitioners) and then further stratified. University students were broken into second- and third-year students (male and female). First-year students were not included as it was deemed many had not yet decided to study PR as a Major. Practitioners were broken into the following groups (government PR, not-for profit PR, private practice).

Because the number of elements in the sub-groups were unknown and could not be individually identified, the sampling design of these groups meant initial surveys were conducted using non-probability purposive sampling, which is used in certain circumstances, as outlined by Trochim (2002) "where it is not feasible, practical or theoretically sensible to do random sampling." Miles and Huberman (1994) and Merriam

(1998) also agree that "non-probability sampling is the method of choice for most qualitative research . . . to solve such problems as discovering what occurs, the implications of what occurs, and the relationships linking occurrences". For me, this method was used, not because it was convenient, but because it meant all sub-groups had an equal opportunity to provide details.

As the aim is not to show bias (Kumar, 1999) every university, practitioner and government department was contacted and given the opportunity to provide details. The sampling frame list covered the entire population. The methodology was also deemed purposive, as I judged those sub-groups could "provide the best information to achieve my study's objectives" and that the people in the groups listed "are likely to have the required information and be willing to share it" (Kumar, 1999, p.276). These are features of many qualitative studies. The size of the professional census reflected the relatively small number of practitioners in Perth.

Instrument design

The primary measurement devices to examine PR practitioners' levels of knowledge and opinions of the issue, were two initial surveys − one each for professionals and students − focus groups and interviews. These attitudinal questionnaires used a mix of closed (75 per cent) and open-ended, unprompted questioning. The aim was to gauge people's attitudes, beliefs and opinions about gender in PR. The questionnaires were first pilot-tested on a group of 10 PR professionals and 10 PR second and third-year students (five male and five female of each). Surveys were also validated by consultation with supervisors and two Perth-based academics, Dr Doug McGhie and Vince Hughes (then an MBA, now Dr). Survey construction was analysed and tested by Brisbane PR consultant Sonia Palazzo and Sydney communications professional Paul Ellercamp. The statistical validity and reliability of the data was verified by Kevin Murray, from the mathematics department at the University of Western Australia.

The key constructs being measured in the surveys included:

- the population's level of awareness of gender imbalance,

- the level of importance the population attached to gender in PR,

- the attitude of the population to gender imbalance.

The procedure of measurement in the survey contained a mix of nominal and ordinal scales. The first third of the surveys contained questions designed to give a nominal measurement by building profiles of individuals in terms of sex, years in the profession, income, level of experience and areas of specialisation. In the second part of the surveys, respondents had to provide answers based on an ordinal (scaled or ranked) level of measurement, relating to aspects of the careers/study such as levels of satisfaction, areas of interest and perception of gender in PR. These questions used a mix of itemised and comparative ratings.

The final 12 questions contained a mix of closed questions (yes/no options) but with additional space for respondents to make open-ended comments on the reasons for their answers. No questions made any statements about aspects of the PR industry. This was considered the best way to avoid misunderstanding and to elicit unbiased answers, and follows the thinking of Davis and Cosenza (1985), who state that "different people attribute different meanings to the same word and all individuals have a different frame of experience when reading and interpreting questions." The use of open-ended sub-questions also worked in tandem to produce a more in-depth understanding of respondents' thoughts, beliefs and attitudes.

A second survey of students was conducted from mid-January to mid-February 2005. This web-based survey consisted of 10 questions, designed to further expand on the year's worth of research undertaken (at that time). The additional survey was prompted by two factors: (a) It had become apparent that the focus of my study should be students, as they are the sub- group where the phenomenon is taking place and will be most influential on the industry in the coming years, and (b) influenced by separate pieces of research conducted in 2005 by two US students, Rebecca Folmar and Gina Noble, on the same topic. It should be noted that these students' questions were not used directly (merely as guidelines), as many of them I thought not worthwhile (such as asking students if they would interrupt their careers to have children – this because students probably would not be thinking about having children). In any event, most of their questions had been framed in my initial survey. Questions are contained in the annexes. The overall aim, however, was to consider what influences students to major in PR, and what (if any) differences are there between gender with regard to this.

In order to reach an even more in-depth understanding of the complex issues of my study, an "active interview" methodology for focus groups was used to research the way professionals view the industry. This approach to qualitative interviewing, outlined by Holstein and Gubrium (1995), recognises that interviews are not free from subjectivity and that the researcher is integral in creating meaning and understanding through a loosely-structured format with the participants. The researcher guides the conversation according to the research agenda, and the questions presented are intended to provoke responses that address these agenda.

The aim of the qualitative process (interviews and focus groups) was to study some of the results that have turned up in the quantitative survey in depth, but also to bring out some new perspectives and to review them as they were seen by PR professionals and students.

In the professional focus group, practitioners discussed [what they thought were] the most interesting problems brought to light by this study. The result of this discussion may provide further inspiration by putting the new results of the surveys into perspective.

This approach allowed for flexibility in the research process, allowing the researcher to ask additional questions that explore the research questions in further detail than a formal, structured interview methodology. PR academic James Grunig (1992) specifically recommended qualitative methods for gaining deeper, more candid responses with research participants than quantitative research can assess, especially for groups such as PR practitioners, who may not respond to a survey. According to Grunig, the semi-structured and in-depth interview may also advance a researcher's ability to understand what the interviewee really thinks about an issue. This allows for a measure of introspection and more detailed answers than would have been provided if a formal process was followed. Also, the act of interviewing the participants face-to-face in their own environment was intended to increase the comfort level of the subjects, and increase the flow of communication.

The method of collecting and collating initial survey data was labour-intensive. No research assistant was used. An initial e-mailing announcing my study was sent in May 2005 to 146 potential practitioners. (Methods were outlined in chapter 3). This was the maximum number possible, due to privacy limitations imposed by the PRIA and by companies and government departments who could not provide personal details of employees, or pass on details to them. My study was also publicised on the PRIA's national web site and in the WA Branch's newsletter. A total of 63 Perth professionals eventually participated, with 40 indicating their intention to be interviewed, and a 11 being available for a focus group.

In collecting professional survey data, the following procedure was followed:

1.   Surveys were received by e-mail and the data collated in MS Excel, from where all responses were calculated.

2.   Copies were made of the original MS Word surveys, with the originals being filed. From the copied files, questions 1–15 (multiple choice) were deleted. Questions 16–26 were edited and converted to text-only format for importation into HyperResearch, a Mac-based qualitative data analysis program.

3.   Separate projects for both the professional and student surveys were set up in HyperResearch.

4.   The analysis depended on defining coding (key words or phrases) which were identified in the editing process and then applied to each survey response.

Each (initial professional and student) survey return took about one hour to process. After analysis, the results were then written into the thesis.

A total of 128 responses were received for the final web-based and "in-house" (student-only) survey, which was limited to 10 questions, seeking further information on the personality traits of PR students. A total of 30 responses were also received via a web-based survey, hosted by Web Monkey, from a contact list of 57 students, giving a response rate of 66 per cent. A further 116 surveys of second- and third-year students were conducted at the two major universities (Curtin and ECU) in March 2006. A total of 18 were invalid.

The choice of qualitative interviews opens the possibility of gradations, as well as more intricate studies, updated regular interpretations, and the raising of important issues. The use of personal interviews has also been used to generate ideas, and provided room for wider analysis of the phenomenon, due to the interviewees being allowed to raise subjects themselves. Furthermore, the subjects were able to express wishes and make recommendations in other areas of PR, which, while not central to, is an important aim of this project.

The dialogue with the practitioners and students was mostly informal, but comprised questions chosen and formulated on the basis of results from the surveys. This increases the possibility of making a comparison of the interviews, which were all conducted by myself. This minimised any differences that may have occurred if several interviewers were used. Questions and locations were standardised in order to assist in the production of unbiased data. The selection of respondents who can participate in the qualitative survey (interviews and focus groups) was limited to the people forming part of the quantitative section, and who have agreed to take part in the qualitative survey.

For the purpose of being able to identify generalised patterns in motives, attitudes and opinions in connection with being a PR professional or student, a number of themes were selected. The interpretation of the interviews was systematised by reviewing, editing and analysing the interviews in relation to the following themes:

- What motivated the subject to enter PR.
- Their opinions on imbalance.
- Did they think males or females were better-suited to PR?

The identifiable patterns that can be "generalised" in relation to these themes are supported by and built up in the report around selected quotations from the interviews, but new and interesting points of view are also presented. Thereby this part of the analysis is also used to generate ideas.

Because much of the research (interviews, focus groups, open-ended questions) was qualitative, and therefore subjective, it has been recommended that my "personal experience be recognised prior to such analysis" (Morse and Richards, 2002). Accordingly, it should be noted that as the primary researcher in this study, I am a public relations and journalism professional, with more than 20 years experience, both in the public and private sectors. While conducting this study I was working initially part-time as a PR Officer for the Army, and then fulltime contract work for the Australian Maritime Safety Authority, WA Office for Seniors Interests, WA Department of Agriculture, Australian Bureau of Statistics (mid to late 2006). I completed my thesis while working fulltime as the senior PR Officer for RAAF Air Command in Sydney (September-November 2006).

Limitations

Due to the small size of the population, subjects were drawn from a purposive (judgmental) sample. There are limitations with this method. However, the relatively low response is indicative of a combination of the small numbers in the Perth PR industry and the limited amount of time people have to devote to being involved in such a study.

As with any study of this type, it will always be a problem to find the extent to which the results of qualitative interviews can be "generalised", but by using interviews it is possible to search for patterns in the respondents' attitudes, opinions, and descriptions of the profession.

As explained elsewhere, the final number of people willing to participate in focus groups and interviews was relatively low. In surveys with so relatively few respondents, a choice has always to be made between few or many selection criteria. In the light of the aim of the survey, relatively few criteria have been chosen. It also proved problematic to obtain detailed data on individuals and their work, because they were promised anonymity in connection with the quantitative survey.

Summary

Chapter Three outlined the methodologies and techniques used to conduct the research. This included an initial census of the population, surveys, focus groups and interviews. A summary of the process appears in figure 17. While survey numbers were relatively low (particularly with regard to PR professionals) they are indicative of the small size of the Perth PR industry. However, the actual response rate, being high, should provide an accurate picture of the industry nationally. This is particularly the case with the extensive open-ended answers, interviews and focus groups, which form the main source of information for this study.

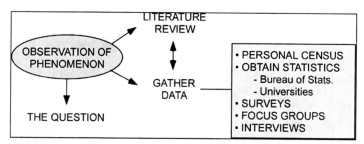

Figure 17: An overview of the way the research was structured.

4 Statistics

Phase One (a population census) was conducted between 21 February and 18 March, 2005. It included an initial survey of:

a. The PRIA (State and Federal bodies)

Because the PRIA did not have past years' membership statistics, it was impossible to gauge membership trends. However, national membership of the PRIA (2005) comprises 2560 females (73%) and 967 (27%) males. This reflects almost identically, membership of the WA Branch, which comprises 269 female (74%) and 80 males (26%). As a result of this study, and following private correspondence (March, 2005) with the then national president, the PRIA will now maintain regular membership statistics.

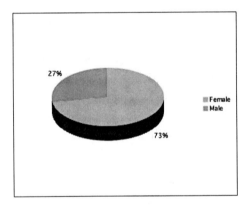

Figure 18: Gender breakdown of national PRIA membership, 2005.

b. National practitioners

A total of 28 practitioners (from 126 e-mailed) responded, giving a response rate of 16 per cent. They were asked to supply the male/female breakdown of fulltime employees, which was 239 female (74%) and 86 males (26%).

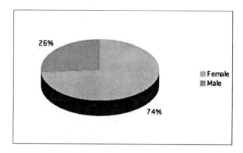

Figure 19: National private PR practice professionals.

c. Perth-based PR practices

A total of 21 (of 47) practices responded, giving a response rate of 69 per cent. Statistics only included those staff directly involved in the PR function. There were 86 females and 30 males involved in private PR practice. The percentages were identical to the national figures.

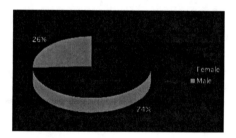

Figure 20: Private practice professionals in Perth.

d. State Government PR Departments

From the census of all 30 WA PR departments, there were a total of 235 PR professionals, with 203 females (74%) and 82 males (26%). Once again, females were measured as 74 per cent of the sub-group.

e. Registered charities (non, or not-for profit)

There are 72 charities listed in the Perth Yellow Pages. Of these, only 16 have fulltime PR practitioners. A phone census of all 16 was conducted, with all 16 providing information, giving a 100 per cent return. There were 21 females (75%) and seven males (25%) working in this PR sector.

f. Perth universities

The four universities all presented their data in different ways. Some differentiate between journalism and PR; others define PR and journalism as "communication". Of the universities, Murdoch's figures were the most detailed, with 'communication' enrolments for BA PR/journalism, BA Multi Media and Bachelor of Communications (Marketing). For this study, I used the PR/journalism course statistics. However, all three courses at Murdoch showed a distinct predominance of female students.

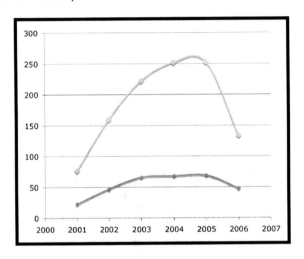

Figure 21: Murdoch University PR/journalism enrolments from 2001–2006.

Murdoch also made it easier (via a comprehensive web site) to obtain enrolment statistics as far back as 2001. One university provided only the current year, while another provided figures dating to 1992. If all years are considered, there have been 2275 females (80%) and only 556 males (20%) studying communications at the four institutions. If only the current year is considered, there are 742 students in their first second and third-year of undergraduate study. This comprises 600 females (80%) and 142 males (20%).

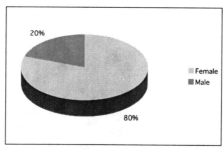

20%

Female
Male

80%

Figure 22: "Communications" (PR/journalism) enrolments at
four Perth universities, 1992–2004.

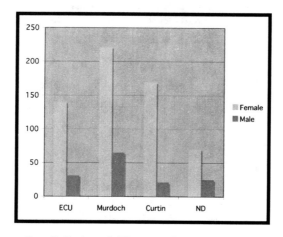

Figure 23: Enrolments in PR courses at Perth universities, 2004.

Due to the PR-specific nature of this study, only Edith Cowan and Curtin Universities have been considered for the final breakdown and analysis of figures, primarily because their statistics can be charted from 2002–2004 (inclusive). In those years there have been 524 female (86%) and 82 male (14%) PR students studying PR. Clearly this demonstrates a predominance of women.

There has been a steady rise in students studying PR at those two universities, as indicated by figure 24 and 25 and table 11. At ECU, the total numbers studying PR increased dramatically from 67 in 2001, to 171 in 2004. The proportion of female students has varied in those years from 82 per cent to 94 per cent, with the average female enrolment at 86 per cent.

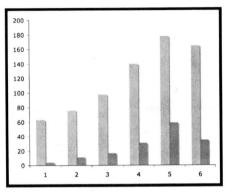

Figure 24: PR enrolments at Edith Cowan University, 2001-2006.

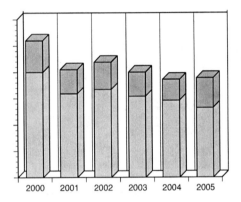

Figure 25: Communication enrolments at Curtin University, 2000-2005.

While women clearly dominate PR enrolments at Curtin University (where women on average comprise 87 per cent of the enrolments) the pattern changed slightly in 2004, with enrolments slightly falling for men and women. This could be a result of declining interest in university study, brought about by higher fees. In fact, correspondence between myself and Dr Trevor Cullen from ECU shows that journalism enrolments there have fallen. Tutorials in the second semester of 2005 were down from 16 to nine. In PR, there were two fewer tutorials in the second semester. When their statistics are combined, the two universities present a clearer indication of the composition of the tertiary PR sector. Overall growth has been high, particularly among women.

	Female	Male	Total
2002	103	14	117
2003	145	23	168
2004	171	35	206
2005	160	57	217
2006	155	42	197

Table 11: Combined PR enrolments at Curtin and Edith Cowan Universities.

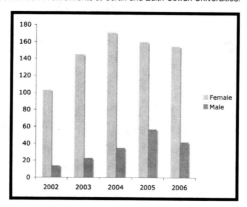

Figure 26: Combined PR enrolments at Curtin and Edith Cowan, 2002–2006.

Looking at a broader picture, combining journalism and PR enrolments, a similar trend is shown (Figure 22). Between 2002 and 2004, the three main universities show similar patterns of women dominating enrolments. Curtin (78 per cent), Murdoch (77 per cent) and ECU (83 per cent).

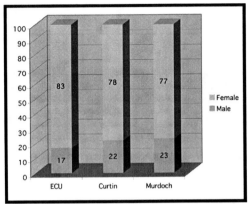

Figure 27: Gender breakdown for Perth university communications enrolments 2001–2004.

g. Summary

The literature review only provided a fragmented amount of data – much of it dated – with most publications citing brief (US) industry and university studies, or anecdotal evidence (in the form of statistics) from educators. This was discussed in Chapter 2.3. US statistics are almost identically replicated in Australia, with this study's census of the industry in Perth showing, on average, women comprising 75.4 per cent of the PR industry, with the breakdown being:

❑ 80 per cent in university courses

❑ 77 per cent of PRIA membership

❑ 75 per cent in charities

❑ 74 per cent in private practice

❑ 71 per cent in government.

Statistics from a variety of sources, both industry, universities and government census in the US, UK and Australia show that there is a consistent (growing, and marked) predominance of women in PR, although the rate of increase appears to be slowing. The statistics merely provide credence to support part of the hypothesis; that there is a predominance of women in PR. What the remainder of this thesis will attempt to present are reasons why this pattern has emerged.

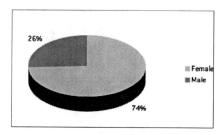

Figure 28: Proportion of PR practitioners (private practitioners, government non-profit in Perth. Source: Author, 2005.

Overall, there was remarkable consistency in the levels of male/female participation in PR (Figure 18). On average, it shows 74 per cent of the population is female. The only slight 'bump' in the numbers was in universities, where women comprise 80 per cent of the numbers. This is due to the lumping together by some universities of students only into communications courses.

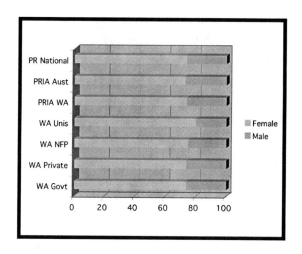

Figure 29: Distribution of males and females across all Australian sub-groups.

Following five separate surveys, there is a consistency in the percentage of women working in PR in Perth, in Australia and in the US, with (Figure 24) best illustrating this phenomenon. The female percentages (Table 12) range from 69–70 per cent.

PRSA (US)	IABC (US)	PRIA (National)	ABS Census	Author survey (Perth)
69	76	73	74	74

Table 12: Percentages of females in PR in the US and Australia

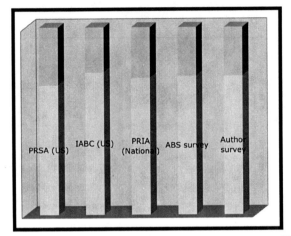

Figure 30: US and Australian employment figures for males and females in PR.

At this point I would like to briefly compare the Perth PR industry figures with those of journalism (previously mentioned). In Perth there are nine major news organisations – *The West Australian, Sunday Times*, Community Newspapers, Channel 7, Channel 9, Channel 10, ABC Radio and TV and two major radio groups. Between them they employ 247 male (57%) and 183 female (43%) journalists. While this is a gender imbalance, it is way below that of PR. Evidence, both from university enrolments, and anecdotally from lecturers at two universities demonstrate that the trend in journalism is following PR, with fewer males interested in journalism as a career.

Conclusion

Chapter Four outlined the population (professionals and students) surveyed, and results from the initial census. This provided statistical proof of the phenomenon, which was shown to be occurring in three countries – Australia (and Perth in particular), the US and the UK. The chapter also compared the trend of PR's 'near-neighbour', journalism, which was found to be experiencing a similar increase in the number of women at university. The figures in journalism have yet to be filter through to the workforce. However, this should be apparent in the next five to 10 years.

The initial census showed that:

❏ The national professional body, the PRIA, did not keep past membership records.

❏ Current statistics for the gender breakdown for employment in PR is virtually identical in Australia, in Perth and in the US at 74 per cent predominance of women.

❏ The gender breakdown in the Perth PR industry is consistent across each sector (government, private companies and non-profits).

❏ University records of communication course enrolments show future trends which have yet to filter through to industry. Enrolments show an average predominance of 80 per cent female, with the figure as high as 86 per cent at one university.

5 Surveys

The second phase of my study was to survey the target groups. Two sets of questionnaires were prepared. One questionnaire was for PR professionals; the other for second- and third-year students. The questions were pilot-tested on several PR practitioners and academics.

Initially, 170 practitioners were contacted. Of these, 55 responded. A slight snowball effect resulted in a further eight completing surveys. A purposive sample produced 63 usable returns with an error rate of nil per cent. The professional PR questionnaires in MS Word format were sent out in the first week of June 2005 by e-mail to the practitioners who indicated their willingness to participate.

The initial statistical analysis of the survey only served as a base on which to gauge certain trends of students and professionals.

With both student and professional surveys attempting to analyse why men and women choose PR as a career, many of the questions in both surveys were similar. Apart from the usual questions about gender and year of study/years spent in PR, eight of the questions shared commonality. For this reason, I have chosen to present the results (answers) this way:

1. 'Student-only' questions

2. 'Professional-only' questions

3. Common questions

5.1 Survey of PR professionals

Of the 63 practitioners surveyed, 41 were female and 22 were male. They had 590 years experience between them, with an average of 10.7 years experience each. Their experience ranged from 1–30 years.

The second part of the survey, consisting of 12 questions, was structured to obtain basic information on practitioners' views, with a view to providing information for interviews and focus groups. In effect, this is a pilot study, as no research of this nature has been done before.

Each question contained two parts – a multiple-choice, lead-in question, followed by an associated question which allows for an open-ended response. I analysed each question, first by the number of responses, then by providing the open-ended answers to each question, based on the coding which was applied manually in the HyperText program. I have included some open-ended answers as in the main body of the thesis, so comments can be seen in light of the questions being asked, and thought processes not be interrupted by having to turn to the Appendix. I have also provided the gender of each respondent. This should help to correct any misunderstanding that some answers may be gender-biased. For whatever reason, not everyone provided detailed answers to all open-ended questions. This may be due to several factors, including: did not have an opinion, did not like the question, did not consider the question relevant, or not interested. A summation of the answers completes the analysis. Additionally, there is an analysis of additional topics which were raised in respondents'
answers, but not directly addressed by
the survey.

All participants were kept informed regularly by e-mail and a regularly-updated web-site (pictured) on progress. The intrusion, however, was minimal, with e-mails sent once every two to three months, advising respondents of the updated web-site information.

[The study's Web address is: www.members.westnet.com.au/gsmith/study]

5.1.1 Sex

From 146 e-mails sent to practitioners, there was a total of 55 responses, giving a return of 40 per cent. There were 21 males (36 per cent) and 34 females (64 per cent). The response ratio reflects the average composition of the population, though there is a slightly higher response by males. This could be simply a result of the random nature of the initial e-mails, as subjects were not identified by gender.

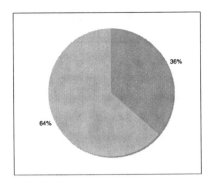

36%

64%

Figure 31: Gender breakdown of responses (females in pink).

5.1.2 Education

Respondents had four choices: Year 10/12, TAFE, Degree, Post-graduate. Most practitioners (71%) in the survey were university-educated, with 20 per cent reaching Year 10/12 level, and the remaining nine per cent attending TAFE.

Proportionally, more females (67%) of the total population attended university. Females also clearly lead the way when it comes to post-graduate study. Of those who have Masters/Honours Degrees, 81 per cent are women.

	High school	TAFE	University
Male	29%	10%	61%
Female	15%	9%	76%

Table 13: Breakdown of professionals' education levels.
Percentages shown reflect the breakdown for a specific gender.

Women are shown to have higher qualifications than men, reflecting community general trends which show more women than men are undertaking tertiary studies. Among young people in Western Australia, females are more likely than males to complete post-compulsory schooling. "In August 2000, the apparent retention rate for females was 77.6%, compared with the male rate of 65.5%" (Gunn, 2002). In higher education generally, women outnumber men by 2:1 in completing a degree. For post-graduate the ratio favours women by almost 3:1. With women now an increasing numerical force in PR, the statistics may merely reflect the growing numbers of women in PR and the fact that more women than men undertake tertiary study. However, it may also indicate that women are more "passionate" about their job, and see a tertiary qualifications as a more useful tool to develop their careers.

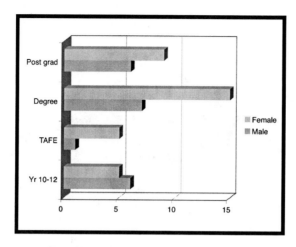

Figure 32: Male/female practitioners' educational levels.

5.1.3 Industry sector

This question presented an opportunity to gauge whether certain industry sectors attract a particular gender. Respondents were given a choice of the four standard industry sectors (government, corporate/in-house, non-profit or consultancy) with a choice to nominate another sector. Overall, the response rate did not truly reflect the numbers obtained in my original Census. For example, my Census (and that of the ABS) clearly shows females as the numerically dominant force across the industry. However, this does not show in the responses to this question, with gender equally spread across all but consultancies, which shows a ratio of 2:1 in favour of women. This is just a result of the relatively small sampling. However, this statistic, as with others in the first section of the survey, does not have an impact on the overall aim of my study, which is to consider the beliefs, attitudes and knowledge of participants with regard to reasons for a gender imbalance.

The breakdown was:

	Corporate	Government	NFP	Consult.	Other
Male	3	6	0	12	1
Female	2	6	2	23	1
TOTAL	5	12	2	35	2

Table 14: Predominant PR work sectors.

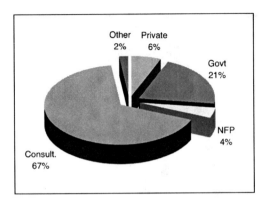

Figure 33: Where PR practitioners are working.

While The numbers in this part of the survey were too small to provide a definite breakdown, the higher proportion of women in PR consultancy work in Perth (66%) compared to 50 per cent in government and corporations, is another area worth further investigation, but is not within the scope of this study.

5.1.4 Type of PR practised

From seven key PR areas of expertise (community relations, media relations, issues management, print/web production, product promotion, investor relations) respondents were asked to nominate in order the three main areas they worked in. Ratings were determined by a system of three points for the leading priority, to one for the third choice. There was also an option to nominate another area. This yielded an additional 10 categories, giving 17 areas of work. The purpose of this question was to see whether males or females are being "herded" into any common roles. Overall, media relations was by far the most nominated area professionals work in (or on). Surprisingly, only one female listed internal communication as a (second) choice. I say surprisingly, because quite a few of the respondents were government practitioners, and internal PR is often assumed to be a necessary part of practice in this sector. Also surprising, was that only one male listed government relations as a second choice.

Other low-scoring categories between both sexes were: investment (6 points), strategy (4), stakeholder management (4), management consultation (4), business development (3) and sponsorship (1). Investment management may be low on the "PR radar" in Perth, due to the city not being regarded as a financial hub, unlike Sydney or Melbourne.

The main types of PR practised were:

Media relations	35%	Events	9%
Issues management	17%	Product promotion	8%
Community relations	11%	Investor relations	3%
Production	10%	Strategy development	2%

For example, among women, events management, product promotion, web/print production and community relations featured prominently. Among men, issues management stood out as a priority function. For women, events management was ranked as the second most practised component (rating 28), compared to males, for whom it rated only four. Women also practised media relations far more widely than men (76 to 39).

Among males, who are generally regarded as being more business-focused, it was interesting to note that only one person listed Industrial Relations, Internal Relations, Business Development or Sponsorship as areas they worked in.

Media relations was the most widely all-around practised function, with female respondents listing it as a first choice. Generally, media relations is regarded as a 'technician' role – one which women predominantly perform. The result simply confirms widely-held views (Seitel, 1998; Donato, 1990; Toth, 2000; Newsom, 2000; Gower, 2001; Grunig, 2001; Hall, 2005) that women are tied to these roles.

At this point there seems to be a discrepancy in the survey. In two previous questions both male and females said they practised strategy, but that it only forms two per cent of their workload. This may mean that strategy is not an ongoing activity (in that plans and results are not constantly monitored).

5.1.5 Years in PR

This question produced a simple numerical answer to gauge the average experience (in years) of practitioners. The 55 respondents had a total of 590 years of experience, ranging from one to 30 years. The average time spent in PR was 10.7 years. Males had an average of 13.6 years in PR, while females had an average of 10.4 years experience. Once again, not too much can be read into these figures, except to say the responses to the open-ended questions were given by some highly-experienced practitioners.

5.1.6 Main role in PR

The purpose of this question was to analyse which role practitioners mostly perform, with the aim of detecting whether some roles attract males, and some females. Respondents could select one of six basic roles, with an option to add others, with the result that a further 10 were added to the list. The given choices were considered as representing the basic PR skills of writing, client liaison, event management, media relations, support/coordination or strategy.

Professionals were asked to nominate the main function/role they performed. In many ways this was similar to the above category. They were given five basic choices (writer, client liaison, event management, media, support/coordination) and were free to list any others, with the result that a further 10 were added to the list. The idea was to test consistency across answers.

Women and men both listed writing, strategy and media relations as their top three preferences. Proportionally, women were more involved in developing strategy than men. It is interesting that strategy features so highly in responses to this question, whereas only two per cent of respondents said they were involved in strategy development (see 3.1.8).

	MEN	WOMEN
1	Writer (32%)	Strategy (37%)
2	Strategy (29%)	Media (18%)
3	Media (19%)	Writer (15%)
4	Events (10%)	Client liaison (9%)
5	Client liaison (5%)	Support (9%)
6	Other (5%)	Events (6%)
		Other (6%)

Table 15: Main roles practised in PR.

The main points were:

❑ Most practitioners considered they worked mostly on strategy

❑ Female practitioners carried out more strategy than males.

It is interesting that in the UK, in terms of roles, media relations is the main form of PR practised by more than 90 per cent of professionals surveyed by the CIPR in 2005, then came planning (87%) and events (73%). "The biggest response from in-house employees was 'media relations', while the biggest response from consultancy respondents was 'communications strategy development' (*PR Today: 48,000 professionals; £6.5 billion turnover. The economic significance of public relations*, 2005).

5.1.7 Level of employment/experience

Levels of employment across four levels were consistent between genders, with the majority working in senior levels. From the statistics, traditional PR stereotypes tended to be reinforced, with women generally performing the more "technician" roles, and men taking management-orientated roles.

	Senior	Middle	Technician	Entry
Male	57	29	14	0
Female	56	27	13	4

Table 16: Percentage breakdown of professionals' level of employment.

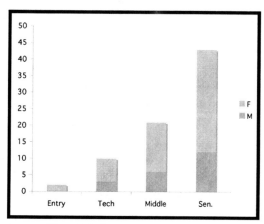

Figure 34: Professionals' level of employment.

5.1.8 Salary

Four levels of salary were presented, roughly equating to the above employment levels. This would give a guide as to earning capacity by gender and help unearth any possible discrepancies between the level of employment and male/female salaries.

Salary levels accurately reflected the levels at which professionals were employed. The most notable point was the lack of salary "discrimination" so often talked of in the literature. Salary levels accurately reflected the levels professionals were employed at. There was only a two per cent difference between males and females in the upper level ($61K-plus) and a three per cent difference favouring males in the second-highest level ($46–60K). At middle ranking ($26–45K), males tended to out-earn females by five per cent, while at the entry level ($20–25K), female salaries were four per cent higher on average.

	$61K–plus	$46–60K	$36–45K	$20–25K
Male	57%	29%	14%	0%
Female	56%	27%	13%	4%

Table 17: Professionals' salary levels.

Due to the small sampling rate, it is difficult to accurately determine salary discrepancies. However, inequity does not seem to be highlighted to any extent. However, the results in this area do not reflect trends in other Australian cities. There is anecdotal evidence that salaries for females in Sydney, for example, are comparably lower than for males.

5.1.9 Hours worked

Most practitioners (44 per cent) worked 8-10 hours per day, with 36 per cent working 6-8 hours, 18 per cent working 10-12 hours and only two per cent working 12 hours or more (only males). Females generally worked fewer hours than males, with the greater percentage (38%) most working in the eight to 10-hour range, compared to males, where 48 per cent worked an average of 10-12 hours daily. UK figures were similar to those in my survey; particularly with regard to men working more hours than women.

In the UK, it was found: "On average, a quarter of public relations professionals work over 48 hours per week. Those who work for a consultancy or agency work the highest average number of hours per week (over 43 hours) whilst those who work in public relations for the public sector work the fewest hours per week (40 hours). Overall, men seem to work slightly longer hours than women; within freelance and in-house not-for-profit organisations, women work longer" (*PR Today: 48,000 professionals; £6.5 billion turnover. The economic significance of public relations,* 2005). Pinker and Spelke (2005) argue that "there are slightly more men than women who want to work long hours. That is, more men than women don't care about whether they have a life".

	12–plus hrs	10–12 hrs	8–10 hrs	6–8 hrs
Male	5%	48%	33%	14%
Female	0%	24%	38%	38%

Table 18: The hours PR practitioners work.

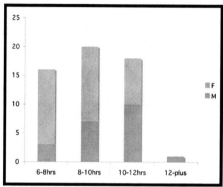

Figure 35: Average daily hours worked by professionals.

5.1.10 PR as a career

Respondents had to nominate in order what made them choose PR as a career. This may help identify possible gender-specific reasons that may make males and females enthusiastic about PR. Are they in it for the money, or is a career the main objective? There were five options, with space for another (if necessary). Answers were based on a points system of five points for the main reason for PR being a good career, down to one for it being least attractive. The options were: money, career, creative, variety, mental challenge. Most respondents (men and women) chose variety as being the main reason for working in PR, with females favouring it more than males. This was followed by creativity and mental challenge (also both males and female).

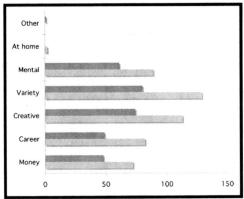

Figure 36: Reasons for choosing PR as a career.

5.1.11 Aspects of PR interest

Are there certain aspects of PR that interest females? What do males like about PR? This question also attempts to identify, from a job-specific (functional) aspect, whether there are any common reasons that might attract either gender to PR. Respondents were given a choice of 12 aspects of PR and asked to list their three main areas of interest, with three points for the first choice, two for the second and one for the third selection. The question is closely linked to choices made in areas of work and the main roles practised. The three questions are similar and aim to detect any differences in types of work preferred by practitioners. The answers of all three indicate women are still associated (whether by choice or management) with the technician-type roles (events, media and writing), whereas men are associated with manager-type functions such as project and reputation management (this equates with answers provide in section 5.1.7). The three areas of most interest to PR professionals are (scores shown in order) media (33) marketing (30) and writing (29). The areas of least interest are budget (1), research (4) and production and investor relations (5).

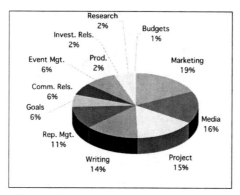

Figure 37: Work areas of most interest to professionals.

Just over half (33) of all 63 respondents said they were interested in media. Proportionally, more men (73%) than women were interested in media and marketing work. However, females (66%) clearly had more of an interest in writing than males – an area in which they are shown to be more gifted academically. In so-called 'traditional' areas of PR, such as events management, females (82%) clearly have more interest than males. In other areas, there was a 50/50 split in interest in community relations, and slightly more females (53%) were interested in reputation management.

Area of interest	Scores		
	Male	Female	Total
Media	9	24	33
Marketing	9	21	30
Writing	10	19	29
Project	11	16	27
Reputation Management	9	10	19
Community Relations	6	6	12
Event Management	2	9	11
Investor Relations	4	1	5
Production	1	4	5
Research	3	1	4
Budgets	0	1	1

Table 19: Areas of most interest to professionals.

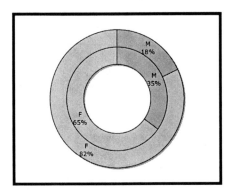

Figure 38: Females are more interested in events management.
The inner circle is the sample population, and the outer circle is the level of
interest in events.

There was an additional area of interest (research) listed in the professional survey. This was deemed necessary as the research component of PR (that is, statistics and focus groups) is usually not fully emphasised at some universities until fourth year and beyond. While the sample was small, it showed that 75 per cent of males preferred research. This would fit with the general consensus of data and literature that suggests men are attracted to the "methodical" side of business. However, it could also be argued that the actual "doing" of research may also be a "technician-type" role. This, in turn may depend on the type of research – qualitative or quantative.

5.1.12 Preferred workplace

With four types of PR workplaces (government, consultancy, non-profit and corporate, or in-house) respondents had to nominate the type of workplace in which they prefer to work. This assumed they read the question carefully and nominated their preference, rather than just the place the type of practice they worked in at the time of the survey. There were respondents who worked in one sector who indicated a preference for another. The overall preference was for consultancy work, followed by corporate (in-house), then government, and non-profit was the least favoured. The overall breakdown was: consultancy (63%), government (20%), private (13%), NFP (4%). Among males the breakdown was consultancy (57%), government (24%), private (19%) and NFP (0). Among females it was consultancy (67), government (18%), private (9%), NFP (6%).

	Consultancy		Govt.		Private		NFP	
Total	63%		20%		13%		4%	
	M 57%	F 67%	M 24%	F 18%	M 9%	F 9%	M 0%	F 6%

Table 20: Breakdown of where practitioners prefer to work.

Among both males and females the percentages who favoured a certain sector were remarkably the same, with a consultancy environment the most favoured at 33 per cent, followed by consultancies (28 per cent) government (21 per cent) and non-profits (18 per cent).

5.1.13 Building client rapport

Most professionals (39%) thought neither gender was better at building rapport with clients. The two graphs below compare female (left) and male responses (right) to the question. Males are evenly divided among their choice of answer. However, when broken down, 40% of females thought they were better at this aspect of PR than males.

5.1.14 Male/female work differences

A total of 75 per cent of respondents said there was a difference in the way males and females worked with clients. Among each gender 81 per cent of male practitioners recognised a difference, while the figure was 71 per cent among females.

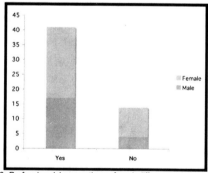

Figure 39: Professionals' perceptions of work differences between gender.

5.1.15 Impact of gender on work performance

A total of 76 per cent said gender did not have any impact on work performance. The figures were identical for males and females. Only three comments were received on this question.

• It depends upon the environment. For example as a woman I have been more effective in male-dominated work environments and less successful in women-orientated organisations and I think this is about complementing each other's strengths and abilities. (F)

• Again, it comes down to individuals not their sex. (F)

• Different skill sets based on how people are nurtured and encouraged through their development and schooling. Different 'drives' according to how genders are nurtured (for example, aggressive macho male stereotype versus the calmer, more creative female stereotype). (F)

5.1.16 Imbalance

Professionals were asked two questions (Nos. 15 and 21):

(1) if they thought there was a balanced workforce in PR, and

(2) if they thought there should be a balanced workforce in PR.

Most professionals (76 per cent) thought there was imbalance. Slightly more females (79%) than males (70%) thought there should be balance. People also commented that balance should not be achieved simply for the sake of balance. The best person for the job should be selected. However, there is general concern that imbalance does create problems, notably "a bias towards women's issues" (M) and "lack of respect for the industry" (F). Also, 73 per cent thought there should be a balanced workforce in PR, with 18 per cent saying there should not, and nine per cent being indifferent. Among males, 76 per cent said there should be a balanced workforce, while only 70 per cent of females thought balance was necessary (18 per cent said it was not necessary, and 12 per cent being indifferent).

The finding of this survey correlates with a recent US study, *Report of the Committee on Work, Life and Gender Issues,* conducted for the PRSA. One comment from the report included: "The men in one group would like to see more professional development workshops around the issues of gender and the profession. One participant said: 'These are big, important issues that cut in a lot of complicated directions" (Toth, 2000).

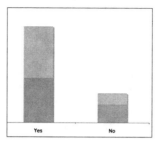

Figure 40: Professionals' levels of concern about imbalance.

Overall, the comments received on positive aspects of having a more balanced workforce (and that includes more women in managerial positions) point to the industry achieving a "better dynamic" (F) and being "better able to represent a more diverse range of clients" (M).

With 24 respondents directly indicating there should be a balance, there is clear evidence of concern. Overall, the feeling is that balance is necessary for a healthy industry.

The fact that women felt quite strongly about the imbalance was perhaps surprising, given that they are the dominant group in the industry. Their comments also generally reflected the statistics, with most of them concerned about the effects that imbalance may have. A common theme throughout, reflected by men and women, was that 'the job should go to the best person'. There was only one comment (from a female) which could be regarded as unbalanced. "This industry doesn't need men." Overall, there was a level of mild concern about what effects imbalance may have, with a reasonable consensus that balance equals diversity.

	Yes %	No %	Irrelevant %
Males	76	19	5
Females	70	18	12

Table 21: Levels of concern regarding industry imbalance.

5.1.17 Should there be a balanced (gender) workforce?

There was a consistent reply across gender. A total of 73 per cent thought there should, with 18 per cent saying it should not and nine per cent saying it was irrelevant. Among males, 76 per cent thought there should be balance, 19 per cent said "no" and five per cent said it was irrelevant. Proportionally, fewer females (70 per cent) said there should be balance, with 18 per cent saying "no" and 12 per cent "irrelevant".

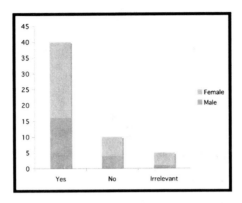

Figure 41: Practitioners' views on whether there should be a balanced
(gender) workforce.

5.1.18 Effects of imbalance on industry

Many respondents (62%) were concerned that a gender imbalance could have an effect on
the industry. There was a marked difference between males and females. Among males,
the concern was higher, at 76 per cent, while only 53 per cent of females were concerned
about an imbalance.

5.1.19 Ethical concerns

Professionals were asked if there were any aspects of working in PR that affects their
ability to work with clients and other professionals within the industry. The responses were
consistent for male and female, with most respondents (64%) saying they had no issues.
However, the fact that 36 per cent had concerns is of interest.

	Yes (%)	No (%)
Male	38	62
Female	35	65
Total	36	64

Table 22: Ethical concerns of professionals.

5.1.20 Confidence

This was a *Clayton's* question, simply asking respondents if they were confident when
making presentations to clients. Its purpose was to let people 'relax' before entering the
second set of questions related to gender. Only two respondents did not answer 'yes' to
being confident. In both cases, understandably, they were 'juniors' and probably had not
yet developed the presentation skills necessary to function at a high level. The question

validates the general opinion of most students and professionals: that one of the main prerequisites for people working in PR is confidence.

5.2 Additional material

This section contains additional analysis of material which was not canvassed as part of the formal survey, but resulted from answers provided by practitioners. Basically, these are key concepts that appeared in answers.

Critical to my study is the ability to try to understand what "makes" a PR practitioner. It was important to learn what practitioners think; for they are the ones that are the industry. Their views and the way they work shape the way the industry operates and is perceived by others – their publics. The most important aspects are the basic building blocks (skills and traits) of practitioners. From my initial attempt at trying to outline an industry profile, these are what (presumably) makes practitioners practise.

Analysis of any answer is open to the reader's interpretation. One (female) participant wrote the following (after reading the summary):

> I was imagining a not-too-professionally appealing headline: 'Study suggests women 'fluff' better than me', or some such horror forever locking women into the perceived 'soft' end of PR. So much of this is just so 'wrong'. The terms self-serving, stereotypical, dangerous, unfounded, appalling, outdated come to mind. Not to mention infuriatingly ignorant.

5.2.1 Common themes

Before addressing each subject area, I would like to present a summary of some recurring themes to emerge from the professional survey. The following table shows common concepts (or themes) and the frequency with which they appeared in the open-ended answers. The frequency of appearance differs from the actual number of answers given. For example, while there were 52 separate references to female skills, only 17 people responded to the question dealing with this aspect of my study. The same procedure was applied to the analysis of interviews with professionals, and this is covered in detail in that section. However, 'themes' common to both the survey and interviews, and the frequency of their occurrence, are highlighted in the following list.

Female traits	91	Male traits	37	Work participation	11
Balanced workforce	82	Effects of imbalance		Knowledge base	11
Gender influence	71	in industry	37	Industry concerns	11
Work differences	58	Perception of PR	35	Male skills	9
Suitability for PR	57	Career barriers	34	Age	9
Image	55	Female skills	22	Qualities	7
Reason for feminisation	53	Gender imbalance	20	PR values	6
Client rapport	48	Performance	17	Uni studies	3
Ethical issues	46	Drawbacks	17	Networking	3
Gender differences	41	Historical aspects	16		

These themes provide an insight into the thoughts of PR practitioners, who are presented with a topic they mostly had not consciously thought about. As such, the themes may represent areas of importance, or concern, they may have about the topic. 'Female traits', for example is mentioned 91 times. This may indicate this topic is central to professionals' thinking with regard to imbalance. Similarly, notions of age and networking, which are mentioned only three or four times respectively, could indicate they are not factors influencing the reasons why people enter the profession.

5.2.2 Female skills/traits

For the purpose of this study, skills are defined as those abilities (physical or mental) which are learned throughout, and contribute to, a person's career. Traits are considered (either scientifically or generally) to be inherent in a person, male or female. In some instances, I had to make a value judgment whether what was being referred to was a skill or trait.

In the areas of natural ability (traits), practitioners (both male and female) believe that women are more "naturally" suited to PR because they possess those traditional "feminine" qualities of empathy, creativity and, indeed, communication. In the area of skills, the responses were predominantly from women, which skews opinions to favour women, making it difficult to make any assumptions. It is interesting to note that two comments from males indicated that women may be better at strategy, which mention they are better both 'tactically' and 'at choosing the way to communicate'. This is also supported by a comment from a female practitioner, who says they may use this tactical advantage by relating better to women, and by 'charming male clients'. Only one female said that males were better at the tactical level. Only one mention was made of suitability to technical aspects of PR, with a female practitioner saying men were better. This, however, would be difficult to fathom, as one of the main reasons women can compete equally with men in PR is the fact that the technical aspects (writing, design, production of materials) do not require physical effort. From the comments, it seems women have the upper hand when it comes to possessing both skills and traits that are suited to PR.

There were far fewer comments relating to male traits and skills, than for those relating to females. It was interesting to note that not many males introduced these concepts into their answers, which may indicate they do lack the "creativity" that would be associated with expanding on answers. From the comments, males are generally perceived to be more direct when dealing with clients.

5.2.3 Qualities

Three people (two of them males) took the opportunity to mention qualities they believe make a good practitioner. The concept is closely related to the skills and traits practitioners should possess, although they are more innate. Once again, the trend indicates that practitioners believe women have those 'human' qualities that make them better suited to PR, as evidenced by these answers:

> If the client is a woman, she is likely to be more trusting of a female rather than a male PR consultant (M).

> Women are more adaptable in getting on with people. And that is necessary (M).

> Everybody is different. I look for someone with integrity, honesty and respect (and a Degree) (F).

5.2.4 Age

I thought it surprising, but important, that nine respondents raised the matter of age as a factor in PR. On refection, this is a valid, and contentious, issue in an industry that thrives to a large degree on image. It is also relevant given the continuing publicity regarding our ageing workforce and the fact that many mature people can not get a job. Age was also mentioned in the following section (twice) as being a drawback in PR, though it is not clear whether it is an advantage/disadvantage to be young or old. I suspect it can be taken both ways, in that older workers can be considered well past their prime and not able to keep pace with modern practice; or that an experienced worker is a valuable asset.

5.2.5 Drawbacks

The concept/theme of "drawbacks" relates strongly to issues that affect how PR work is undertaken. Family issues were prevalent in this theme. From the comments, this predominantly affects females. While phoning consultants for my initial census, many women listed as consultants were no longer working in that role as they were raising children. In the course of interviews for this study, several practitioners mentioned that the reason there are so many female consultants in Perth was that many businesses were set up initially so women could balance family and career. As two practitioners commented:

> PR is a job that is flexible, and you can work at it for 2-3 days a week. That would suit women better. Certainly if women have children, PR would suit them in that regard" (M).

> Women look at it as a means to an end, as in 'I want to do a fun job that's going to get me through to when I leave to have babies'. And I want a job that I can do while I raise kids, and from home, part-time. When the kids are back at school I don't have to re-qualify" (M).

In this regard, the female consultancy would not only be attractive to women (particularly those with young families), its management would be more sympathetic to hiring women with families. An article on the *icBirmingham* web-site in 2004, summarised this aspect: "One of the reasons behind the success of women PR professionals is undoubtedly the flexibility of the profession, as it provides the opportunity for career-minded women to have it all in terms of high powered jobs, while still balancing family life – at least to some degree." Once again, responses to my surveys indicate the way in which PR suits women in this regard:

> Family responsibilities. PR has some odd hours, which make it hard for mothers (M).

> I suspect it is still the woman usually who has to drop work to attend a sick child, and this would impact on performance, although one would expect irregularly (F)..

> As in all careers, it is difficult to balance a family's needs with a full-on career (F).

5.2.6 Historical aspects

Comments here are basically anecdotal in nature, but provide a snapshot of how the industry has developed. As my study attempts to discover why the industry is becoming feminised, the last two comments provide scope for future exploration of this theme along historical lines. However, without PRIA membership statistics it will be difficult to compare the growth of university courses and an increase in female professionals, though the two are inexorably linked.

> In a State of male-dominated industries (mining and agriculture) PR has been one department that females have been encouraged to populate (F).

The preponderance of males in very senior positions is as much an artifact of the 'old-school' PR, when journalists made the move to the dark side (and most journalists were male). This seniority imbalance will progressively shift as these old crusties (self included) drop off the professional twig. Government and corporates are still (in the main) uncomfortable working with female-dominated professionals on equal footing (consider nursing etc) a 'female' PR profession will take longer to gain acceptance (M).

It has traditionally been an area women have been seen to excel (F).

It's been the case for more than 10 years throughout Australia. Same percentage when I studied at RMIT in the early 1990s (F).

PR has been increasingly being perceived as 'female' sector (F).

PR shifted from being a career progression for ex-journalists (mainly men) to a more recognised professional option in its own right with university courses attracting more women (M).

The whole world of (white collar) work is becoming feminised, but PR is the most visible example of this phenomenon. (M).

5.2.7 Image and perception of PR

It certainly seems that the industry's view of itself says that the profession is full of "fluff" (both in looks and content). While professionals' views were not as expansive as students', there was quite a deal of comments on how the industry is perceived. The following selection of quotes demonstrates the common theme that the industry is simply perceived as feminine, thereby discouraging males from entry.

It is perceived as a feminine industry/career. Males' and females' interests vary naturally. Women are more confident in communications (F).

It's seen as a more female occupation due to the perception of events, schmoozing, very tactical work. PR is often perceived by men to be a glorified secretary's role (F).

I think PR has a perception of being a female industry – a bit like nursing – so men are not naturally drawn to it, unless they come in via journalism or publishing (F).

I think it's more of the perception of the industry being more female oriented and that it's a lot easier for a female to get in (M).

People have a false perception of what PR is. Males just think it's a female course (F).

There's a perception of PR as a 'soft' alternative in comparison to journalism (F).

PR tends to be full of good-looking, well-groomed people, so someone who doesn't fit that mould may find it difficult to get ahead (F).

There's been a dumbing-down of the profession. These days a pretty face counts for more than knowledge (M).

PR is seen as 'fluff', while journalism is seen as 'tough' (F).

I believe it is viewed as a 'chicks' field and therefore is not taken as seriously as it would if there were more men (M).

I think it is seen as a 'fluffy' role and equated more to something women would do (F).

The industry is female-dominant because of public perception (F).

There's a perception that the career is 'feminine', as opposed to civil and mechanical engineering, which is (seen as) 'masculine' (M).

Possibly because it's generally perceived as a good job for females – lots of working with people, etc (F).

5.2.8 General concerns

Though there was room for practitioners to express concerns about gender, some deviated from the topic to express general concerns about the industry. While these comments are not directly related to my study's overall aim, I would make one comment with regard to the third and fourth responses, which touch on the industry's professionalism. The placement of PR courses outside business schools does nothing to enhance the discipline's standing among fellow students – future business leaders. Compare this approach to marketing and advertising courses, which are usually located within business schools.

My only concern is the amount of tripe generated by some practitioners (M).

An increasing emphasis on women's lifestyle editorial rather than complex investigative issues. (M).

There are too few good professionals and the PRIA has no real quality assurance program in place - nothing as rigorous as the law or accounting professions. Until we take ourselves seriously, other won't (M).

I think the gender imbalance of females, especially the 40-something generation that heads up the PRIA or the 20-something set that heads up the Young Guns, has a negative impact of the professional reputation of the PR industry in WA as there is a perpetuation of the stereotyped 'big-boobs, big-hair', or 'young buns' 'clique' of the same women - that do not encourage the business marketplace to see PR as a strategic professional skill (F).

I have heard of many young females (with university degrees) who entered the industry with consultancies and were expected to work long hours doing all of the office's general work (little of which is genuine PR work but menial tasks such as taking the boss' dry cleaning in or getting coffees.) They were treated rudely by supervisors and more experienced colleagues. They decided to leave PR. This treatment is not at the hands of males but other females. Others have received this treatment but hang in there and move on within the industry (F).

5.2.9 Would they do it again?

Most professionals (64.5%) if given the option, would again chose PR as a career. There was little difference in the response rate between genders. Among females, 62 per cent said they would. The figure was slightly higher among males at 67 per cent.

5.3 Student surveys

Response by university was:

University	Male	Female	Total
Murdoch	6	40	46
Notre Dame	5	15	20
Curtin	5	30	35
Edith Cowan	1	3	4

Table 23: Response rate for student survey.

There were a total of 116 responses received from second-, third- and fourth-year PR students from four universities, comprising 98 females (84 per cent) and 18 males. The breakdown was 67 (second-year), 45 (third-year) and four (fourth-year) students.

Murdoch results

There were a total of 45 usable surveys from 78 returns. Most of the discarded surveys came from people not studying PR as a Major. There were also several surveys incorrectly completed, making them invalid. Of the completed surveys, there were six males (13% and all second-year students) and 39 females (87%), comprising 15 third-year and 30 second-year students.

Notre Dame

There were a total of 20 usable surveys from 23 returns (all third-year students). There were 15 females (75%) and five males (25%). This equates almost identically to the national and Perth gender breakdown of the industry.

Curtin

There were a total of 35 usable responses from 45 returns. Those not completed correctly came from respondents who were not primarily completing PR Degrees (six), or questions being incorrectly answered (four). Of the usable responses, 86% were from women.

ECU

Due to administrative problems at the university, there were only 16 returns, comprising 14 females (87%) and two males.

5.3.1 Perceptions of PR

In question four, students were asked how they perceive PR – as a career, as a job, or may lead to something else.

	Career	Job	Other
Male	11 (55%)	1 (6%)	7 (39%)
Female	71 (75%)	4 (3%)	22 (22%)

Table 24: Gender breakdown of how students perceive PR.

Overall, 70.7 per cent of students see PR as a career, indicating they are studying it with long-term goals in mind and are serious about the subject. For males, 57.9 per cent see it as a career, 36.8 per cent as leading to something else, and 5.3 per cent as job. As a proportion of the population, more females (73.2%) than males view it as a career. For females, 22.7 per cent see it as leading to something else, and four per cent as a job. Women clearly perceive PR to be a career. It is interesting to note that students at Notre Dame differed from those at the other institutions in that only 33 per cent saw PR as a career. Most (56%) saw it as leading to something else.

5.3.2 Forging a career

In question 10, students were asked what chance of success they thought they had in obtaining work in PR. There were four alternatives, with one choice to be made from: less than 20 per cent, 20–40 per cent, 50–70 per cent, 80-100 per cent. Most students were positive about obtaining work in PR with the majority (57%) believing they had a 50–70 per cent chance of working in the industry. Generally, males and females had the same levels of optimism. As a percentage of the population, females were slightly more optimistic in the upper level, with 27 per cent positive they would get a job, compared to 21 per cent of males.

	20% chance	20–40% chance	50–70% chance	80%+ chance
Male	1	3	11	4
Female	5	11	55	26
% total	5%	12%	57%	26%

Table 25: Gender breakdown of how students rate their chances of obtaining work in PR.

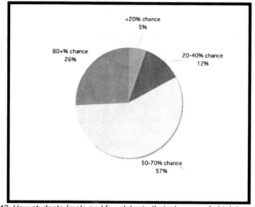

Figure 42: How students (male and female) rate their chances of obtaining work in PR.

5.3.3. How students view PR as a subject

Question 19 contained five Likert-type sub-questions relating to what students thought of PR as a subject. The aim was to see whether females and males thought differently about certain aspects of the discipline; particularly with regard to creative and practical aspects. One of the main aims was to learn whether students were serious about the subject. Students had four levels of choice to rate their level of agreement/disagreement with the propositions presented.

	Strongly disagree	Mildly disagree	Mildly agree	Strongly agree
Male	2 (5%)	12 (63%)	4 (4%)	1 (1%)
Female	26 (27%)	41 (42%)	26 (27%)	4 (4%)
TOTAL	28 (24%)	53 (46%)	30 (26%)	5 (4%)

Table 26: Proposition A – that PR is an easy study option.

If the results of proposition A (that PR is an easy study option) are split between those who disagree and those who do not, then most students (70 per cent) regard the subject as relatively difficult. There is little difference between the sexes. Among males, 68 per cent believe it is difficult, compared to 70 per cent of females. This contrasts to a US study on PR students by Noble (2005), who found "women (71 per cent) were more likely to disagree that public relations courses are easier than the average college course than men (53 per cent). More men (31.4 per cent) than women (17.5 per cent) consider public relations to be an easy major, and men were more likely to say they chose public relations because they couldn't find another major and public relations seemed easy." There is an interesting sidelight here, in that many students commented in open-ended answers to surveys that they found PR involved a lot more writing than they thought. This may contributed to the high number who consider the subject not to be a "soft" study option.

	Strongly disagree	Mildly disagree	Mildly agree	Strongly agree
Male	5 (27%)	4 (21%)	5 (26%)	5 (26%)
Female	24 (25%)	21 (22%)	39 (40%)	13 (13%)
TOTAL	29 (25%)	25 (22%)	44 (37%)	18 (16%)

Table 27: Proposition B – I am mildly interested in PR.

Answers for proposition B (that students are mildly interested in PR) were quite even. If the table is split into those who agree and disagree with the statement, 53 per cent agreed they were only mildly interested in PR. The general trend towards being disinterested came mainly from females (53%). However, double the proportion of males (26%) felt more strongly disinterested in PR than females (13 per cent). The reasons for the lack of interest are not apparent.

	Strongly disagree	Mildly disagree	Mildly agree	Strongly agree
Male	9 (47%)	7 (37%)	3 (16%)	0
Female	34 (35%)	26 (27%)	33 (34%)	4 (4%)
TOTAL	43 (38%)	33 (28%)	36 (31%)	4 (3%)

Table 28: Proposition C – PR will suffice until other opportunities arise.

This question in proposition C also attempts to gauge students' interest in the subject. Most agree that PR is not a "subject in waiting", with 66 per cent disagreeing it will suffice until other opportunities arise (that is, they are serious about the subject). More females (38%) than males (16%) agreed they are considering their options.

	Strongly disagree	Mildly disagree	Mildly agree	Strongly agree
Male	1 (5%)	0	7 (37%)	11 (58%)
Female	3 (3%)	4 (4%)	41 (42%)	49 (51%)
TOTAL	4 (3%)	4 (3%)	48 (41%)	60 (53%)

Table 29: Proposition D – PR allows me to be creative/inventive.

Almost all respondents agreed there was wide scope within PR for them to be creative.

	Strongly disagree	Mildly disagree	Mildly agree	Strongly agree
Male	0	0	7 (37%)	12 (63%)
Female	3 (3%)	3 (3%)	35 (36%)	56 (58%)
TOTAL	3 (3%)	3 (3%)	42 (36%)	68 (58%)

Table 30: Proposition E – PR offers good practical skills.

As in the previous proposition, the clear majority of students agreed that PR taught them good practical skills (above) with little variation in the statement that PR offered good practical skill between males (63%) and females (58%).

5.3.4 Perceptions of teaching

In question 12, students were asked whether they perceived any differences in the way their male and female tutor and/or lecturers taught. Most students (62%) did not perceive any difference. Within the gender grouping, a greater percentage of females (64%) thought there was no difference, compared to 52.6 per cent of males. There certainly seems no imbalance as far as the gender of tutors and lecturers in Australia is concerned. The survey showed that 57 per cent of tutors were male. While the statistic is by no means "alarming", it could also be the focus of a separate study, although my results show this is of little concern to students.

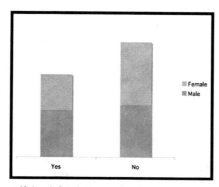

Figure 43: Level of student perception about teaching differences.

	Yes	No
Male (within gender)	47.4%	52.6%
Female (within gender)	36.1%	63.9%
TOTAL	37.9%	62.1%

Table 31: Perceived differences between male and female tutors.

5.3.5 Technician roles

As much of this research is about perceptions, it is important to gauge how students perceive themselves progressing once they enter the workforce. Students were asked whether they thought males or females would be more likely to be in a technician (that is, writing, editing, design, web/print) role. While both genders have the same degree, their views differed. Most students (60%) thought men and women would be considered for these roles equally. However, when looking at the gender responses, proportionally more males (26 per cent) thought they would be in this role, while 22 per cent of females thought they would. This contrasts with a year 2000 US study, which showed women believed they would be more likely to be hired for technician roles.

	Men %	Women %	Equally %
Male	26	15	58
Female	18	22	60
Total	19	21	60

Table 32: Students' views on being hired for "technician" roles.

5.3.6 Imbalance

Among students, 63 per cent thought there was an imbalance in gender. Among males, 58 per cent thought there was imbalance, while among females the figure was 64 per cent. There was a higher awareness of imbalance (73%) among professionals, with males (76%) more aware of the trend than females (70%).

	Level of awareness
PROFESSIONALS	
Total	73%
Male	76%
Female	70%
STUDENTS	
Total	63%
Male	58%
Female	64%

Table 33: Awareness of imbalance.

5.3.7 Pay discrepancies

More than three-quarters of students (88%) were not aware there were pay discrepancies, favouring men, within PR. Male students' lack of recognition was 74 per cent, while among females it was 76 per cent. This was based on statistics from a 2002 *PR Week* survey. However, since that survey, and in the time my research was undertaken, there is some doubt that the level of pay discrepancy exists. Evidence is starting to emerge that salaries are now more equitable. This is what I found in my survey of Perth professionals (Table 17).

	Yes (%)	No (%)
Male	26	74
Female	24	76
Total	24	76

Table 34: Students' levels of awareness regarding pay discrepancies.

5.3.8 Socio-economic group

Most students (41.7 per cent) came from families in the above-average income group (as defined by the Australian Bureau of Statistics and being in the $58k–$70k income bracket). The breakdown was as follows:

Low ($6k-$21k)	Middle ($22k-$58k)	Above Av. ($58-$70k)	High ($70k-plus)
8.3%	37.5%	41.7%	12.5%

Table 35: Socio-economic group origins of PR students

5.3.9 Traits

Students were asked to select which one of the following traits best described them. The aim was to determine whether there was any particular general personality type that was attracted to PR. Of course, the limitation is this might not be correct, as it is the student's own impression of their personality. Most students (42 per cent) described themselves as outgoing. This was followed by personable and creative (each at 17 per cent), positive and organised (each at 8 per cent), decisive and quiet (both at 4 per cent).

5.3.10 Type of student in PR

Is there a stereotypical student in PR? According to this survey, most students (67 per cent) like to "weigh up their ideas against others", indicating they are what is commonly called "team players". Of the remainder, 20 per cent said they preferred to produce their own ideas, and 13 per cent said they preferred to implement others' ideas.

5.3.11 Favourite (school) subject

As outlined, much of the literature suggests that women are better at English (and communicating) than men, and this in turn causes those people with a predisposition to that subject to enter PR. Did university students favour English at school, thereby already having a PR-centric focus? From a list of seven core subjects, English was the most favoured subject at school (29 per cent), followed by history (26 per cent), politics, science and other languages (equal at 12.5 per cent), drama and geography (6 per cent), PE and maths (3 per cent). The results are also reflected in a survey (McCurdy, 2005) of 169 third-year south-east Queensland university PR students in which 6.3 per cent of females said English was the reason they undertook PR, while no males listed this as a factor. That English is the most favoured subject at school correlates to the study of PR students conducted by McCurdy (2005).

5.3.12 Influence on PR study

Students were given six alternatives from which to choose one that most influenced their decision to study PR. Most students (37 per cent) said they "knew and enquired about PR". This was followed by 20 per cent saying they switched to PR after starting university, and a further 17 per cent expressing a general interest in the subject. Some 13 per cent said a friend or relative told them about PR. Importantly, no students were influenced by the three other choices: someone in the industry, school careers counselors or the media.

5.3.13 People's views of PR

As much of the focus groups and interviews pointed towards the perception of the industry having a possible effect on students selecting or avoiding the profession, students were asked about their view on how the public might perceive PR (How do you think most people perceive PR?). From four choices, the students were evenly split between the public 'thinking it's about spin' and 'they're a little unsure about it'. No students thought the general public had a positive impression about it.

This has implications for the industry, in that (a) it needs to better promote itself among possible candidates, and (b) needs to correct misconceptions among the public perception (and probably other professions).

5.3.14 Is PR 'fuzzy'?

The question was precipitated by a point raised by some during interviews and a focus group that because PR is hard to measure it can be hard to grasp, or 'fuzzy' in its logic. Students were asked if they agreed with the statement: 'PR is fuzzy in its logic'. However, the high proportion of women respondents makes this result would be skewed, with 63 per cent disagreeing with the statement.

Strongly agree	Mildly agree	Mildly disagree	Strongly disagree
4%	33%	29%	33%

Table 36: Students' views on PR's 'fuzzy' logic

5.4 Second student survey

> I thought PR was about providing ideas and information at a senior corporate level, as well as playing a lot of golf. I now know it's a bloody hard-working industry. (Male student).

5.4.1 Gender and university breakdown

There were a total of 175 surveys completed from three universities, Curtin, Edith Cowan and Murdoch. Due to an altered course structure at Notre Dame, students from that institution were not surveyed in class. The four surveys from Notre Dame were of students who were third-year and participated in the on-line component. The overall gender breakdown was 38 males (22 per cent) and female 137 (78 per cent). These figures (once again) reflect the general states of earlier (2005) surveys and censuses that showed a 74 per cent predominance of women in the industry (comprising professionals and students). At Murdoch and ECU, the ratio of males to females was much higher than the industry average (see below), while Curtin reflected the industry average. It is not clear why Murdoch and ECU have a higher ratio of females to males. The fact that these figures correlate to earlier statistics should further demonstrate the changing nature of the state of the industry.

5.4.2 Gender and socio-economic group

(These groups are based on the four groups defined by income by the Australian Bureau of Statistics – ABS). Most students (38 per cent) came from an average socio-economic group, followed by 25 per cent from above-average and high-income families. Low-income students represented only 12 per cent of the population. There was little variation between males and females, except that slightly more males (38%) than females (22%) from above-income families did PR. However, this was counter-balanced in the high-income group, in which 27% of females studied PR, compared to 16% of males. Overall, it could be concluded that students from low-income backgrounds do not study PR. However, this is a general trend across all university courses.

	Low	Average	Above average	High
Male	11%	35%	38%	16%
Female	113%	38%	22%	27%
Total	12%	38%	25%	25%

Table 37: Socio-economic background of students.

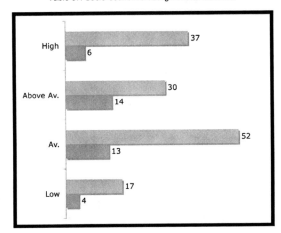

Figure 44: Breakdown of students' socio-economic groups.

5.4.3 Personal traits

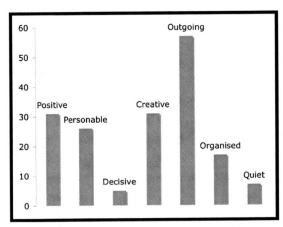

Figure 45: How students view their personality traits.

Students were asked to describe which personality traits best described them. Short of asking students to undertake psychometric testing (not within the budget, or timeframe), this was the only way to discover whether there is a certain personality trait/s that belong to those about to enter the profession. Simpson (2005) cites Holland (1959, 1962, 1966, 1982) who highlighted the importance of fit between an individual's personality and career choice. Also known as the 'trait theory' (Zaccaria, 1970, as cited in Simpson, 2005), this suggests that the choice of occupation is likely to be an expression of one's personality and that members of certain occupations are likely to have similar personality characteristics. Medical staff have found to be analytical, non-conforming and introspective with strong altruistic motivations.

A total of 57 students (32 per cent) said they were outgoing. The next two most common traits both had equal responses; those being positive and creative (31 students each, or 18 per cent). Being personable was next on the list, with 26 students (15 per cent), followed by organised (17 females only), quiet (four per cent) and decisive (three per cent). The fact that not many students said they were decisive is probably due to the fact they are students and probably finds with regard to PR that they lack the knowledge to express strong opinions.

	Positive	Personable	Decisive	Creative	Outgoing	Organised	Quiet
M	19%	23%	40%	35%	19%	0	14%
F	81%	77%	60%	65%	81%	100%	86%
Total	18%	15%	3%	18%	32%	10%	4%

Table 38: Students' overall views of their personality traits.

When responses are considered among males and females separately, a clearer picture emerges of how the genders perceive their personalities. In all but two categories, the answers were similar. Table 38 (above) indicates how closely aligned male and female PR students believe their personalities are across all but two categories. The two exceptions were "creative" and "organised". A total of 30 per cent of female respondents believe they are creative, compared to only 15 per cent of male respondents. Females also considered themselves to be much more highly organised than males, with 12 per cent of females considering this their dominant trait, while no males believe they are "organised". The answers demonstrates that females believe their personalities are both highly creative and organised. No males indicated they were organised – a trait commonly mentioned as being important in PR, and generally regarded as being indicative of women.

As these quotes from surveys and interviews of students indicated, the industry regards "being organised" as a female trait.

Women tend to be more creative, organised and focused on finer details –
all aspects needed for success in the industry (F).

Females tend to be more strict and attentive to detail, well prepared and
organised (M).

Females are more strict and organised (F).

The stereotypical PR person needs to be organised, methodical, a very
good communicator and network easily. That implies an outgoing person
(F).

Creativity also is regarded as a necessary commodity in PR, and one which some believe
fits women better than men in PR. "This new way of working, particularly when applied to
public relations, is ideally suited to women, who ... can exercise their penchant for
language, creativity and communication" (Chater and Gaster 1995). In her unpublished
Master's thesis, which studied 159 [US] students, Noble (2004) found "women (73.8 per
cent) were more likely to agree they selected public relations as a major because of the
creative aspects than did men (51.4 per cent)." Noble based her survey on a study
undertaken by Fullerton and Umphrey (2001) on advertising students at two US
universities. Based on that study and her own findings, Noble (2004) said: "Public
relations students and advertising students possess very similar traits" (p. 5). Students, both
males and females also regard creativity as a female trait, as these comments show:

I feel that generally females tend to be more creative than males (M).

Males are typically interested in and excel in numbers-based occupations,
and females are typically more creative (F).

Women like being creative (M).

The field appeals to females more because it is creative and fun and
includes creative writing, which I always thought females excelled at,
compared to males (M).

Males tend to do commerce in general, and girls are more interested in the
creative side, for example, PR (F).

PR is probably more suited to females because of the creative or
communication aspects, which women tend to be better at (F).

Women are better-suited as they are more creative, persuasive and
dedicated to their career (F).

Women are more creative, better at multi-tasking and communicating (F).

Similarly, professionals also believed creativity is a major factor in why females choose to study PR. As one Perth male professional commented in an interview: "Female high school students often have PR suggested [to them] because of basic psychometric assessment which identifies the creative/intuitive aspects of the profession as suitable for women."

	Positive	Personable	Decisive	**Creative**	Outgoing	**Organised**	Quiet
M	16	16	5	**30**	30	**0**	3
F	18	15	2	**15**	34	**12**	4

Table 39: Comparison (in percentages) on how male and female student perceive their personalities.

Table 39 (above) lends credence to the thoughts of Anne Parry, IPR Midlands group chair and deputy MD of Quantum PR in Birmingham, UK, who said in a 2004 interview with the business website *icBirmingham*:

> Women also tend to be more practical than theoretical, particularly when it comes to attention to detail. Dare I say it, but one of the main reasons behind our growing dominance is that as a general rule we are better than men at thinking on different levels all at the same time. It's just part of our make-up. I could also argue that women are better listeners, more methodical in their decisions, less confrontational and less likely to go off in unproven directions, but I might be in danger of offending my only male colleague and business partner at Quantum and the handful of top PR men that I have enormous respect for.

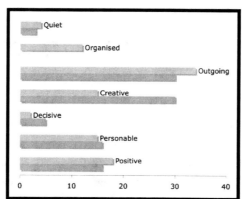

Figure 46: Self-defined personality traits.

5.4.4 Subject at school

English was listed as the subject most students (34%) excelled in at school. This correlates to a US study by Noble (2004) who found 48 per cent of students listed English as their "favorite or second-favorite subject in high school". The only variations between the two surveys was that this study showed drama (14 per cent) as the second-favourite subject, while the US study showed history as second. However, history (7 per cent) was the third selection in Perth. (Note: the results in the two surveys would vary markedly, as the US study only provided four subject choices – English, history, maths and journalism; further demonstrating that study's limitations).

	Science	Maths	**English**	Lang.	History	Econ.	Art	Drama	Other
Male	3	3	**10**	2	2	0	1	3	5
Female	6	7	**44**	9	14	4	12	20	13
Total	9	10	**54**	11	16	4	13	23	18
	(6%)	(6%)	**(34%)**	(7%)	(7%)	(10%)	(4%)	(14%)	(11%)

Table 40: Students' best subjects at school.

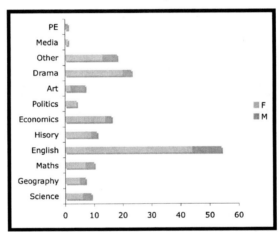

Figure 47: English stands out as PR students' best subject at school.

The breakdown by gender for subject showed both males (27 per cent) and females (35 per cent) said English was heir best subject at school. That is where the similarity stopped. For females, the second subject chosen was drama (16 per cent), while 14 per cent of males chose art. Interestingly, economics rated third choice for females (11 per cent), while it was only seventh choice for males (6 per cent). Table 44 provides a comparison of all choices. (Note: "other" subjects included cultural and media studies, home economics, music [2], accounting [2], physical education [3], marketing and legal studies).

FEMALES		MALES	
English	35%	English	27%
Drama	16%	Other	14%
Economics	11%	Art	14%
Other	10%	Drama	8%
History	7%	Maths	8%
Maths	6%	Science	8%
Science	5%	Economics	6%
Geography	4%	History	6%
Politics	3%	Geography	6%
Art	2%	PE	3%
Media	1%	Politics	0%
PE	0%	Media	0%

Table 41: Male and female breakdown of best subject at school.

5.4.5 Influence to study PR

The most common reason for students selecting PR at university was that they knew about it and had made enquiries (26 per cent). A further 22 per cent said they were interested, indicating they probably had also made enquiries. This indicates there seems to be a good deal of information about PR available, and that students are aware of it as a subject option. However, if there is information available, it is not coming from school careers counselors, with only five students (three per cent – four females and one male) saying they received information on PR this way. In fact, all categories, except industry contact, provided more information than school counselors. The media (at eight per cent) was a better source of information, even if the general consensus is that it provides a distorted picture of PR.

(Note: "Other" categories (17 per cent) included: 'PR was closest to events', 'suited my personality', 'thought it would be interesting' [2], 'the women', 'didn't want to do accounting', 'complimented (sic) advertising' [2], 'internship manager', 'fits in well', 'my sister' [2], 'uni lecturer', 'needed to get into uni', 'uni guide book', 'parents' [2], 'I liked writing, so I thought of PR', 'an elective that suited me', 'part of Masters', 'wanted to mix it with marketing', 'through employment'.

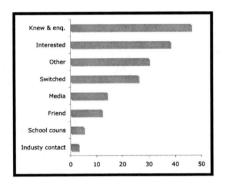

Figure 48: Most influential sources of information about PR.

Reason	Responses
Knew and enquired	26%
Always interested	22%
Other	17%
Switched course	15%
Media	8%
Friend	7%
School counsellor	3%
Industry contact	2%

Table 42: Reasons why male and female students choose PR.

There were few differences in the way in which male and female students obtained their information (table 46). Most females (27 per cent) and males (26 per cent) knew about PR and made enquiries. Proportionally, slightly more females (9 per cent), compared to three per cent of males, obtained their information about PR from the media. This demonstrates males and females get information on PR from the same sources.

FEMALE		MALE	
Knew and enquired	27%	Knew and enquired	26%
Always interested	22%	Always interested	22%
Other	16%	Other	21%
Switched	15%	Switched	14%
Media	9%	Friend	8%
Friend	7%	School counsellor	3%
School counsellor	3%	Media	3%
Industry contact	1%	Industry contact	3%

Table 43: Areas of PR influence to male and female students.

5.4.6 Gender and the way people view PR

Most students (40 per cent) believe people believe PR is mostly about 'spin'. A further 32 per cent think most people are unsure about PR, with 13 per cent not knowing anything about PR. Only 11 per cent of students thought the public had a positive impression of PR.

Male students were more skeptical of the public's views about PR, with 54 per cent believing the public though it was about 'spin', compared to only 36 per cent of female students. This was reflected in the fact that 13 per cent of females thought the public had a positive impression of PR, while among male students it was only three per cent.

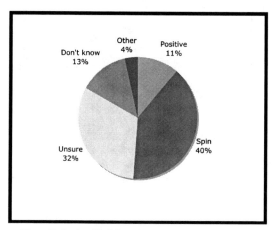

Figure 49: Students' beliefs on the way the public perceives PR.

5.4.7 Gender and preferred work situation

In a work situation (university) the majority of students (65 per cent) preferred to balance their ideas against others, followed by 21 per cent, who prefer to follow others' ideas. The remaining 14 per cent prefer to follow their own ideas. Slightly more males (43 per cent) prefer to follow their own ideas, compared to only 31 per cent of females. This is a surprising statistic (particularly as there was such as strong female sampling). The inference is that males may be slightly more confident (and perhaps assertive) in the university work situation, or perhaps more individualistic, rather than team-orientated. Both males (49 per cent) and females (51 per cent) like to have a balanced approach.

	Own ideas	Other's ideas	Balance of ideas
Male	43%	8%	49%
Female	31%	18%	51%
Total	14%	21%	65%

Table 44: Students' preferred method of work.

5.4.8 Is PR 'fuzzy' in its logic?

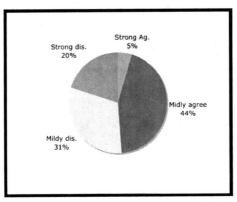

Figure 50: Students, PR and 'fuzzy' logic. Half agree PR is 'fuzzy'.

Students were evenly split (51 per cent agree to some extent, and 49 per cent disagree to some extent) on whether PR is "fuzzy" in its logic (meaning some of its outcomes are hard to measure). However, the majority viewpoint was that 44 per cent mildly agree with the statement.

The level of disagreement among males and females was the only area of difference. When males' and females' attitudes are considered separately, proportionally more males (38 per cent) than females (15 per cent) strongly disagree with the statement. Most females (34 per cent) only mildly disagree that PR is "fuzzy".

	Strongly agree	Mildly agree	Mildly disagree	Strongly disagree
Male	5%	35%	22%	38%
Female	4%	47%	34%	15%

Table 45: How each gender feels about PR being 'fuzzy'.

5.4.9 Students' (pre-study) perception about PR

If the public is misinformed about PR, are students also influenced by perceptions of the profession? According to students, the answer is 'yes', with 58.3 per cent saying they study the subject because of their perceptions of it. What those perceptions are is a question which is canvassed in the survey's open-ended answers. Figures were virtually identical across the genders (58% "yes" for females, and 59% for males).

	Yes	No
Male	22	15
Female	79	58
Total	101	73

Table 46: Perception of PR prior to study.

5.4.10 Does perception of PR influence students to study it?

As for the above question, students were split equally, with half saying their perception of the subject did influence their decision to study it. There was also an equal split across gender.

	Yes	No
Male	18	19
Female	69	68
Total	87	87

Table 47: There is an even split among males and females on perception as an influence.

The responses to the open-ended question produced some clearly-defined themes, including: students' surprise at the amount of work involved in PR; that PR involved a lot of writing, and that their initial perception about PR was wrong (that probably relates more to the amount of work involved, and that they actually had to write essays and prepare communications plans). It is in the area of their perception that mostly relates to my hypothesis that people enter PR because of the perceptions about it – that it is perceived to be a female job, and that it is seen as an easy study option – and that these perceptions are a result of societal conditioning, created largely by the media, which portrays the industry as something anyone can do.

5.5 Common (survey) questions

Some questions from the first two surveys featured similar themes. I have included them at the end of the chapter in order to better compare responses.

5.5.1 PR sector specialisation/interest

Question five presented students with a list of 11 areas of PR specialisation. Students were asked to list their top three preferences. This was meant to indicate the sector of PR in which they would like to specialise. This has limitations in that their views of PR, and therefore their area of interest, will more than likely change during their course of study. Professionals were asked a similar question – which area is of most interest?

	Overall %	Male % (order)	Female % (order)
Entertainment	28	38 (1st)	27 (1st)
Fashion	17	6 (=4th)	20 (2nd)
Tourism	17	11 (=3rd)	18 (3rd)
NFP	12	17 (2nd)	11 (=4th)
International	11	11 (=3rd)	11(=4th)
Health	3	0	3 (5th)
Food	3	6 (=4th)	2 (=6th)
Financial	2	0	2 (=6th)
Industrial	2	0	2 (=6th)

Table 48: Type of PR in which students would prefer to specialise.

Responses differed markedly among males and female students. This is to be expected, given the high number of women in the survey.

Entertainment PR is clearly an area in which all students want to work. It was the leading choice overall (28%) and among males (38%) and females (27%). Noble (2004) also found "sports public relations (29 per cent) and entertainment public relations (24 per cent) were the most popular choices for public relations careers [among US students]."

While beauty and tourism were the second choice overall (at 17% each), there was a clear difference among males in the selection of fashion (ranked fifth choice at 6%) and females (ranked second choice at 27%). Both males (11%) and females (18%) ranked tourism as their third choice.

Working in the not-for-profit sector was selected by 12 per cent of students as the overall fourth choice. Males indicated a greater desire to work in this sector, with 17 per cent of men selecting it (and as their second choice), compared to 11 per cent of women (equal fourth choice). This is interesting, as it says men (at least those studying PR) do have those 'innate' qualities of compassion, empathy, which are so often associated with women.

The International PR sector comprises work within government and quasi-government organisations such as the United Nations. It was the fourth choice by 11 per cent of all students, both males and female. It also ranked similarly for males (equal third choice) and females (equal fourth).

Health and the food industry PR each only registered three per cent interest. No males were interested in health. For food, six per cent of males were interested, compared to three per cent of females.

Financial and industrial PR did not register among males, and only two per cent of females chose both of them as their main areas of interest.

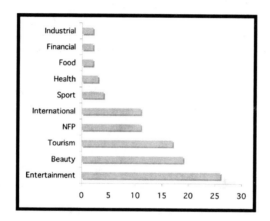

Figure 51: Female students' industry sector of interest.

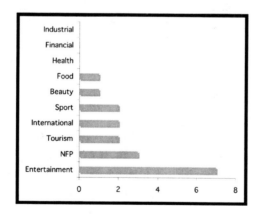

Figure 52: Male students' industry sectors of interest.

Professionals, like students, rated entertainment highly (second choice) as a sector in which they were interested (Figure 38). However, this result is skewed. Of the 18 per cent of the population that selected this as an option, 15 per cent were women. Clearly, however, women like to work in the entertainment PR sector. The leading sector of interest for professionals was Information Technology, with 22 per cent of respondents selecting it. The financial and government sectors were equal third choice (10 per cent). Women did not register interest in the following sectors: travel, health, sports, mining and property.

5.5.2 Areas of interest

> I could walk into a university and ask who wants to work in entertainment or tourism and the hands would shoot up. And I could ask who wants to work in investor relations, and no hands would go up. Then I'd ask who wants to earn $100K in eight to 10 years? The hands would go up. Of those, I'd ask who would want to work in investor relations, and the hands would drop. So I'd walk out and say none of you are going to earn much.
> – MD of a Perth PR consultancy.

The areas of interest were reflected in question 5 to students, and in question 12 to professionals. Students were asked what three areas of PR (in order) interested them most, from 12 choices.

	Total%	Male%	Female%
Events	40	6	34
Media	26	4	22
Project	17	3	14
IMC	8	2	6
Com. Relations.	4	1	3
Goal-setting	4	1	3
Writing	4	1	3
Rep. Mgt.	3	0	3
Investor	2	0	2
Budgets	1	0	1
Production	1	0	1

Table 49: PR sectors of interest to students, expressed as a percentage of the gender group.

Both male and female students agreed on their five first areas of interest (in order): events management, media relations, project management, community relations and integrated marketing communication. The only noticeable difference (and this was marginal) was that more females (37 per cent) selected events management as their first choice, compared to 27 per cent of males. This follows traditional employment patterns within PR, in which females have traditionally performed that function.

Males did not choose any of the following as a first, second or third choice: community relations, reputation management, investor relations, budgets and production. While this may indicate they have yet to develop any interest in these areas, it may also demonstrate that females have a better all-around appreciation of the many facets of PR.

Noble (2004) found that in the US, sports public relations (29.4 per cent) and entertainment public relations (23.8 per cent) were the most popular choices for public relations careers. Her comments pose an interesting sidebar to this study, regarding the image/perception of the profession as created by the media (both through entertainment (TV shows such as *Absolutely Fabulous*, *Spin City* and *Absolute Power*) and the way the news media portrays PR people (that is, as 'spin' merchants).

> Why are students selecting these aspects of public relations? We are all consumers of the media, and students' selection of sports and entertainment public relations fields may be due to their greater familiarity with these via the news media and television. Students may gravitate to these specific areas of public relations because these areas receive more news coverage. What part do the apparent glamour, fame and fortune of the sports and entertainment fields have to do with student interest? Further studies may differentiate between the interests of students who wish to be in the sports and entertainment public relations fields versus those interested in other aspects of the public relations industry (Noble 2004).

Professionals are mostly interested in Integrated Marketing Communication (24 per cent), media relations (23 per cent) and reputation management (17 per cent).

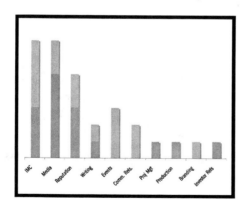

Figure 53: Professionals' areas of interest.

5.5.3 Preferred workplace (sector)

Students and professionals were asked the type of PR in which they would prefer to work, and had to select one sector from several alternatives. The common sectors were: consultancy, government, non-profit and corporate (in-house). Because students are not working they had two additional choices – 'anything I can get', and 'undecided'. Most students (52%) list corporate PR as their first choice. Nineteen per cent were undecided, and nine per cent said they would work at any PR job. Consultancies, non-profit organisations and government were highly unpopular choices.

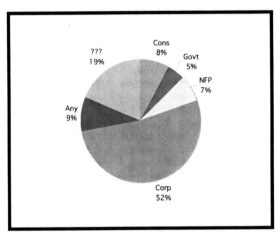

Figure 54: Students' preferred workplaces.

5.5.4 Influence of gender

Both groups were asked if they thought gender might influence a person's entry into PR. Apart from the basic statistical outcome, the aim of this question was to elicit respondents' views on the fact that being either male or female might influence people in commencing a PR career. There was a marked difference in the way the questions were presented to each group. The professional survey, which was sent earlier than the students survey, did not have the option of a "not really" response. My original intention was to force respondents into making a distinct choice, therefore prompting comments in the open-ended answer (which happened). This decision was also a result of the fact that there was likely to be a relatively low response to the survey, and the priority was to obtain as much qualitative data as possible.

	Yes (%)	No (%)	Not really (%)
STUDENTS			
Male	53	0	47
Female	27	18	55
Total	31	15	54
PROFESSIONALS			
Male	65	35	
Female	50	50	
Total	56	44	

Table 50: Students' and professionals' opinion on gender as an influence into PR.

5.5.5 Awareness of imbalance

Students and professionals were provided with statistics showing the gender balance of PR and asked if they were aware of it. Professionals were more aware of the imbalance. Female students and professionals were more aware of the imbalance than their male colleagues. This gap was slightly more pronounced among professionals (6% among students, and 11% among professionals).

	Yes (%)	No (%)
STUDENTS		
Male	58	42
Female	64	36
Total	63	37
PROFESSIONALS		
Male	71	29
Female	82	18
Total	78	22

Table 51: Students' and professionals' awareness of gender imbalance.

Note: among the universities, Murdoch students were more aware of the imbalance (39.7%), followed by Curtin (30.2), Notre Dame (17.2) and ECU (12.9).

A total of 78 per cent of professionals said they were aware most of the industry was female. As the chart (below) shows once again, women were more aware of the trend, with 82 per cent aware of it, compared to only 71 per cent of males being aware. This question tried to get to the heart of my study, which is why feminisation has occurred. There was a good response (31) in the open-ended answers. The most common reason put forward was that the industry is simply perceived as being feminine, with 10 respondents directly stating that. In conjunction with that theme, it is perceived as being glamorous (three), a "soft" career option (three). The next most popular (eight answers) theory was that women have better skills.

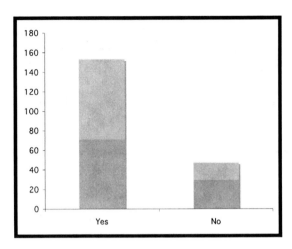

Table 52: Professionals' awareness of imbalance.

Across both groups, females were more aware of the gender imbalance than males. Is this in itself an indication of what many papers, textbooks and practitioners are saying: that women are more intuitive and can pick up on issues?

Only 43 per cent of professionals were aware of the imbalance, compared to 63 per cent of students. Female professionals had a higher awareness (82%) compared to males (71%). Among students, 64 per cent of females were aware, compared to 58 per cent of males.

	Awareness %
PROFESSIONALS	
Total	43
Male	71
Female	82
STUDENTS	
Total	63
Male	58
Female	64

Table 53: Level of awareness of imbalance.

5.5.6 Ability to build rapport

This question attempts to gauge whether people believe men or women are better at building rapport with clients. Results varied markedly between the two groups. Students (both male and female) almost overwhelmingly said neither men or women would be better at building rapport with clients. Most (90%) said neither would be better, with the remaining 10 per cent split between men and women. However, professionals were evenly split, both overall and by gender, with 25 per cent saying men would be better, 26 per cent saying women and 39 per cent neither.

	Men (%)	Women (%)	Neither (%)
STUDENTS			
Male	5	5	90
Female	5	25	70
Total	5	22	73
PROFESSIONALS			
Male	29	33	38
Female	24	38	38
Total	25	36	39

Table 54: Students' and professionals' opinions on building client rapport.

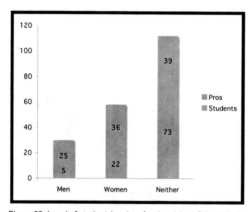

Figure 55: Level of students' and professionals' confidence in the ability of males or females to build rapport with clients

5.5.7 Qualities of PR practitioners

Students had eight choices. They could choose three. The top choices, scored on a three-two-one points basis were:

1. Verbal skills   65
2. Organisational   55
3. Strategic skills   46
4. Planning   39
5. Writing   33
6. Media   17
7. Listening   15

147

5.5.8 Reasons for entering and working within PR.

Students were given nine choices. The result of their responses (in order of importance) was:

1. Work with people   28%
2. Job satisfaction   21%
3. Variety   21%
4. Creative   17%
5. Current affairs   6%
6. Money   3%
7. Prestige   2%
8. Perceived benefits   1%

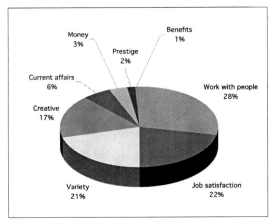

Figure 56: Students' reasons for studying PR.

Among males, the order and percentage of respondents who selected a particular reason for studying PR was:

1. Creativity   44%
2. Variety   23%
3. Job satisfaction and working with people   9%
4. Benefits, current affairs and prestige   5%

Among females the results showed:

1. Working with people   32%
2. Job satisfaction   24%
3. Variety   21%

4.	Creativity	12%
5.	Current affairs	6%
6.	Money	4%
7.	Prestige	1%

The responses varied among males and females. The clear difference is that males and females clearly have different reasons for studying PR. This is reflected in the top two choices, which differed. Forty-four per cent of males chose creativity and variety as their leading selection (compared to only 12 per cent of females), with variety (23 per cent) the second choice. The top two choices for women were working with people (32 per cent, compared to 9 per cent for males) and job satisfaction (24 per cent, compared to nine per cent for males).

	People	Money	Satisfaction	Benefits	Current Affairs	Variety	Prestige	Creative
M	9	0	9	5	5	23	5	44
F	32	4	24	0	6	21	1	12
T	33	4	25	1	7	24	2	20

Table 55: Summary of reasons why students study PR;
expressed as a percentage of the population.

Additional points of interest were:

- Males across all universities do not consider working with people to be important when considering a PR career, with only two males selecting this.
- Money is not an important consideration for students choosing PR as a career. Only four females chose this. No one from ECU thought money was important.
- An interest in current affairs was higher among women than men, particularly at Notre Dame and Murdoch Universities. No one at Curtin and only one male at ECU thought this a consideration in selecting a PR career.
- While creativity is a factor considered by most students to be important, only one female student at ECU selected this as a factor. This is surprising, as the PR course is part of the School of Creative Industries.

			Reasons for studying PR								Total
University			Work with people	Money	Job satisfaction	Benefis	Current affairs	Variety	Prestige	Creative	
Notre Dame	Gender	Male	1					1		4	6
		female	3	1	2		2	3		3	14
	Total		4	1	2		2	4		7	20
Murdoch	Gender	Male	1		2				1	2	6
		female	13	1	8		4	7		7	40
	Total		14	1	10		4	7	1	9	46
Curtin	Gender	Male				1		2		2	5
		female	10	2	8			8	1	1	30
	Total		10	2	8	1		10	1	3	35
ECU	Gender	Male					1	1			2
		female	5		5			2		1	13
	Total		5		5		1	3		1	15

Table 56: Students' reasons for studying PR (by university).

Perth PR professionals were asked to choose (in order) what made PR a good career. The phrasing was different to reflect the fact that professionals had time to consider and evaluate what was driving their careers. The choices were also different, and included money, career, variety, creativity, and mental challenge, along with room for respondents to add another aspect of their choosing, of which only one did (a flexible workplace). Job satisfaction was found to be highest among females. When asked if they would choose PR as a career again, 72 per cent of women said they would, compared to 50 per cent of males.

For professionals, the reasons for choosing PR were:

1. Variety   31%

2. Creativity   29%

3. Mental challenge 25%

4. Career   15%

5. Money   5%

There was no variation in order of selection between either gender, which contrasts starkly to the different reasons male and female students gave.

Clearly, variety and creativity are important factors for choosing PR among students and professionals. However, among female students these two factors were third and fourth choices respectively. Female students chose "working with people" and "job satisfaction" as their top two choices.

	Money	Career	Creativity	Variety	Mental	Other
M	10	11	27	29	21	2
F	13	16	24	25	22	0
Total	12	14	25	27	21	1

Table 57: Professionals' opinions on what makes a good PR career,
expressed as a percentage.

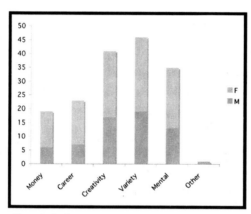

Figure 57: Professionals' views on what makes a good career.

5.5.9 Career barriers

Respondents simply had to answer yes or no as to whether they perceived any barriers to
their careers. There was a marked difference in the overall response between students and
professionals in what they thought were barriers to their careers.

Students were split evenly on whether there were barriers that could affect their careers.
Among male students, 63 per cent thought there were impediments, while only 53 per cent
of females held that opinion.

Among professionals 75 per cent listed barriers – 12 per cent higher than students. This
may simply reflect the naivety of youth and/or the years of experience/cynicism that
practitioners have. Unlike the students, the percentage response among professionals was
consistent across gender, with 76 per cent of males saying there were barriers, while
among females it was 74 per cent.

	Yes (%)	No (%)
STUDENTS	50	50
Male	63	37
Female	47	53
PROFESSIONALS	75	25
Male	76	24
Female	74	26

Table 58: Respondents' concerns about career barriers.

5.5.10 Suitability for PR

Both students and professionals were asked if they thought men or women were better suited to a career in PR. It was a contentious question designed to get people thinking. Contrary to some respondents' replies, this was not designed to be sexist. Judging by the responses, most professionals (70 per cent, and three of them men) thought women were better suited to be in PR. Four per cent thought men were better suited, and 42 per cent said gender either did not, or should not, enter into it. One woman thought men were better suited to PR. Even though most people made a choice, they also qualified it in their open-ended answers, with 13 of the 28 open-ended answers qualified by saying gender should not really enter into the equation.

	Men%	Women%	Neither%
Students (total)	3	36	61
Male	14	53	33
Female	3	73	24
Professionals (total)	4	42	70
Male	5	26	69
Female	4	38	59

Table 59: How students and professionals ranked each gender's suitability for PR. Results are expressed as a percentage of the group.

5.6 Conclusions

The statistics, which proved the phenomenon and provided further impetus to conduct this study, show the trend of increasing female predominance across three countries (the US, UK and Australia) to be similar, and prove that there has been a rapid increase by women into PR in the past 20 years.

While I initially thought the survey data would act more as a guide for the "rich" nature of the qualitative phases of the study (i.e., what I could put towards participants in interviews and focus groups) it yielded a wealth of material and showed distinct trends about the way the profession is perceived by students and professionals.

The results of each question are, by themselves, self-explanatory and therefore, in effect, mini conclusions. However, some of the more notable aspects of the surveys were:

- Both groups are aware of the gender imbalance, with females in both groups more aware of it than males.

- Both professionals (70%) and students (63%) thought women were better suited to PR.

- Variety was among the most highly-ranked reason why both professionals and students undertake PR. Money is not an important consideration among both groups.

- Not many students consider an interest in current affairs to be important in PR.

- Both males and female students both list entertainment PR as their main area of PR sector interest.

- Females still seems to be "pigeonholed" into technician-type roles. While at university, they either think this is what they will end up doing, and those in the workforce tend to either gravitate to it, or are merely allocated those roles.

6 Focus groups and interviews

> A big issue is when you try to find out what PR is. They don't tell you
> much. Maybe if they tell you more at the start it might correct the problem
> of so few guys doing it. Then again, it might work the other way. But I
> wouldn't have been able to say what it was when I started. But then, I
> can't tell you what it is after two years (male student).

The aim of interviewing the industry (professionals and students) was to gain "rich" information that might not be apparent from the surveys. Statistics can only tell so much, and do not give a clear indication of the insights into what people think of the industry, and even as to why people choose PR as a career.

6.1 Student focus groups

6.1.1 Focus group 1, ECU

The first student focus group was held at Edith Cowan University in a lecture theatre, from 7.45pm to 8.30pm. It consisted of 10 fourth-year PR students (eight female and two male) and was observed by tutor, Mr Vince Hughes, MBA. There was a mix of students, with two from Norway (1M, 1F), one from India (M), two from China (F) and one (F) from Hong Kong. For responses, students are identified by number (from left to right, and by gender (M or F). The format was to put forward results of earlier surveys and to ask students to respond to the results. All students were informed their identities would remain anonymous and that participation was voluntary. The main points to emerge from the focus groups:

6.1.2 Student interviews

> I was the only male in my tute of 25 this semester. In lectures it's
> dominated "majorly" by females. You look around and you might see 10
> guys among 50 or 60 females. So I did think at some stage why there were
> so many females (male student, 2005).

The interviews with students were, as it turns out, the key to the process. Professionals, in the main, could not provide reasons why the phenomenon was occurring. They key had to be with students; particularly the males. This sub-group is where the trend is apparent. The old days of entry to PR via journalism (previously a male-dominated profession) have long and truly passed.

From the transcripts of the interviews, a common theme among males was that PR was seen as "ambiguous", "fuzzy" and generally lacked direction. (This feedback prompted the question in the second student survey about PR being "fuzzy in it logic"). One male student I interviewed was so disillusioned with PR, after two years, that he decided to switch to advertising in 2006. The following comment from a male student was typical.

> To be honest, one of the things that has turned me off PR is that it seems ambiguous compared to marketing and advertising. It's hard to measure PR, and you don't know if the work you are doing is working or not. If you're doing marketing and advertising you have a better gauge. Sometimes you feel as though you've been studying for two years and don't know if you've done anything. I think this is one of the big issues we come across. Everyone likes to measure things at the end of the day to see how they're going. Males like that sense of competition and they try to beat other individuals, so they like to be measured. That's where it's frustrating because PR is hard to measure. We have sat down and talked about it. And it just seems you never know where you're at with it.

And another comment from a male student:

> The internship proved to me what I had started to think about the industry. I'd say that it true that the industry isn't very black and white. When I was doing my internship, I'd be there and ask them: 'exactly what do you do? What's involved?' They were connecting A to B, jumping up in the air and saying they were brilliant. It's very grey. And that's why I'm switching to advertising/marketing, because PR is not very definite. You don't exactly know what your role is. I think that anyone that hasn't done PR would see it a female-dominated industry. And that's a turn-off for guys, I think. I think one of the main skill to have in PR is to be able to be able to say something without saying anything, and I think women are pretty good at that. That does make it [PR] fuzzy. I think that's a motherly instinct (every woman has a chance to be a mother) and it's ingrained in females. Of course guys can have that ability, but it's more apparent in females.

Some of the female subjects (as the following comment illustrates) were aware of the different ways men and women thought about PR and its place in the business world.

> The males did have a different approach. They tended to come from a marketing or political perspective. I always feel that men do marketing and women do PR for some reason. It is just my perception. Generally, men that do PR often give it a title so it doesn't look like they're doing PR. I've always thought of it as a profession that women do, like nursing. I wouldn't think of women becoming marketers. I don't think they do it consciously. It's just that they have this ideas that there are certain roles men do, and some that women do. It's like when they enroll, at uni someone says: 'what are you doing?' And they get the reply that 'oh, that's for girls.

With PR not seen by students not be a particularly serious business subject, it is perhaps is an area in which ambitions do not play an important role. If we follow the reasoning of Moir and Jessel (1996), in that "ambition simply means different things to the different sexes", then PR probably suits women, more than men.

6.2 Professionals' focus group and interviews

6.2.1 Focus group – professionals

Due to the relatively low numbers in the focus group, and the short time frame, there were fewer topics mentioned (15), compared to the interviews (26 topics). There was a marked difference in the main topics being raised. The main differences were:

- Only one person in the focus group raised the issue of looking at the educational system, whereas 10 mentions were made of this in the interviews.

- The focus group did not broach the subject of imbalance. The interviews raised this topic 11 times.

- Other issues not raised by the focus group, but mentioned (times in bracket) in interviews were: female skills (6), abstract nature of PR (4), comparison to HR (3), creativity (3), and gender differences (2).

- Interviews did not raise the issue of PR being glamorous, or of women being better at multi-skilling.

Overall, the most mentioned topics were: perception of PR (14), influence of education (university) on PR, general imbalance (11), image of PR (8), women as better communicators, female skills, compassion (6), women [general], family issues, abstract nature of PR (5). There were another 11 topics, rating four mentions and below). These topics are simply based on the number of times they were mentioned. The statistics may vary somewhat in some categories. For example, if the topic of image in taken to be part of people's perception of PR, then the area of perception would increase markedly to 22 points.

The most-mentioned topics in the professionals' interviews were: imbalance/balance (11), university (10), perception of PR (8), "soft" nature of PR, (6), female skills 6, abstract nature of PR (4), comparison with human resources (4). There were another 19 concepts/themes raised, ranging from three to one mentions.

The most-mentioned topics in the focus group were: perception of PR (6), writing (4), males and men (3), glamour (3), "soft" nature of PR (3), women as better communicators, power. There were a further seven topics raised.

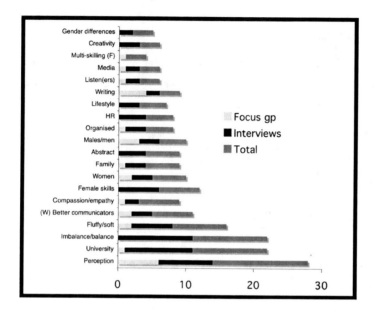

Figure 58: Most talked-about professional interview and focus group topics.

6.2.2 Professionals' interviews

The first round of interviews began in November 2005 and concentrated on professionals. Interviews were largely conducted at venues of the subject's choosing, which usually was a coffee lounge, or the subject's workplace. This proved to be convenient and allowed to subjects to be at ease in an informal situation, thereby facilitating participation. In-person interviews were necessary, as in most instances I had not met the subject. The personal contact helped facilitate the discussion and opened the door to additional contact at a future date. Ethics approval was gained by subjects earlier signing a form (in the survey) to signal their intention to participate. They were informed before the interview that it would be recorded, that their involvement was voluntary and that they or their company would not be identified. Interviews were stored on my personal computer at home and later transcribed. Files were converted to MP3 format and are included on disc in annex S.

After the first two interviews it became apparent that professionals, despite their years of experience and wide knowledge of the industry, could not precisely identify why the industry had become female-dominated. This was simply explained by the fact that they had never thought of the issue until it was put before them in this study. However, as evidenced by the above, there was a good deal of discussion, which should form the basis of further research into the subject. All agreed that my study was interesting and were interested in the outcomes.

The more experienced male practitioners had extremely strong opinions on the way the industry had developed, with most agreeing the calibre of female practitioner was generally poor, as evidenced by comments such as:

> If someone could answer me why is it more difficult for females to pick up the 'corporate' reins of an account, I'd love to hear it. I could actually develop and education package that could be slotted into the universities. It just seems to me that the young guys have a better understanding of business. That's probably a slight on female practitioners, and it's not meant to be. It's just that when they come through, it is a significant effort to get them thinking about corporate reins, particularly investor relations. Things like profit, triple bottom line and such mean nothing to them (senior consultant).

A senior government PR manager was much more forthcoming in his observations of the way the industry has developed.

> There's a whole lot of blondes out there in black dresses who are very good at functions, but when they come to write press releases they create 'lobsters' (with a whole lot of shit at the head). They just can't nail it in the first three paragraphs.

And this, from another private industry practitioner:

> I attended a national PRIA event about five or six years ago, at which 212 people attended. Six were male. I worked as an in-house 'associate' with one of (the city's) largest PR operations a year or so back for about 12 months. This company occupies 80 per cent of the 18th level. They employed a mix of 30-plus full and part-time staff of which only myself, the MD and three others were males (two of which often did crisis management seminars on-site at coal mines etc). That's more like an 88 per cent female dominance by my reckoning. This gender imbalance by itself didn't really bother me. It is, however, the lack of any real 'humour' in and about the workplace – everything all serious and self-important.

Whatever one's views, these three practitioners have a combined 74 years experience between them, and their opinions can not be ignored. However, none could answer why the industry had become female-intensive.

Respondents, both students and professionals, commented on the characteristics of PR practitioners in the survey questions and interviews. Both groups had similar opinions of what comprised the typical characteristics of people entering the profession. This correlated to research uncovered in the literature review, which found that females possessed certain qualities deemed necessary to be successful in PR. Respondents agreed that PR practitioners possessed the following characteristics: ability to listen, good communicators, organised and can write well. This was in evidence, given the following excerpts from interviews.

> *FEMALE STUDENT:* Males in PR seem to be a little bit more sensitive than other males students in other disciplines. They are more organised and methodical. The majority of them, I guess, seem to have more feminine characteristics. You can talk to them more easily than some of the other male students. They possibly don't fit in with what might be termed the general male culture. They're very creative, with innovative ideas and very helpful, when I've done group work with them. I haven't had to ask for their work. They're quite organised. But they're not quite as helpful as females. I just think those qualities are needed for a PR person to be successful, and women generally have them more than men.

> *MALE STUDENT:* When I was the only guy in a group I was constantly trying to get them to do things my way. I found a lot of their writing was a lot more flowery. I guess if you're trying to make things positive for the client they could do it. But I found myself better at organising or managing things in the group situation. Maybe they were better at the creativity, and I was better at managing. Maybe that comes back to the view that men lean towards more business-related subjects.

> *MALE PRACTITIONER:* Women are very good communicators (in general), they have an ability to articulate information in a manner that is often easily understood and coherent. As such they actually have the starting point for being a PR practitioner. They are excellent communicators; they are good at telling a story, they are good at writing, they actually enjoy writing. And writing is the critical aspect, whether male or female, which takes people down a potential career in PR.

> *MALE PRACTITIONER:* I think physiologically and mentally (left-brain, right-brain) there are differences in the way males and females work, and their approach to things. But some of the planning women do are better than men; particularly event management. They have that attention to detail (such as colour) and I don't mean that to be sexist. But things like that can add value to an event.

MALE PRACTITIONER: Men and women do communicate differently. Women are naturally better communicators. I think women are certainly generally more empathetic than males, and that certainly helps in PR. One of the other areas that women excel in is that they are better organisers. Most of them, when they try to tell us why they want to be in PR, they name event management as the reason. Either they have an interest in organising things, or they have an interest in parties. That's fine. Either interest is valid, but they're in it for their organisational ability. It's one of the reasons women thrive. They are good documenters and they are thorough. The people who are good at PR are usually somewhere in the centre. The good males have some of the feminine characteristics: the ability to build relationships, have empathy, communicate clearly The very good women also have some of the necessary robustness to be tough and use in negotiations, and some of the slight aggression you need to have to work with the media. It's a hybrid type of person.

One thing is clear: PR has changed over the years, reflected not only in the number of women but in the way it is learnt and the way it is practised. This was borne out in an interview with one of Perth's most senior male professionals, who observed:

The lifestyle stuff is still mainly the women's preserve. This, of course makes them valuable in PR, because that's where the modern marketing style of PR find its outlet. To me that is the major part of PR today and that's where women are fitting in. It's the lifestyle aspects of PR that is emphasised.

This view seems to resonate with Rickertson (1999) who points to the growth in newspaper 'lifestyle' sections. He compared editions from Melbourne's *The Age* newspaper in 1956 and 1996. "There was the same amount of 'hard' news, despite a three to fourfold increase in the paper's size." It poses the question of whether the rise in the 'fluffy' side of journalism, as a possible consequence of our clamour for material things, has prompted a subsequent rise in the 'fluffy' side of PR, often mentioned by this study's respondents.

6.3 Conclusions

The interviews with students and professionals provided a more detailed insight into the mindset of today's PR participants, in line with the 'rich' nature of the research. While limited by their sample size, they nevertheless contain the opinions of the local industry's most senior 'players', and those of future practitioners. In keeping with the 'rich' nature of this study's research, all interviews are fully transcribed within the annexes. Quite clearly, imbalance is something that both groups are well aware of. There was a common theme among males that PR was seen to be "ambiguous" and/or "fuzzy". This fits in with a general perception that males are attracted to more business-like subjects where results are measurable. The material gleaned from students was, at best "sketchy"; possibly due to them being not used to present their opinions. On the other hand, the professionals were, as expected, more forthcoming in their answers. In general, both students and professionals agreed that PR suffers from a perception that it is "soft". Both groups highlighted the way PR is perceived, which, for me, seems to be at the core of the problem. The subsequent interviews also reinforced these views, with both groups agreeing that PR practitioners need certain qualities (also reflected in the literature). These qualities included listening and writing ability, which were accepted by most participants as inherently feminine qualities.

7 Summary

My study has contributed immensely to my personal and professional learning and development. It has further developed my research, interviewing and academic writing skills. It has expanded my view of the workplace, and allowed me to look at fields I had not previously considered in my academic career: most notably the field of work and gender, and subjects including sociology and psychology. Additionally, it has also honed my ability to work to deadline and enhanced my organisational skills. This was achieved by an almost-daily routine of either reading or writing something, and by being meticulous in recording Readings and making relevant notes. From a methodological viewpoint, I gained further understanding of how to gather, analyse and present statistical information, with widespread use of programs used to present data (notably SPSS and Excel). I also became adept at using a textual qualitative research program, HyperResearch. Most importantly, it has allowed me to explore a subject I was intrigued by, and present that information to a (mostly) receptive audience – the people involved in my study: PR professionals.

The staff at Central Queensland University most influenced by the research are my supervisors, Prof. Alan Knight and Kate Ames. Like the industry professionals and students, both Prof. Knight and Ms Ames were interested in the subject from the start, and continued their enthusiasm (and support) throughout. The high level of involvement, I put down to the fact that the research was not only original, but was about something that people in the profession knew was occurring, but had not been explored in any detail. Being the first Study of its type, this thesis has provided a starting point for other academic studies. Prof. Knight has commented several times of different aspects of my study which have surprised him – apart from the obvious gender imbalance. These included the fact that professionals and students are not primarily driven by money; that there is (alleged) gender discrimination within PR, and that tourism and entertainment are the two most preferred areas of PR that students want to work in. These are, no doubt, all subjects for separate research projects.

From an industry perspective, practitioners and students have been influenced by this Study. This was evident from the start, with the strong numbers responding to the surveys, and their willingness to follow progress with regular updates. There were a total of 63 practitioners who received regular updates. E-mail feedback from the approximate bi-monthly updates was encouraging, although spasmodic (but not expected). Academics at all universities were interested, cooperative and encouraging, with all four universities involved in my study providing statistics and allowing me to personally present pre-survey information on my study to students. Some even collected the information for me.

Students, in Australia and overseas, also showed interest. I was interviewed by two Canadian students for a post-graduate course; by a journalism student at Notre Dame for an assignment, and provided information to a UK-based male post-graduate student in the UK.

Further interest was demonstrated by the PRIA, which published several of my articles on its national web-site and in the Western Australian and Queensland branch magazines. I was also invited to present my findings to the Queensland branch of the PRIA (at a date yet to be arranged). The journal *PRism*, published by Bond and Massey Universities, printed an article, as did the UK PR magazine, *Beyond Spin*.

One of the most positive aspects of my study has been that is has brought about a change in policy of the Public Relations Institute of Australia, which will now maintain membership statistics, with a gender breakdown. As mentioned, prior to this study this was not the Institute's practice. The collection and archiving of membership statistics will enable future gender trends to be tracked more easily. It has also made the PRIA more aware of the trend and of possible implications for the profession.

The research undertaken can certainly contribute to the wider body of knowledge about the PR industry. While my study raises more questions than it answers, it acts as a catalyst for future research, which needs to be conducted over ensuing years and with a wider range of subjects. The inclusion of the PRIA and all major tertiary institutions that teach PR are necessary for a full picture to emerge. This thesis will act as a base that will serve to inform and help guide subsequent PR industry gender studies. The fact that this is the first major project on this subject provides original findings that should be used to better understand the motivations and aspirations of PR students. Industry research on the changing gender composition of PR is also necessary. Questions also need to be asked concerning whether feminisation is affecting the industry.

The surveys were the first among the 'PR industry' in Australia (and to date the most comprehensive in the Western world) to examine people's views on this topic, and to gauge their opinions on the reason for the phenomenon. There were three surveys undertaken, among the Perth "PR industry". These consisted of two surveys among industry professionals (consultants, government, non-profits and in-house practitioners) and one survey (on-line and print) among 116 second and third-year PR students.

8 Conclusions

> I have only just recently been exposed to this (increasing number of
> women in PR). At a recent course I conducted for the PRIA there were
> only 12 women. So I asked them why there were no men, and they replied
> that they 'were much cheaper than men'. They went on to explain that at
> the top end of town, in financial PR, however, most, if not all the
> practitioners were men. But I don't know if that was just "gender-talk". I
> have no evidence to back it up (Male university lecturer in Sydney).

If only it was that simple. However, the reasons for the growing number of females, and decline in males, can not be simply attributed to one simple reason. There are numerous factors – some more obvious than others.

From the literature, the following findings emerge:

The changing nature of our society, from industrial to information-dominated, ideally suits the infusion of women into knowledge-based industries such as public relations

That women numerically dominate in all areas within the industry

They are ideally suited to roles within public relations as a result of sociological and psychological factors.

However, the literature (particularly the PR literature) falls short when trying to fully explain the reasons for women's rise to prominence within PR. The public relations industry should (if it's doing its job) be able to reflect many of the changes in gender relations and roles affecting society; particularly as immense changes in gender are sitting right on its doorstep. Accordingly, an important, but unrelated, finding from this literature review is that the field of gender and its relationship with PR provides an opportunity for the advancement of knowledge within an important but relatively uncharted field.

When I began this study there seemed to be little information. On conclusion of the literature review, I have found that still to be true. The lack of material certainly lends credence to the notion that PR does not lend itself to being studied.

> It's difficult to study the careers of women in the field because public
> relations careers are not high profile. The role of PR in fact often requires
> avoiding the spotlight. The result is that public relations history has only
> produced a few identifiable personalities (Newsom, Turk and Kruckeberg,
> 2004, p38).

Certainly, from the literature (and as you will read later, from the opinions of professionals and students) women seem better suited emotionally and psychologically to work in public relations. This may explain the high proportion of women in the field. Men, perhaps, have yet to grasp and use the qualities which seem to have put women at the forefront of the profession. "The next generation of public relations workers will see a leveling of perceived differences between how men and women public relations workers think and behave" (Mackey, 2003). This may then see a more even spread of males and females in the profession. As Indian and UK professional Prema Sagar, of Genesis PR, said: "Public relations is still a field that is looked down upon. The simplest example of this is that there are very few men doing this job" (Newsom, Turk and Kruckeberg, 2000). Sagar, the first Indian to be inducted into the International Communications Consultancy Organisation's (ICCO) International Hall of Fame, reflects on a pessimistic future for the industry if it remains unbalanced:

> Many public relations practitioners fear that the presence of increasing
> numbers of women in the field is already causing corporate "layering" that
> lowers the status of the PR function on the corporate ladder. Others
> believe that, in a global society where women have lower status than men,
> delegating the PR function to women will denigrate the profession. Few
> critics are brave enough to voice these concerns loudly, but their
> murmurings can be heard.

In her 2005 survey of PR professionals in northern England, Hall recommended that it was most important an investigation be undertaken into why the profession remains so attractive to women, to encompass the current and future impact caused by the feminisation of the field. "The argument is that this is important if the industry wishes to maintain its growing reputation and continue to be taken seriously in future" (Hall, 2005). Has feminisation brought about collaboration, sensitivity towards audiences and better two-way communication? Certainly PR has become more open and two-way. But perhaps this may be just a result of media fragmentation and the development of the Internet, which encourages PR practice to be more "in tune" with its target audiences.

While it may be the opinion of most writers that women seem more suited to a career in PR, I do not believe this to have been scientifically justified. Much of the limited amount of industry-specific research was conducted at a time when currently outdated perceptions of males' and females' roles, and of the way males and females think, held sway.

The rise in the number of females in PR may simply reflect the changing nature of the Australian education system. Maushart (2005) outlines the way that the system has, in the past 10–15 years, been designed to even the imbalance in the system, which favoured boys. What is happening now is that females are playing catch-up, and, it seems, surpassing boys' academic achievements. Some academics believe education, like PR, has been feminised. Others argue it has been 'verbalised', with a growing emphasis on self-expression, verbal analysis and information-processing. Certainly the two of the key competencies necessary in PR – written and verbal expression – favour women. According to Maushart (2005): "It is true that females hold a slight edge in these areas. On average, Australian boys do not perform – and never have performed – as well as girls in any of the main literacy strands, especially writing and speaking . . . yet perform no worse than their peers in comparable countries." So it seems that what holds true in Australia, in education and PR, would also apply in the US, the UK and Canada, where the same trends are evident.

One of the more practical explanations of the rise of women is that simply because there are more women studying the subject, there are more entering the profession. It may well be that simple. However, that does not explain why there are so many women (and so few men) studying the subject. As Brown, 1998 said: "Maybe public relations is merely the first portion of that industry to witness some gender equity. In an information economy, where communication is increasingly vital, perhaps that's not such a bad place to start."

With regard to the subject of brain differences, I can not see that this has a much influence on whether males or females would choose PR, other than to generalise and say that because language (written and verbal) is such a major component of PR, it naturally follows that females would be better suited and/or more attracted to the subject, given that the research in this area shows that females are predisposed to language skills. But that is clearly a nonsense because "if boys are more able in mathematics and girls have a greater verbal ability, it is hard to see how men can be better fitted for political life and their dominant role there" (Sayers, as cited in Bland, 2005).

In summary, there seems to be little consistent evidence for significant differences between men and women in ability to nurture, communicate, or in the way brain patterns function. As Kimmel (2004) so succinctly put it: "In most cases, brain researchers (like many other researchers) find exactly what they are looking for" (p. 32). Or, as (Bland 2005) said:

> It is suggested that men and women may tend to think in different ways, but every individual thinks in his or her individual way. Let us not come to believe that all women think in one way and all men in the other.

As with all findings, some are more relevant than others.

Salary certainly could not be considered a reason for more women than men studying PR, as this study found little difference in salary between men and women. This is supported by Hutton (2005) and Hall (2005). Hutton stated: "Detailed statistical analysis of a major salary survey and a review of existing studies both indicate that there is no empirical reason to believe that there is gender-based salary discrimination in the PR field" (pp. 73-83). Hutton's findings were based on a 2001 study on salary by *PR Week* which showed "there is little or no gender-based salary discrimination". Hall's survey of PR professionals in northern England produced a similar result to mine: that there was little difference in earnings between males and females. Hall said: [There was] "only a minor discrepancy in salary . . . possibly around £500–£1000 ($1000–$2000) per annum (if this can be classified as minor). Female practitioners seem to be earning slightly less than male public relations professionals, despite the fact they appear to hold more qualifications (both industry and non-industry-related)."

Despite some of the negative comments with regard to hours, the issue of a balance between family and work as a reason for the number of women in PR, indeed, in any occupation, can not be dismissed. American psychologist Steve Pinker says economists who study employment practices have long noted that:

> Men and women differ in what they state are their priorities in life. Men, on average, are more likely to chase status at the expense of their families; women give a more balanced weighting. Once again: think statistics. The finding is not that women value family and don't value status. It is not that men value status and don't value family. Nor does the finding imply that every last woman has (Pinker, 2005, np).

In line with that train of thought, Pinker also raises another aspect (related to the above) that was mentioned by women practitioners in surveys and focus groups. "There are some things in life that the females rated higher than males, such as the ability to have a part-time career for a limited time in one's life" (Pinker, 2005). Female practitioners mentioned this (in PR) being a flexible occupation and allowing them to have children, then perhaps work from home. Several (male) consultancy principals also discussed this aspect of the profession, which is covered elsewhere in the thesis. This aspect is raised by many scholars, and most recently by Walters (2006) in *Business Review Weekly*, which looked at the decline of women in IT; for those very reasons. "IT does not attract females because of its culture, in which long hours are the norm. This in turn "means giving up an active social life, forgoing hobbies and delaying marriage" (p. 31).

In Germany, studies have shown that cultural professions (for example, journalism and design, "might serve as a model for less gendered forms of work and work and life arrangements [and that] it is more likely that we find women making the trade-offs between work and family in the sense of 'dual earner/female part-time career' or 'dual earner and marketised career' patterns, a finding similar to studies of professionals in other countries" (Gottschall 2002).

The gap in the three main areas chosen by respondents as the reason they work in PR – variety, creativity and mental challenge – (Figure 28) show that women may possess a more 'creative' bent toward the profession, as indicated by Cline (as cited in Aldoory, 2001) who said: "Women's interest in more creative pursuits are examples of socialization." This brings into play the notion of whether PR is still seen as a 'soft social' discipline, in which creative concepts are more favoured than hard-nosed business skills. This may have it roots in the fact that many PR courses are embedded into university social science departments, rather than business schools and/or faculties. Does this fact simply attract more women, who are attracted by the "social" side of PR? In the analysis of surveys, some respondents raise this aspect. (Folmar, 2005) points to this. Results of my surveys prove that 72 per cent of the women surveyed listed creativity as why they choose PR as a career.

> Evident in extensive research is the perception that the female majority in the field of public relations 'softens' the image of the field and causes it not to be seen as a legitimate, management-driven profession. Noted public relations practitioner Philip Lesly (1988) noted that the impact of a largely female field would have such consequences as lowering professional aspirations because women wanted to perform technical rather than managerial duties, lowering income levels because fields that became "female" experienced such losses, and creating the image of public relations as a soft, rather than "heavy-hitting top management function *(Sha, 2001, p. 5).*

One of the most relevant 'snippets' to shed light on the theory (as cited by Folmar, 2005) was written by Linda R. Silver, who in 1988 speculated:

> The reason feminised professions are often seen by social scientists and the public at large as 'semi-professions' can be attributed to the differing goals male and female professionals have in regard to relationship management. While male professionals work to advance themselves through their professional lives, using their knowledge to define their clients' needs and hence to place themselves above their clients, women professionals place primary importance on filling the needs of others (p. 26).

Most importantly, according to Silver, is that "this difference in management style manifests itself in the perceptions people have of certain professions", which is what I have argued in this study. It also holds that it is not just the perception the public holds about PR, it is also the perception that the industry, and those about the industry, have about PR.

From comments from males and females in this study, the industry view of the industry says that the profession is full of "fluff" (both in looks and content). From my perspective, I think the issue of image is more than "skin deep". I believe the industry as a whole suffers from lack of credibility because its image is still one of being gimmicky, rather than offering substance. This, in part, is due to the early days of PR, when it was long lunches and parties – a fact well known by any journalist or PR practitioner who has been around for more than 20 years (this includes myself). In the wake of the Brian Burke lobbying scandal in WA, Stewart (2006) looked at lobbying and also PR (as many PR firms have specialist lobbyists). He refers to the "guns for hire provided by dedicated PR and lobbying firms", and interviews Adam Kilgour, CEO of the PR and lobby group, CPR. "The work of most lobbyists is far less exciting than the public perception. 'Instead of lunches of Cristal and Krug in Italian restaurants in Perth, lobbing mostly involves research, strategy, analysing data, turning it into digestible messages and sharing it with governments'," Andrew Parker of Parker and Partners says (p. 27).

I and many others believe the issue of the perception and image of PR is more than "skin deep". I believe the industry as a whole suffers from lack of credibility because its image is one of being gimmicky, rather than offering substance. This, in part, is probably a 'hangover' (no pun intended) from the early days of PR, when it was long lunches and parties.

Folmar (2005) proposes that it might be that males are simply 'unattracted' to public relations. Data from her survey of university students "reflected that students perceive a certain degree of ambiguity associated with public relations, because public relations does not have one definition by which it is known, which was evident in both of the texts analysed, the profession carries with it a stigma of being somewhat nebulous in nature. In other words, the very nature of public relations might be a turn-off for males" (p. pp. 88–89). This was in evidence in my interviews, with words like 'soft' and 'fuzzy' being used (by males) to describe the practice of PR. In general, male students see PR as being unable to deliver the necessary 'business' outcomes that can be achieved in subjects like marketing, which, as one student said, can be measured more effectively.

> There's a perception in PR that you are always only a spokesperson for whoever you work for, and that you never really get involved with driving the business. So that could be a disincentive for males not doing PR. I guess it gets back to me thinking that it's an inadequate subject (Male student in 2006 interview).

This attitude, which seems to be prevalent among the wider number of male students (and it is difficult to ascertain, based on the relatively small sample in this study) ties in with the theory put forward by Game and Pringle (1983) who believe "Men who do 'women's work' may be seen as weak, effeminate or even homosexual. Men's work has to be experienced as empowering" (p. 16).

The image and perception of PR is considered by males to be 'feminine'. The general consensus among males was that PR is a 'soft' subject. PR, it seems, does not suit conform to what male students' perceive to be a business subject. Primarily this means that they do not see the value PR contributes to a business, and nor can they measure the outcomes of PR programs. As outlined in the interviews and in answers to my surveys, males regard the process and outcomes of PR as being intangible. Males continue to prefer what have traditionally been regarded as male business subjects, such as economics, marketing and advertising. There are numerous reasons for this. Principally, students are still socially-conditioned by the media, both news and entertainment, to view PR in a less-than-serious light.

If we use a feminine/masculine traits analysis on PR, we find that those skills and traits most people believe belong with PR are 'feminine'. These include all those already mentioned, and then some. According to Deaux (1976): "studies show that women are much more willing to disclose information about themselves than men. . . . Men like other men who disclose relatively little information about themselves, whereas women consistently show a preference for those women who are willing to discuss personal information" (pp. 60-61). If so many women are working in PR may indicate that this "information-rich" nature of women may also be another reason why they may be ideally suited. As shown in this study, men do not perceive PR to be a 'serious' subject. In the business world, having a tendency towards self-disclosure (that is, being overtly verbose) would probably be seen by many men in management as a weakness; therefore those entering PR could be seen as a vacuous or flighty and not possessing the competitive traits necessary for 'pure' business (accounting, marketing).

8.3 Conclusions from student surveys

While it is not documented, it is common in the industry that women have been allocated events organisation. This may be a hangover from the early days of PR when males dominated the industry and women were seen as only suitable for the "froth and bubble" aspects of PR (launches, lunches, concerts). The perception (there's that word again) among students that this is an important aspect of PR is worrying, and only serves to reinforce the stereotype. However, this phenomenon (along with the emphasis on media relations) may be a byproduct of the industry in Perth, which is small and does not attract the large corporates that are present on the east coast. This in turn leads to a "dumbing down" of the industry, which is forced to revert to gimmicks and media stunts to attract publicity.

Many of the small to medium-sized business in Perth either do not consider, or understand modern PR practices such as stakeholder relations, issues management and Integrated Marketing Communication. This simply compounds the problem of academics being unable to present the relevance of these aspects to students.

The way students perceive PR is, I believe, a worrying aspect borne out by this study. Students' perceptions is also the critical factor in helping to shape future directions for the profession. Today's students are tomorrow's practitioners. Many students (particularly males) initially perceive PR to be a "soft" option. This begs the question of whether universities are attracting the right type of person into the industry. This study has shown that PR attracts people (particularly students) for the variety, creativity, mental challenges and career path it offers. Money was a fifth choice. So while there may be negative perceptions of the profession as a whole, people are still drawn to it for reasons other than financial gain.

This study's surveys clearly show that men and women have different areas of interest with PR, and that they are utilised (by management) in different areas of PR. Women are still associated (whether by choice or management) to the technician-type roles (events, media and writing), whereas men are associated with manager-type functions such as project and reputation management, reputation management.

In her US study, Noble (2004) found most students "majored in public relations because [they] find it interesting". Students also agreed strongly with the following statements, indicating their focus on life after college: "I majored in public relations because this major will give me the skills that will lead to a job when I graduate"; "I majored in public relations because it combines creativity and business". Women (73.8 per cent) were more likely to agree they selected public relations as a major because of the creative aspects than did men (51.4 per cent). In my survey, the main reason for choosing PR was variety (53 per cent of respondents), followed closely by creativity 47 per cent). My survey also found that of those who listed creativity as a reason for working in PR, 72 per cent were women. The same applied to variety, with 63 per cent of those choosing it as their main motivation being women.

With imbalance being the cornerstone of my thesis, professionals' responses to questions relating directly to imbalance were critical. Despite the fact that 73 per cent of respondents said there should be balance in the industry, and that balance is necessary for a healthy industry, there were few concerns from those surveyed. This may reflect the attitudes of those in 'power', who probably do not see beyond today and the long-term effects imbalance may have. In many ways, PR professionals are no different from the general population when it comes to future thought. There was general consensus that imbalance in itself is not necessarily a good thing for any industry, and particularly PR, which is about promotion and providing a balance of views. If there was any concern, it was only by a few (and then from a literary research viewpoint) that salaries may decrease. This is what has been shown to happen when an industry become predominantly female. In summary, there was quite an unreflective response from industry.

Is it merely that, despite PR's early beginnings as a male-dominated field, we have now come to recognise, through natural selection, because of our brain patterns (and differences), females are naturally more suited to PR? It may be that certain (more business-focused) sections of PR, such as investor relations and political lobbying, will remain in the male domain. This may eventually see PR split to produce separate fields in their own right, as we have witnessed in the case of Integrated Marketing Communication, which is now offered at one Australian university as a separate post-graduate degree. According to Moir and Jessel (1996): "the connection between masculinity, prestige and status is a dynamic one; when traditional male jobs come to be filled by women, the jobs lose their status in men's eyes" (p. 162). If this is the case, then here is another reason why men simply avoid entering PR.

For me, there were several important points raised by the literature that crossed over into the surveys and interviews and point towards the reasons why more women than men are entering PR.

It is clearly shown that the way our culture 'socialises' us (that is, imparts its mores, values and customs) is a crucial factor in developing our gender perceptions of all facets of our lives; from how we play to what we regard as male or female roles and careers. "Some experts, believe physical differences in the brain may not be there at birth but are gradually sculpted. This is because social conditioning begins from the first day of life" (Midgley, 2006). Our socialisation leads to the way we perceive things, including occupations. The media, in turn – also a product of our society – merely serve to reinforce these perceptions. In the case of PR, the media presents the profession in various negative guises, as dodgy, glamorous, flaky, secretive, fuzzy and unscrupulous – hardly the light a profession would seek to advertise itself. Yet this is how PR is being 'advertised' consistently.

Part of the perception is that PR is inherently 'feminine' in nature. This thesis has shown that PR requires certain basic skills, most of which appear to be better performed by women, and are shown to be aspects of work that women enjoy more than men. The study has presented evidence that shows women perform better than men in written and spoken English, and the ability to listen. These attributes are generally perceived by men to be 'female' subjects. This study's participants have also indicated in their responses that they perceive PR to be 'feminine'. It naturally follows that if women are proven better performers in these areas, they are better suited to a career in PR. Similarly, if the perception is that the industry is feminine, then it will remain that. This, I believe, ties in with evidence showing there has been a rise in the number of 'soft' industries, such as ecology and psychology. PR is simply just one more of those 'soft' industries experiencing large growth. Sue Webb, who is completing a PhD at ECU on the issue of declining female participation in IT, believes that the "biggest problem is misperception [about] the public image of IT jobs" (Walters, 2006, p. 32).

There is also the consideration of how the historical nature of communications (journalism and PR) is changing. As shown, PR initially was the domain of former journalists, mostly male. About 10-12 years ago, with the rise in communications courses and the changing nature of the workforce, more women entered the profession. PR has now turned almost completely around in its gender structure, and the signs are that journalism is not far behind. The conclusion is that the entire communications profession will become female-intensive.

8.4 Recommendations and observations

> End of the road for top spin doctor ...

> Paul Willoughby, one of the Government's highest-paid 'spin doctors', will leave the public service today, after his position at the Roads and Traffic Authority was abolished ... The Opposition Leader, Peter Debnam, has vowed to cut 75 per cent of spin doctors from the police media unit" (Dick and Kennedy, 2006).

PR's portrayal in the media is cause for concern; particularly if PR wants to be taken more seriously and the indications are that it is not – by both students and the public. The above example is typical of the way journalists perceive PR practitioners – until they become one themselves. How the industry deals with this is up to the industry. However, I believe the profession should look at ways of rectifying the misconceptions. An advertising campaign similar to the *Numbers* campaign conducted in late 2005 to early 2006 by Certified Practising Accountants (CPAs) may be warranted. However, this is probably not achievable, due to the high cost and the PRIA's low membership base, which (at the time of writing) is slowly being expanded. Certainly, the PRIA could be more pro-active in performing some 'PR for PR'.

From both a personal and professional viewpoint, I do not consider that a growing imbalance is necessarily a healthy thing. All the imbalance will do for the profession is simply attract more females (and deter males). Some may argue that the profession may be better served by people who are interested in it, and if they are females, so be it.

Other industries (notably, mining, engineering and IT) are concerned about male dominance and have actively sought to recruit females. The mining industry in WA, and the national IT sector, launched such campaigns in 2006. My view is that the imbalance in PR should be addressed by the PRIA and institutions by rectifying the false impressions of the profession among students and the public.

The IT industry has interesting parallels to PR, in that the percentage imbalance is roughly the same, but in reverse. The difference is that the IT industry seems to be taking strong steps to correct the imbalance (Hilderbrand, 2005). Australian IT managers and peak bodies are now calling for the industry to try to attract more females. The Australian Computer Society has taken the dramatic and controversial step of sponsorship the 2006

Screen Goddess Calendar, which depicts women working in IT in various bikini-clad poses which replicate scenes from famous movies, such as an Ursula Andress scene from *Dr No* (pictured).

Writing in *The Australian,* the Society's president said:

> Women are grossly under represented in the ICT sector and strong
> measures are required to attract more women into this industry ... the
> ACS Foundation has a number of scholarships designed to encourage
> women in to ICT. We are constantly looking for opportunities to promote
> the interest of women. My hope is that the maelstrom over the Screen
> Goddess calendar will at least stimulate some positive discussion that will
> lead to effective ways of addressing the ICT gender imbalance. (Argy
> 2006)

The CIO (Chief Information Officer) of the Executive Council (an organisation with offices in Australia, Canada and the US) is encouraging universities in Victoria, NSW and Queensland to standardise their courses. Writing in Sydney's *Daily Telegraph,* Hilderbrand reports the courses will help reshape IT students' perceptions about the profession, particularly focusing on how IT contributes overall to how a business works. The [Australian] Council's executive director, Con Colovos, said:

> Females are articulate, excellent communicators and very good at
> analysis. Without them IT will be without the balance that will be required
> for it to mature as other industries have. We do not want to see our
> industry be stereotyped as males doing geeky, nerdy work (Hilderbrand
> 2005).

Hilderbrand's observations are backed by McCurdy (2005), who found in her survey of third-year Queensland PR students that 'communication' was listed by 12 per cent of women as the reason they were studying PR, while no males listed it as a reason. This may simply indicate that females like to communicate. While it may seem a blindingly-obvious question, it is, after all, the reason for PR's existence – to communicate. This theme was explored further by Walters (2006). Writing in *Business Review Weekly* about the decline of women in IT, she said women have the skills that IT needs (communication, organisational and analytical ability). However, because of the 'blokey' culture of IT, the long hours and the nerdy image, they are drifting into other occupations. Certainly these qualities are essential in PR. It may be that many current PR graduates could be the very people the IT industry is letting slip through the net.

From an educational viewpoint, perhaps the way PR is taught and promoted may need to be addressed. Clearly, many students (and indeed, some professionals) have misconceptions about PR. A first step would be for educational institutions to correct the negative image PR has, particularly among males. This relates to the perceptions that PR is a 'female' profession, that is not 'serious' and is simply about spin. If balance is to be restored, or even slightly corrected, PR needs to be presented in a more serious light in order to attract more males. Educators may have to question the choice of materials (texts, in particular) that are being presented to students. Are texts mostly written by males for males in countries where the industry is male- or female-dominated? I believe universities may need to take a better look at the way PR is portrayed in promotional material. Rather than show females doing PR, why not show males, or at least a balance?

While students may soon discover that the study of PR is subject to most of the normal disciplines of any university course, the fact that many enter it with little knowledge (and some of that knowledge quite distorted) is a situation that needs to be addressed by universities, and by the industry, through the PRIA. Public relations could certainly do no worse than, at the minimum, supply career information to prospective students through a direct campaign at State education authorities. Beyond that, it may look at increasing its profile with another direct campaign aimed at leading businesses, which may highlight campaign successes. There is, however, a clear need for industry bodies, particularly the PRIA, to maintain a watch on trends.

There are several questions that arise from this research and which could be addressed by further study. The most important is: will this trend affect the way information is interpreted? In other words, is there a female bias that presents in PR communications? Other salient points are: will an imbalanced PR profession alter the public's perception of the subjects it seeks to promote, advertise and report on?

One of the main considerations is to consider whether the profession, and individuals, will be greatly affected by the change in gender construction. This study showed that 62 per cent of professionals are concerned about what effects imbalance may have on the industry, but none indicated what effects these might be. The inference is that while professionals are concerned, until the situation affects them directly, they are not worried about it.

Finally, is the PR industry even aware of the phenomenon of increasing numbers of females entering the industry? If so, does it at all care? I would answer, "yes", the industry is aware of the phenomenon, but, "no", it does not care enough to have it on the agenda for discussion at any official level. The profession should be asking itself if and/or how the increasing number of women in PR has impacted, or will impact, on the profession. And what are the long-term implications, if any, for the profession as a result of such an imbalance.

As shown, other industries are well aware of gender imbalances and possible problems that may arise from that. Some, notably IT and engineering, are taking steps to correct the situation. While many PR professionals (mostly from Queensland) have shown interest in this study, no-one from the national body, or academia, has come out and said "yes, there may be a problem and we should be analysing a response" – if one is necessary. Only time will tell whether this trend will have any effects on the industry. However, as someone who has observed the phenomenon over many years, at the very least, I believe the profession needs to be prepared for a possible change in the way PR is practised. Whether this will be detrimental is hard to say at this stage.

The overall aim of my study was the examine the reasons for the growing number of women entering PR. Based on the evidence, I believe that while there are many factors which contribute to the predominance of women in PR, it is our cultural view of PR (our socialisation) which is the dominant force in determining whether males or females enter PR.

A growing female presence may serve to enhance or hinder the industry; although this will depend on the level on influence women will exert at upper management levels – something that seems not to have happened yet. Whatever the eventual outcome, the composition of the profession should be no different from what we seek to achieve in many aspects of life – balance.

As Dan Edelman said: "We need balance" (2002).

References

Aalito, I and Mills, A 2002, 'Organisational culture and gendered identities in context', in I Aalito and A Mills (eds), *Gender, identity and the culture of organisations*, Routledge, London, p. 4.

Aires, E 1997, 'Women and men talking. Are they worlds apart?' in MR Walsh (ed.), *Women, men and gender. Ongoing debates*, Yale University Press, New Haven, pp. 91–9.

Aldoory, L 2001, 'The standard white woman in public relations', in E Toth and E Aldoory (eds), *The gender challenge to media: diverse voices from the field*, Hampton Press, Cresskill, NJ.

Allison, B, O'Sullivan, T, Owen, A, Rice, J, Rothwell, A and Saunders, C 1996, *Research skills for students*, Kogan Page, London.

Alvesson, M and Billing, YD 2002, 'Beyond body-counting. A discussion of the social construction of gender at work', in I Aalito and A Mills (eds), *Gender, identity and the culture of organisations*, Routledge, London, pp. 72–88.

Andsager, JL and Hust, SJT 2004, 'Differential gender orientation in public relations: Implications for career choices', *Public Relations Review*, vol. 30.

Argy, P 2006, 'Tacking the hi-tech gender imbalance', *The Australian*.

Australian Bureau of Statistics 2006, *Western Australian Statistical Indicators*, Perth.

Balnaves, M and Caputi, P 2001, *Introduction to quantitative research methods: an investigative approach*, Sage, London.

Barnett, R 2004, 'Gender differences and similarity in personality and social behaviour'.

Barnett, R and Rivers, C 2004, 'Men are from earth, and so are women. It's faulty research that sets them apart', *The Chronicle of Higher Education*, vol. 51, no. 2, p. 11.

Beasly, M 1999, 'Newspapers: is there a new majority defining the news?' in C Pamela (ed.), *Women in mass communication: changing gender values*, Sage, Newbury Park, pp. 180–94.

Becker, L, Vlad, T, Hu, J and Mace, N 2003, *Gender equity elusive, surveys show*, Grady College of Journalism and Mass Communication, University of Georgia, viewed 4 May 2005, http://www.grady.uga.edu:16080/annualsurveys.

Becker, L, Vlad, T, Hennink-Kaminski, H & Coffey, A 2004, *Annual Survey of journalism and mass communications enrolments*, Henry Grady College of Journalism, University of Georgia, Athens.

Benbasat, I and Zmud, R 1999, 'Empirical research in information systems: the practice of relevance', *MIS Quarterly*, vol. 23, no. 1.

Bland, J 2005, 'About gender: sex differences', *About gender: towards a balanced account of human gender and sex differences*, viewed 29 December 2005, www.gender.org.uk/about/07neur/77_diffs.htm.

Broom, G and Dozier, D 1990, *Using research in public relations*, Prentice Hall, Inglewood Cliffs.

Brown, J 1998, 'Spin sisters: Why is PR the only high-tech field that women run?' *Salon*, vol. 12, no. 1, viewed 21 Dec 2003, http://archive.salon.com/21st/feature/1998/12/cov_03feature.html.

Chater, K and Gaster, R 1995, *The equality myth*, Allen and Unwin, Sydney.

Childers-Hon, L 1995, 'Toward a feminist theory of public relations', *Journal of Public Relations Research*, vol. 7, no. 1, pp. 27–88.

Childers-Hon, L 2003, *Feminism And Public Relations*, 2003, viewed 16 February 2005, http://www.prsa.org/_Resources/profession/6k029520.html.

CIPR London, 2005, *PR Today: 48,000 professionals; £6.5 billion turnover. The economic significance of public relations*, 2005, CIPR, London.

Cline, C 1999, 'Public relations: the $1 million penalty for being a women', in C Pamela (ed.), *Women in mass communication: changing gender values*, Sage, Newbury Park, pp. 263–77.

Cline, C, Smith, H, Johnson, N, Toth, E and Turk, JVS 1986, *The velvet ghetto: summary report*, IABC, 2004, viewed 20 March 2005, http://www.iabc.com/fdtnweb/pdf/VelvetGhetto.pdf,

Cockburn, C 1991, *In the way of women: men's resistance to sex equality in organisations*, Macmillan, London.

Couch, J and Sigler, J 2001, 'Gender perceptions of professional occupations', *Psychological Reports*, vol. 88, pp. 693–8.

Creedon, P 1989, *Women in mass communication: changing gender values*, Sage, Newbury Park.

Cross, S and Bagilhole, B 2002, 'Girls' jobs for the boys? Men, masculinity and non-traditional occupations', *Gender, Work and Organization*, vol. 9, no. 2.

Cumming, J 1997, 'Attracting girls and women students to non-traditional areas', *Queensland Journal of Educational Research*, vol. 13, no. 1, pp. 6–16.

Davis, D and Cosenza, R 1985, *Business research for decision making*, PWS-Kent, Belmont, California.

Deaux, K 1976, *The behaviour of men and women*, Brooks/Cole, Monterey.

DeRosa, D and Wilcox, D 1989, 'Gaps are narrowing between male and female students', *Public Relations Review*, vol. 15, no. 1, pp. 80–9.

Dick, B 1993, 'You want to do an action research thesis?' *Action Research Theses*, viewed, 12 July 2006, http://www.scu.edu.au/schools/gcm/ar/art/arthesis.html.

Dick, B 1997, *Approaching an action research thesis: an overview*, viewed 22 August 2006, http://www.scu.edu.au/schools/gcm/ar/arp/phd.html.

Dick, T and Kennedy, L 2006, 'End of the road for top spin doctor', *Sydney Morning Herald*, 4 August.

Donato, K 1990, 'Keepers of the corporate image: women in public relations', in B Reskin and P Roos (eds), *Job queues, gender queues: explaining women's inroads into male occupations*, Temple University Press, Philadelphia, pp. 129–43.

Dorer, J 2005, 'The gendered relationship between journalism and public relations in Austria and Germany. A feminist approach', *Communications*, vol. 30, pp. 183–200.

Dozier, D 1988, 'Breaking public relations' glass ceiling', *Public Relations Review*, vol. 14, no. 3, pp. 6–14.

Eaton, BC 2001, 'I'm a femininst, but ... a response to sexism, racism and class elitism in mass communication', in E Toth and E Aldoory (eds), *The gender challenge to media: diverse voices from the field*, Hampton Press, Cresskill, NJ.

Farmer, A 2003, *Women rule at Channel 13*, Maynard Institute for Journalism, viewed 8 December 2005, http://www.maynardije.org/news/features/030110_channel13.

Farmer, B and Waugh, L 1999, 'Gender differences in public relations students' career attitudes: a benchmark study', *Public Relations Review*, vol. 25, no. 2, p. 235.

Faulkner, R, Maanen, J V and Dabbs, J 1984, *Varieties of qualitative research: studying organisations*, Sage, Beverley Hills.

Fernandez, WD, Lehman, H and Underwood, A 2002, 'Rigour and relevance in studies of IS innovation: a grounded theory methodology approach', paper presented to European Conference of Information Systems, Gdansk, Poland.

Folmar, J and Boynton LA 2005, 'Why are more women than men attracted to the field of public relations? Analyzing students' reasons for studying PR', Paper presented to the AEJMC conference, San Antonio, Texas, August.

Game, A and Pringle, R 1983, *Gender at work*, George Allen and Unwin, Sydney.

Glick, P, Wilk, K and Perreault, M 1995, 'Images of occupations: components of gender and status in occupational stereotypes. ' *Sex Roles: A Journal of Research*, vol. 32, no. 9, pp. 565–83.

Gottschall, K 2002, *New forms of employment in Germany: labor market regulation and its gendered Implications*, University of Bremen, Bremen.

Gower, K 2001, 'Rediscovering women in PR', *Journalism History*, vol. 27, no. 1, pp. 14–22.

Grunig, J 1992, *Excellence in public relations and communication management*, Lawrence Erlbaum and Associates, Hillsdale.

Grunig, L 2001, *Toward the truly inclusive public relations classroom: determining students' expectations*, Department of Communication, University of Maryland, 2004, viewed 16 January 2005, http://www.crge.umd.edu/resources/Grunig_paper.pdf.

Grunig, L, Toth, E and Childers-Hon, L 2000, 'Feminist values in public relations', *Journals of Public Relations Research*, vol. 12, no. 1, pp. 49–68.

Grunig, L, Toth, E and Hon, L 2001, *Women in public relations: how gender influences practice*, Guildford Press, New York.

Gunn, J, 2002, *Educational participation in Western Australia*, Australian Bureau of Statistics.

Hakim, C 1987, *Research design. Strategies and choices in the design of social research*, Allen and Unwin, Boston.

Hall, S 2005, 'Examining the manager-technician roles in public relations: is gender discrimination still an issue? A study of PR practitioners in northern England.' MA (Marketing) dissertation thesis, Newcastle Business School, University of Northumbria at Newcastle.

Hamilton, P 1999, 'Journalists, gender and workplace culture', in A Curthoys and J Schultz (eds), *Journalists. Print, politics and popular culture*, University of Queensland Press, St Lucia, pp. 103–5.

Hilderbrand, J 2005, 'Women escaping nerdy IT', *Daily Telegraph*, 29 December, p. 18.

Holstein, J and Gubrium, J 1995, *The active interview*, Sage, Thousand Oaks.

Hopkins, S 2004, *Women in economics departments in Austraian universities: Is there a gender imbalance?*, Curtin University, Perth.

Hughes, V 2005, 'An examination of facilitators and inhibitors to knowledge-sharing in a policing environment: lessons from intelligence-led crime management units of the Western Australia Police Service', Edith Cowan University.

Hutton, J 2005, 'The myth of salary discrimination in public relations', *Public Relations Review*, vol. 31, no. 1, pp. 73–83.

icBirmingham, 2004, *Why women dominate PR*, viewed 15 March 2005, http://icbirmingham.icnetwork.co.uk/0150business/womeninbusiness/tm_objectid=14780965and method=fullandsiteid=50002andheadline=why-women-dominate-pr-profession-name_page.html.

Jacob, E 1988, 'Clarifying qualitative research: A focus on traditions', *Educational Researcher*, vol. 17, no. 1, pp. 16–24.

Kimmel, M 2004, *The gendered society*, 2nd edn, Oxford University Press, Oxford.

Klein, HK and Myers, MD 1999, 'A set of principles for conducting and evaluating interpretive field studies in information systems', *MIS Quarterly*, vol. 23, no. 1, pp. 67–94.

Kolb, D 1997, 'Her place at the negotiation table: gender and negotiation', in MR Walsh (ed.), *Women, men and gender. Ongoing debates*, Yale University Press, New Haven.

Kumar, R 1999, *Research methodology – a step-by-step guide for beginners*, Sage, Thousand Oaks.

Lee, A 1994, 'Electronic mail as a medium for rich communication: an empirical investigation using hermeneutic interpretation', *MIS Quarterly*, no. June, pp. 143–57.

Leggeter, B 2005, *Is it gender or the way we sell?*, Bite PR, viewed 15 December 2005, http://blog.bitepr.com/2005/09/is_it_gender_or.html.

Lesly, P 1989, 'PR's downward spiral', *Public Relations Journal*, vol. 45, no. 5, pp. 40–41.

Levy, GD, Sadovsky, AL and Troseth., GL 2000, 'Aspects of young children's perceptions of gender-typed occupations', *Sex Roles: A Journal of Research*, vol. June, p. 993.

Lukovitz, K 1989, 'Women practitioners. How far, how fast?: Progress of women in the public relations profession', *Public Relations Journal*, vol. 45, no. 5, pp. 14–21.

Mackey, S 2003, 'Changing vistas in public relations theory', *PRism*, vol. 1, no. 1.

Manpower Research and Statistics Department, *Occupation segregation: a gender perspective*, 2000, Ministry of Manpower, Singapore.

Martin, P 1993, 'Feminist practices in organisations: implications for management', in E Fagenson (ed.), *Women in management: trends, issues and challenges in managerial diversity*, Sage, Newbury Park, pp. 274–91.

Maushart, S 2005, 'What's wrong with boys', *Weekend Australian Magazine*, April 8–9, 2004.

McCurdy, F 2005, 'The feminisation of public relations: views of students and practitioners in south-east Queensland', Honours thesis, Griffith.

McNiff, J, Lomax, P and Whitehead, J 2003, *You and your action research project*, 2nd edn, RoutledgeFalmer, London.

Merriam, S 1998, *Qualitative research and case study applications in education*, Joey-bass, San Francisco.

Midgley, C 2006, 'Why we're hemispheres apart', *The Australian*, 19–20 August, p. 26.

Midgley, C 2006, 'Lobal warfare', *Time On Line*, viewed August 2006, http://www.timesonline.co.uk/tol/life_and_style/article603199.ece?token=null&offset=12.

Miles, M and Huberman, AM 1994, *Qualitative data analysis*, 2nd edn, Sage, Thousand Oaks.

Miller, L 2002, 'Tough issues, tough world', *PR Watch*, vol. 8, no. 1.

Miller, L, Neathey, F, Pollard, E and Hil, D 2003, *Occupational segregation, gender gaps and skill gaps*, UK Equal Opportunities Commission, London.

Moir, A and Jessel, D 1996, *Brainsex*, 2nd edn, Mandarin, London.

Moran, M 2005, *Odd behaviour and creativity may go hand in hand*, Yale University, viewed 29 December 2005, http://exploration.vanderbilt.edu/news/news_schitzotypes.htm.

Morse, J and Richards, L 2002, *User's guide to qualitative methods*, Sage, Thousand Oaks.

Muoio, A 1998, 'Women and men, work and power', *Fast Power*, no. 13, p. 71.

Newsom, D, Turk, JV and Kruckeberg, D 2000, *This is PR. The realities of public relations*, 7th edn, Thomson Wordsworth, Belmont CA.

Newsom, D 2004, *This is PR. The realities of public relations*, 8th edn, Thomson Wordsworth, Belmont CA.

Noble, G 2004, 'Why do students major in public relations? A study of factors influencing a student's choice of major, and gender similarities and differences.' Unpublished thesis, Oklahoma State University.

O'Neill, L and Walker, E 2001, 'Women in the information technology industry: a Western Australian view', paper presented to The 9th European Conference on Information Systems, Bled, Slovenia.

Ohlott, P 2005, 'Same difference: how gender myths are hurting our relationships, our children, our jobs', *Personnel Psychology*, vol. 58, no. 4, pp. 1062–6.

Oliver, R 2004, *Research paradigms*, Research methodology course notes (ECU).

Pockcock, B and Alexander, M 1999, 'The Price of Feminised Jobs: New Evidence on the Gender Pay Gap in Australia', *Labour and Industry*, vol. 10, no. 2, p. 75.

Pinker, S and Spelke, E 2005, *The science of gender and science. Pinker vs Spelke: a debate*, Harvard University, viewed 9 January 2006, www.edge.org/3rd_culture/debate05/debate05_index.html.

Practitioner, A 2005, *'Grimbos': humourless times in the office*, 23 November, E-mail.

Rakow, L 1989, 'Feminist studies: the next stage. Critical studies in mass communication'.

Rea, J 2002, *The Feminisation of Public Relations: what's in it for the girls?*, Victoria University, Melbourne.

Reason, P 2001, *Learning and change through action research*, Sage, London.

Reciniello, S 1999, 'The emergence of a powerful female workforce as a threat to organisational identity: what psychoanalysts can offer', *The American Behavioral Scientist*, vol. 43, no. 2, pp. 301–24.

Rickertson, M 1999, 'Newspaper feature writing in Australia', in A Curthoys and J Schultz (eds), *Journalists. Print, politics and popular culture*, University of Queensland Press, St Lucia, p. 178.

Robson, C 2002, *Real-world research: a resource for social scientists and practitioner-researchers (regional surveys of the world)*, Blackwell, London.

Rozier, C, Thomson, M, Shill, J and Vollmar, M 2001, 'Career paths of male physical therapist students entering a female-dominant profession', *Journal of Physical Therapy Education*.

Rush, R and Grubb-Swetnam, A 1996, 'Feminist approaches', in M Stacks and D Stacks (eds), *An integrated approach to communication theory and research*, Lawrence Erlbaum Associates, Mahwah, NJ.

Sarantakos, S 1993, *Social Research*, Macmillan Education Australia, Melbourne.

Scrimger, J 2001, 'Women in public relations: how gender influences practice', *Canadian Journal of Communication*, vol. 26, no. 4, pp. 107–8.

Seitel, F 1998, *The practice of public relations*, 7th edn, Prentice Hall, Upper Saddle River.

Sha, B-L and Toth, E 2005, 'Future professionals' perceptions of work, life, and gender issues in public relations', *Public Relations Review*, vol. 31, no. 1, pp. 93–9.

Shute, N 2005, 'His brain, her brain', *US News and World Report*, vol. 138, no. 8, p. 36.

Simpson, R 2005, 'Men in non-traditional occupations: career entry, career orientation and experience of role strain', *Gender, Work and Organisation*, vol. 12, no. 4.

Stewart, 2006, 'Out of the shadows', *The Weekend Australian,* 17-18 March, p. 27

Student, Anon 2005, *Discrimination in PR*, 3 November, E-mail.

Tavris, C 1992, *The measurement of women*, Simon and Schuster, New York.

Toth, E 2000, *Year 2000 gender study. Report of the committee on Work, life and gender issues*, Public Relations Society of America, New York.

Toth, E and Aldoory, E 2001, 'The gender challenge to media: diverse voices from the field', in E Toth and E Aldoory (eds), *The gender challenge to media: diverse voices from the field*, Hampton Press, Cresskill, NJ.

Trochim, W 2002, *Research methods knowledge base*, 2nd edn, Atomic Dog, Cinncinatti.

Tymson, C 1998, *Gender games: doing business with the opposite sex*, Tymson Communications, Sydney.

US Department of Labor 2004, *Occupational Outlook Handbook*, viewed 12 September 2006, http://www.bls.gov/oco/ocos086.htm.

Wahlstrom, B 1990, 'The brain, gender and human communication', in R Rush and D Allen (eds), *Communications at the crossroads. The gender gap connection*, Ablex, Norwood, pp. 20–46.

Walsh, MR 1997, *Women, men and gender. Ongoing debates*, Yale University Press, New Haven.

Walters, K 2006, 'EX I.T.', *Business Review Weekly*, July 27–August 2, pp. 26-32.

Wikipedia 2006, *Definitions of socialization*, viewed 17 March 2006, http:www.wikipedia.org/socialization.html

Wilcox, D, Ault, P and Agee, W 1998, *Public relations: strategies and tactics*, 5th edn, Longman, New York.

Willams, LC 2002, *Profile 2002: a survey of IABC membership*, International Association of Business Communicators.

Wootton, B 1997, 'Gender differences in occupational employment', *Monthly Labor Review*, vol. 120, no. 4, pp. 15–25.

Zawawi, C 2000, 'History of public relations in Australia', in J Johnston and C Zawawi (eds), *Public relations theory and practice*, 1st edn, Allen and Unwin, Sydney.

Bibliography

Aldoory, L 2004, 'Leadership and gender in public relations: perceived effectiveness of transformational and transactional leadership styles', *Journal of Public Relations Research*, vol. 16, no. 2, pp. 157–83.

Aldoory, L and Toth, E 2002, 'Gender discrepancies in a gendered profession: a developing theory for public relations', *Journal of Public Relations Research*, vol. 14, no. 2, pp. 103–26.

Allen, D 1990, 'Women transforming communication', in D Allen and R Rush (eds), *Communications at the crossroads. The gender gap connection*, Ablex, Norwood, pp. 59–76.

Alloway, N and Gilbert, P 2004, 'Shifting discourses about gender in higher education enrolments: retrieving marginalised voices', *International Journal of Qualitative Studies in Education*, vol. 17, no. 1.

Arndt, B 2003, 'Jobs for the boys', *Sydney Morning Herald*, 20 March.

Australian Bureau of Statistics 1996, *Trends in the female-male earnings ratio*, ABS, viewed 29 April 2005.

Australian Bureau of Statistics 2005, *Australian economic indicators*, vol. April, Australian Government.

Australian Bureau of Statistics 2005, *PR workforce from 1991, 1996 and 2001 Census*, Australian Government.

Bailey, R 2004, *Our PR future is well-educated, business focused – and female*, Institute of Public Relations (UK), viewed 19 February 2006, http://www.ipr.org.uk/news/stories/192.htm.

Bailyn, L and Etzion, D 1986, 'Experiencing technical work: a comparison of male and female engineers', *On Line Ethcis*, viewed 5 Oct 2005, http://onlineethics.org/div/abstracts/Bailyn-study.html#discussion.

Barbie, E 1986, 'The logic of sampling', in E Barbie (ed.), *The practice of social research*, 4th edn, Wadsworth, London, pp. 136–77.

Beasly, M 1999, 'Newspapers: is there a new majority defining the news?' in C Pamela (ed.), *Women in mass communication: changing gender values*, Sage, Newbury Park, pp. 180–94.

Becker, L, Huh, J and Vlad, T 1998, *Predictors of diversification of journalism and mass communication faculties (1989–1998)*, Grady College, University of Georgia.

Becker, L and Kosicki, G 1996, *Annual survey of journalism and mass communications enrollments*, Henry Grady College of Journalism, University of Georgia, Athens.

Becker, L and Kosicki, G 1997, *Annual survey of journalism and mass communications enrollments*, Henry Grady College of Journalism, University of Georgia, Athens.

Becker, L, Kosicki, G, Hammatt, H, Lowrey, W, Shin, SC and Wilson, J 1998, *Annual survey of journalism and mass communications enrollments*, Henry Grady College of Journalism, University of Georgia, Athens.

Becker, L, Vlad, T, Hennink-Kaminski, H and Coffey, A 2004, *Annual Survey of journalism and mass communications enrollments*, Henry Grady College of Journalism, University of Georgia, Athens.

Becker, L, Vlad, T, Hu, J and Mace, N 2003, *Gender equity elusive, surveys show*, Grady College of Journalism and Mass Communication, University of Georgia, viewed 4 May 2005, http://www.grady.uga.edu:1680/annualsurveys.

Becker, L, Vlad, T, Huh, J and Prine, J 2000, *Annual survey of journalism and mass communications enrollments*, Henry Grady College of Journalism, University of Georgia, Athens.

Becker, L, Vlad T, Huh J, Prine J 2001, *Annual Survey of journalism and mass communications enrollments*, Henry Grady College of Journalism, University of Georgia, Athens.

Becker, LB, Kosicki, G, Lowrey, W, Prine, J and Punathambekar, A 1999, *Annual Survey of journalism and mass communications enrollments*, Henry Grady College of Journalism, University of Georgia, Athens.

Berdie, D and Anderson, J 1974, *Questionnaires: design and use*, Scarecrow Press, Methchen, NJ.

Blattel-Mink, B 2002, *Gender and subject decision at university*, Heidelberg University, Heidelberg.

Blättel-Mink, B 2002, 'Gender and subject decision at university', *Equal Opportunities International*, vo 21, no. 2, pp. 43–64.

Blättel-Mink, B 2002, 'Gender and subject decision at university', *Equal Opportunities International*, vo 21, no. 1, pp. 43–64.

Blustain, S 2000, 'The new gender wars', *Psychology Today*, vol. 33, pp. 42–9.

Bradley, M 2004, 'Women with attitude beat boys for the jobs', *Sydney Morning Herald*, 13 November 2004.

Brandell, G, Nyström, P and Sundqvist, C 2003, 'Mathematics – a male domain?' paper presented to ICME 10, Sweden.

Braund, M 1999, 'Police-public relations in Canberra: does gender make a difference?' paper presented Second Australasian Women and Policing Conference, Emmanuel College, University of Queenslanc Brisbane, viewed 16 March 2005, http://www.aic.gov.au/conferences/policewomen2/Braund.html.

Centre for Economics and Business Research 2005, PR Today: *The economic significance of public relations*, CIPR, London.

Chao, A and Utgoff, K 2004, *Women in the labor force: a databook*, US Department of Labor, Washington.

Chatterjee, C 1999, 'Gender pressures add up', *Psychology Today*, vol. 32, no. 4, p. 12.

Childers-Hon, L 2003, *Feminism And Public Relations*, 2003, viewed 22 February 2005, http://www.prsa.org/_Resources/profession/6k029520.html.

Choi, Y and Hon, L 2002, 'The influence of gender composition in powerful positions on public relatior practitioners' perceptions', *Journal of Public Relations Research*, vol. 14, no. 3, pp. 229–63.

Clory, MN 2001, 'A personal reflection on television messages and images, and a challenge to future practitioners', in E Toth and E Aldoory (eds), *The gender challenge to media: diverse voices from the field*, Hampton Press, Cresskill, NJ.

The gender puzzle 2005, TV, Australia, 24 July. Distributed by ABC.

Corbin, J 1990, *Basics of qualitative research*, Sage, Newbury Park.

Cotter, DA, DeFiore, JM, Hermsen, JM, Kowalewski, BM and Vanneman, R 1995, 'Occupational gend desegregation in the 1980s', *Work and Occupations*, vol. 22, no. 1, pp. 3–22.

Creedon, P and Henry, S 1999, 'Changing media history through women's history', in *Women in mass communication: changing gender values*.

Currie, J and Thiele, B 2001, 'Globalisation and gendered work cultures in universities', in A Brooks a A Mackinnon (eds), *Gender and the restructured university*, SRHE and Open University Press, Buckingham, pp. 90–116.

Cutlip, S, Center, A and Broom, G 2000, *Effective public relations*, Prentice-Hall, Upper Saddle River.

Debussy, N 2001, *Women set to dominate PR but earn less than men: survey*, Curtin University, Perth.

Densem, Y 2004, *Where have all the boys gone?*, NZ Journalism Online, viewed 20 March 2005, www.jeanz.org.nz.

Department of Anthropology, 2005, 'Definitions of anthropological terms', Oregon State University, viewed 18 August 2006, http://oregonstate.edu/instruct/anth370/gloss.html#S

DeVaus, D 1995, *Surveys in Social Research*, 4th edn, Allen and Unwin, Sydney.

Dolan, D 1990, 'The developing role of women in communications industries: can technology be the turning point?' in R Rush and D Allen (eds), *Communications at the crossroads. The gender gap connection*, Ablex, Norwood, pp. 106–19.

Eagly, AH and Karau, SJ 2002, 'Role congruity theory of prejudice toward female leaders', *Psychological Review*, vol. 109, no. 3, pp. 573–98.

Eddleston, KA, Baldridge, DC and Veiga, JF 2004, 'Toward modelling the predictors of managerial career success: does gender matter?' *Journal of Managerial Psychology*, vol. 19, no. 4, pp. 360–85.

Employment Research Institute 2004, *Gender Stereotyping in career choice: pupils' perceptions of their suitability for jobs*, Napier UniversityEmployment Research Institute, Edinburgh.

Farmer, B 1997, *Using SPE context analysis in the public relations campaigns class*, viewed 9 February 2004, http://lamar.colostate.edu/~aejmcpr/44farmer.htm.

Fielding, R 2001, *Government gears up to get women into IT*, viewed 20 March 2005, http://www.accountancyage.com/news/it/1118802.

Flintoff, J-P 2005, 'Of course women don't rule the world: just don't let them tighten their grip', *Sunday Times*, 21 August.

Frank, T 2002, *Onward and upward. A study of the progress made by women in the communications sector*, Canadian Women in Communication, 2004, viewed 19 March 2005, http://www.cwc-afc.com/pdfs/en/Research_Tema_Frank_Report.pdf.

Frewin, L 2001, *Closed minds shut women out of IT*, viewed 20 March 2005.

Goode, W and Hatt, P 1952, *Methods in social research*, McGraw-Hill, Tokyo.

Goodman, M 2003, *Corporate Communication practices and trends*, Corporate Communication Institute, Farleigh Dickinson University, Madison, NJ.

Grafisk, S 2000, *The circumstances of women entrepeneurs*, Danish Agency for Trade and Industry, viewed 18 April 2005, http://www.ebst.dk/publikationer/rapporter/women_entrepreneurs/kap10.html.

Gregory, H 2005, 'Management: where are all the men?' *PR Week*, 2 September.

Grennan, H 2005, 'Few women at the top', *Sydney Morning Herald*, 19 July.

Grunig, L 1999, 'The 'glass ceiling' effect on mass communication students', in P Creedon (ed.), *Women in mass communication: changing gender values*, Sage, Newbury Park, pp. 125–47.

Grunig, L 2001, *Toward the truly Inclusive public relations classroom: determining students' expectations*, Department of Communication, University of Maryland, 2004, viewed 15 March 2005, http://www.crge.umd.edu/resources/Grunig_paper.pdf.

Grunig, L 2003, 'The feminisation of public relations', paper presented to Women in public relations, Marshall University, 6 October 2003.

Gunn, J, 2002, *Educational participation in Western Australia*, Australian Bureau of Statistics.

Haines, V and Wallace, J 2003, 'Gender-role attitudes, perceptions of engineering, and beliefs about women in engineering – having it all: are male and female engineering undergraduates really so different?' *Alberta Journal of Educational Research* vol. 49, no. 4, p. 376.

Henry, S 1999, 'Changing media history through women's history', in P Creedon (ed.), *Women in mass communication: changing gender values*, Sage, Newbury Park, pp. 34–58.

Hopkins, S 2003, *Women in economics departments in Australia: is there a gender imbalance*, 2005, http://www.ecosoc.org.au/women/docs/Gender%20Balance.pdf.

Horin, A 2004, 'Shame at the top: old boys' network keeps women out of the boardroom', *Sydney Morning Herald*, 1 Dec 2004.

Horin, A 2005, 'Men out of work: why families are falling apart', *Sydney Morning Herald*.

Iliffe, J 2002, 'Time to address nursing's gender imbalance', *Australian Nursing Journal*, vol. 9, no. 11, p. 1.

Jackson, C 1999, 'Men's Work, Masculinities and Gender Divisions of Labour', *Journal of Developmental Studies*, vol. 36, no. 1, p. 89.

James, G 2002, *Qualitative methods for assessing relationships between organizations and publics*, Institute for Public Relations, viewed 12 April 2005, ttp://www.instituteforpr.com/pdf/2002_Qualitative_Methods_Assessing_Relationships.pdf .

Kolb, D 1997, 'Her place at the negotiation table: gender and negotiation', in MR Walsh (ed.), *Women, men and gender. Ongoing debates*, Yale University Press, New Haven.

Krupnick, C 1985, 'Women and men in the classroom: inequality and its remedies', *On Teaching and Learning*, vol. 1.

Kulik, L 1998, 'Life orientation and work attitudes of Israeli males who make atypical career choices', *Journal of Psychology and Judaism*, vol. 22, no. 2, pp. 101–14.

Lafky, S 1999, 'Economic equity and the journalistic workforce', in C Pamela (ed.), *Women in mass communication: changing gender values*, Sage, Newbury Park, pp. 164–79.

Lee, B 1993, 'The legal and political realities for women managers: The barriers, the opportunities and the horizon', in E Fagenson (ed.), *Women in management: trends, issues and challenges in manageri diversity*, Sage, Newbury Park, pp. 246–69.

Leeds Metropolitan University 2004, *The 90 per cent club*, viewed 19 February 2006, http://www.leeds.ac.uk/pr/blog/student_feedback.htm

Locke, J 2005, 'Public relations and women a better fit', *AEJMC Reporter*, 11 August.

Locke, J 2005, *Public relations and women make a better fit*, Association for Education in Journalism a Mass Communication, viewed 12 December 2005, http://aejmc.net/SAT05/?20050811.

Lupton, B 2006, 'Explaining men's entry into female-cncentrated occupations: issues of masculinity an social class', *Gender, Work and Organisation*, vol. 13, no. 2, pp. 103–27.

Lusetich, R 2005, 'Sex and the brain', *The Weekend Australian*, 1–2 October, p. 19.

Lyness, K and Thompson, D 1997, 'Above the glass ceiling: a comparison of matched samples of fema and male executives', *Journal of Applied Psychology*, vol. 82, no. 3, pp. 359–75.

Lyness, K and Thompson, D 2000, 'Climbing the Corporate Ladder: Do Female and Male Executives Follow the Same Route?' *Journal of Applied Psychology*, vol. 85, no. 1, pp. 86–101.

MacKendrick, S 2004, *The old boys had it right*, Canadian Women in Communication, 2004, viewed 2 July 2006, http://www.cwc-afc.com/show-content.cfm?section=res-art.

MacKendrick, S 2004, *Hairy-chested notions of how companies function*, Canadian Women in Communication, 2004, viewed 20 July 2006, http://www.cwc-afc.com/show-content.cfm?section=re art.

MacKendrick, S 2004, *A phantom menace? Not yet*, Canadian Women in Communication, 2004, viewe 20 July 2006, http://www.cwc-afc.com/show-content.cfm?section=res-art.

Madden, J 2000, 'The economic consequences of pay equity for female-intensive occupations: a multiregional CGE analysis', paper presented to International conference of input-output techniques, Macerata, 21–25 August 2000.

Manpower Research and Statistics Department 2000, *Occupational segregation: a gender perspective*, Singapore Government.

Masterton, M 1983, *But you'll never be bored. The five Ws of Australian journalism*, South Australian College of Advanced Education, Adelaide.

McKenna, M and Roberge, RA 2001, 'Restructuring, gender and employment in flux: A geography of regional change in Cornwall, Ontario', *Canadian Geographer*, vol. 45, no. 2, pp. 223–37.

McLoughlin, LA 2005, 'Spotlighting: Emergent Gender Bias in Undergraduate Engineering Education', *Journal of Engineering*, vol. 94, no. 4, pp. 373–82.

Mediawatch 2004, *Where have all the young men gone?*, TV New Zealand, 8 August.

Merriam, S 1998, *Qualitative research and case study applications in education*, Joey-bass, San Francisco.

Metz, I 2004, 'Do personality traits indirectly affect women's advancement?' *Journal of Managerial Psychology*, vol. 19, no. 7, pp. 695–707.

Morgan, C, Isaac, J and Sansone., C 2001, 'The role of interest in understanding the career choices of female and male college students', *Sex Roles: A Journal of Research*, vol. March.

Murphy, T 2004, *The PR gender bias*, PR Opinions, viewed 19 February 2006, http://www.natterjackpr.com/2004/01/19.html#a893.

National Advisory Council on the employment of women 2004, *Women's access to industry training*, NZ Government.

Newmarch, E, Taylor-Steele, S and Cumpston, A 2000, 'Women in IT – What Are the Barriers?' paper presented to Network of Women in Further Education, Australia.

Noble, GJ 2005, 'Why do students major in public relations? A study of factors influencing a student's choice of major, and gender similarities and differences', paper presented to AEJMC Conference, San Antonio.

Nobles, S 2005, 'TV portrayals of women are bad for our industry', *PR Week*, vol. 8, no. 30, p. 8.

Northcraft, G and Gutek, B 1993, 'Discrimination against women in management – going, going, gone or going but never gone?' in *Women in management: trends, issues and challenges in managerial diversity*, Sage, Newbury Park, pp. 219–41.

O'Connor, T 2004, *Qualitative research methodology*, NC Wesleyan College, viewed 18 May 2005, http://faculty.ncwc.edu/toconnor/308/308lect09.htm.

O'Neil, J 2004, 'Effects of gender and power on PR managers' upward influence', *Journal of Managerial Issues*, vol. 16, no. 1, pp. 127–45.

Panigyrakis, GG and Veloutsou, CA 1998, 'Sex-related differences of public relations managers in consumer goods companies in Greece and Italy', *Women in Management Review*, vol. 13, no. 2, pp. 72–82.

Parpas, E 2005, 'Does gender matter?' *Adweek*, vol. 46, no. 46, pp. 16–8.

Patton, M 1990, *Qualitative evaluation and research methods*, Sage, Newbury Park.

Peters, C 2002, 'Gender in communications: micropolitics at work', paper presented to AARE 2002 International Education Research Conference, Brisbane.

PRSA Georgia 2003, *Women in PR*, viewed 24 July 2006, http://www.prsageorgia.org/newsletter/back/june01/pres.html.

Rakow, L 1986, 'Rethinking gender research in communication', *Journal of Public Relations Research*, no. Autumn, pp. 11–26.

Rakow, L 1992, *Women making meaning. New feminist directions in communication*, Rotuledge, New York.

Rakow, L 1996, *All university curricula are political*, Middle Tennessee University College, viewed 28 June 2005, http://www.mtsu.edu/~masscomm/seig96/blanchrd/rakow.htm.

Rask, K and Tiefenthaler, J 2004, 'Too few women? Or too many men? The gender imbalance in undergraduate economics', Colgate University.

Reis, J 1995, 'Public relations: absolutely fabulous or absolutely serious', Unpublished thesis, RMIT.

Rivera-Ciudad, R 2002, *The public relations industry*, US Department of Labor, Washington.

Robinson, P 2003, 'Women at top would prevent corporate calamity, says expert', *Sydney Morning Herald*.

Rogers, D 2005, 'Gender Balance will come with maturity', *PR Week*, 2 September.

Rush, R and Allen, D (eds) 1990, *Communications at the crossroads. The gender gap connection*, Ablex Norwood.

Sankaran, S 2001, 'Methodology for an organisational action research thesis', *Action Research International*, vol. Paper 6, viewed 17 September 2005, http://www.scu.edu.au/schools/gcm/ar/ari/p-ssankaran01.html.

Schember, L 1999, 'Women in mass communication education: who is teaching tomorrow's communicators?' in P Creedon (ed.), *Women in mass communication: changing gender values*, Sage Newbury Park, pp. 148–63.

Sha, B-L 2001, 'The feminisation of public relations: contributing to a more ethical practice', in E Toth and E Aldoory (eds), *The gender challenge to media: diverse voices from the field*, Hampton Press, Cresskill, NJ.

Shaw, M (ed.) 1995, *Man does, women is*, Faber and Faber, London.

Shim, SH 2005, *Feminisation of the field*, viewed 12 April 2006, http://sunnyshim.blogspot.com/2005/12/feminisation-of-field.html.

Shim, SH 2005, *Why women dominate PR profession*, viewed 12 April 2006, http://sunnyshim.blogspot.com/2005/12/why-women-dominate-pr-profession.html

Simpson, R 2000, 'Gender mix and organisational fit: how gender imbalance at different levels of the organisation impacts on women managers', *Women in Management Review*, vol. 15, no. 1, p. 5.

Spykerman, S 1997, *Gender roles and work: recent research*, Hope College, Michigan, School of Psychology, viewed 11 November 2005, http://www.hope.edu/academic/psychology/335/webrep/genroles.html.

Stevens, J 2003, *IT gender gap continues to widen*, viewed 20 March 2003, http://www.accountancyage.com/analysis/it/1138753.

Still, L 1993, *Where to from here? The managerial woman in transition*, Business and Professional Publishing, Sydney.

Sullivan, L 2005, *Gender imbalance in engineering education*, 2005, unknown publisher.

Susman, G and Evered, R 1978, 'An assessment of the scientific merit of action research', *Administrative Science Quarterly*, vol. 23, pp. 582–603.

Taff, H 2002, *Times have changed? The Velvet Ghetto study revisited*, International Association of Business Communicators, New York.

Tanton, M 1994, *Women in management: a developing presence*, Routledge, London.

The Weekend Australian 2005, 'Women slap BBC veteran', 20–21 August, p. 24.

The West Australian 2002, 'Women lead surge in full-time jobs', 13 September.

Toth, E 1991, 'Public relations practitioner attitudes towards gender issues: a benchmark study', *Public Relations Review*, vol. 17, no. 2, pp. 161–74.

Toth, E and Aldoory, L 2000, *Year 2000 gender study. Report of the committee on Work, life and gender issues*, Public Relations Society of America, New York.

Toth, L 2000, 'An exploratory look at graduate public relations education', *Public Relations Review*, vol. 26, no. 1.

vanRuler, B and deLange, R 2002, 'Barriers to communication management in the executive suite', *Public Relations Review*, vol. 29, no. 2, pp. 145–58.

Vella, F 1993, 'Gender roles, occupational choice and gender wage differentials', *Economic Record*, vol. 69, no. 207.

Walter, N 2005, 'A waste of women', *Australian Financial Review*, 1 July.

Wanzenried, G 2003, *How feminine is corporate America?*, University of Connecticut Economics Department, viewed 27 April 2005.

Ward-O'Neill, J 1999, 'Positioning women as "outsiders within" the public relations profession', paper presented to AEJMC Convention, Commission on the Status of Women, Michigan, viewed, 21 October 2005, http://list.msu.edu/cgi-bin/wa?A2=ind9909BandL=aejmcandF=andS=andP=5220.

Weidman, L 2001, 'Tales from the testosterone zone', in E Toth and E Aldoory (eds), *The gender challange to media: diverse voices from the field*, Hampton Press, Cresskill, NJ.

Weiss, E 2002, *Publishing: fact and fiction*, viewed 19 October 2005, http://www.nla.gov.au/events/weiss.html.

Wilcox, D, Ault, P and Agee, W 1998, *Public relations: strategies and tactics*, 5th edn, Longman, New York.

Wilcox, D, Ault, P and Agee, W 2003, *Public Relations: strategies and tactics*, Allyn and Bacon, Boston.

Wrigley, B 2002, 'Glass ceiling? What glass ceiling? A qualitative study of how women view the glass ceiling in public relations and communications management.' *Journal of Public Relations Research*, vol. 14, no. 1, pp. 27-55.

Annexes

Sent via e-mail to PR course co-ordinators mid-June 2005

SUBJECT: PR GENDER SURVEY

Hi, (Name of course co-ordinator)

I am undertaking a PhD through Central Queensland University. The project is a gender study of the PR industry. To that end, I would like your permission to conduct a survey of second- and third-year [University name] PR students.

All I request is time at the end of a lecture to present the survey and to distribute questionnaires. All up this should take 30 minutes (that includes time for the students to complete the survey, which I have attached).

The methodology has been approved by the CQU Ethic Committee (Ref. H05/05-54 of 2 June 2005).

Any assistance is appreciated, [name]. Thanks for your consideration.

Regards,
Greg Smith

Sent via e-mail to University Heads of Communication, June 2005

SUBJECT: REQUEST FOR ENROLLMENT STATISTICS

I am a Perth-based PhD student (Central Queensland University) researching the predominance of women in communications (PR) in Perth.

I am in the stages of initial research and would like to know if your School would be able to provide statistics of course enrolment, preferably for as many years as possible, please?

Could you also indicate to whom I should address future requests for possible participation of [University name] students in survey and/or focus groups, please?

The research has been approved by the CQU Ethic Committee (Ref. H05/05-54 of 2 June 2005).

Your assistance would be greatly appreciated.

Sincerely,
Greg Smith

2005 gender survey into the public relations industry

This survey is the second stage of research into the predominance of women in public relations (primarily in Perth) and is being conducted as part of a PhD in Communications through the School of Infomatics and Communication at Central Queensland University, Rockhampton. The supervisors are Professor Alan Knight, and Kate Ames.

It is intended to form the basis for interviews and focus groups, to be conducted later in 2005 and 2006.

In brief:

- o   All information in this survey is confidential.
- o   No names are being used.
- o   No-one will be identified.
- o   There is no compulsion for you to complete the survey.
- o   All surveys will be destroyed once the results have been collated.

You will be advised of the survey results by e-mail. These will also be published at the web site http://members.westnet.com.au/gsmith/study. If you require further information, please contact me at gsmith@westnet.com.au.

I thought it necessary to ask a question about income. While I realise for many people this is "private", its inclusion will help show the relationship between gender and earning capacity. Again, I assure you that this information is strictly confidential. No person is identified, and all responses will be destroyed. Results will be used only in this study.

Finally, thank you for your continued interest and participation in this study, which, as far as I am aware, is the first of its type. It should form the basis of future research. Your involvement will contribute to knowledge about our industry, particularly in Perth.

Sincerely,

Greg Smith

Greg Smith
3 June 2005

INSTRUCTIONS

This survey should take no more than 25 minutes. Please answer all questions. To answer multiple choice questions, highlight the box, and click your mouse. For answers which require wording or numbering, type in the grey area. Please save your document and return by e-mail to gsmith@westnet.com.au. Thank you.

1. Sex
   ■ M   ■ F

2. Highest schooling
   A ■ High School
   B ■ TAFE
   C ■ Uni

3. Highest qualification
   A ■ School Cert/HSC/Leavers
   B ■ TAFE Cert/Diploma
   C ■ University Degree
   D ■ Post-Grad
   E   ■   Other

4. In order, list the three areas you mostly work in.
          Community relations
          Media relations
          Issues management
          Event management
          Product promotion
          Other (specify)

5. What sector of the industry do you mostly work in?
   A ■ Private company (in-house)

B ■ Government

C ■ Non-profit

D ■ Consultancy (in-house)

E ■ Other

6. How many years have you worked in public relations?

years

7. What type of role best describes the work you do?

A ■ Writer

B ■ Client liaison

C ■ Event management

D ■ Media

E ■ Support and co-ordination

F ■ Strategy development?

G ■ Other

8. What level are you employed at?

A ■ Junior/entry

B ■ Technician (writer, media, events)

C ■ Middle (some client liaison, some strategy)

D ■ Senior (strategy only)

9. What is your salary range?

A ■ $20,000–$35,000

B ■ $36,000–$45,000

C ■ $46,000–$60,000

D ■ $61,000–plus

10. On average, how many hours a day do you work?

A ■ 6–8 hours

B ■ 8–10 hours

C ■ 10–12 hours

D ■ 12–plus hours

11. Several factors may influence the choice of PR as a successful/good career. Number (in order) what you believe makes PR a good career?

      Money

      Career path

      Creative aspect

      Variety

      Mental challenge

      Other (specify)

12. What three aspects of PR interest you most (number 3 only, in order):

      Goal-setting

      Marketing and branding

      Project management

      Budgets/cost control

      Graphic design

      Writing

      Media liaison

      Events management

      Investor relations

      Reputation management

      Research

      Community relations

13. In order, what type of PR would you/do you prefer to work in:

        Consultancy

        Government

        Corporate/in-house

        Non-profit

14. Do you think there is a balanced workforce in PR (as it relates to gender)?

■ Yes   ■ No

15. A census of the Perth PR industry and universities this year showed that on average that 74 per cent of the industry is female. Were you aware of this?

■ Yes   ■ No

Why do you think this has happened?

16. Do you think men or women are better suited to a communications career?

■ Men   ■ Women

Why?

17. Do you think a person's gender influences his/her entry into PR?

■ Yes   ■ No

If yes, in what way/s?

18. Do you think men or women (or neither) are best able to build rapport with clients?

■ Men   ■ Women   ■ Neither

Why?

19. Are there any barriers that you believe could hinder a person's career in PR?

■ Yes   ■ No

What are they?

20. Do you think there should be a balanced workforce in PR?

■ Yes   ■ No

Why

21. Do you think gender impacts on individual performance in PR?

■ Yes   ■ No

Why?

22. Do you think gender imbalance might have any effects/s on the PR industry?

■ Yes   ■ No

If yes, what effects might they be?

23. Do you think there is a difference in the way males and females work with clients?

■ Yes   ■ No.

If so, how?

24. Are there any aspects of working in this industry that affect your ability to work with clients and other industry professionals, media, target audiences?

■ Yes   ■ No

What are they

25. Are there any ethical issues that effect your work within the industry?

■ Yes   ■ No

What are they?

26. Does this differ between males and females?

■ Yes   ■ No.

What are they?

27. Will you be available for an ■ Interview   and/or   ■ Focus group?

28. What day and time best suits you for:

a. An interview   Preference: ■ In-

person   ■ Phone

b. Focus group

29. Do you have any comments or questions about this survey?

Thank you for your participation

- Greg Smith

June 2005

PR GENDER – STUDENT SURVEY

This survey is the first stage of research into the predominance of women in public relations.

This questionnaire is being conducted as part of a PhD in Communications through the School of Infomatics and Communication at Central Queensland University.

It is intended as a guide towards more in-depth interviews and focus groups, to be conducted late in 2005 and 2006. Supervisors are Prof. Alan Knight, and Kate Ames.

In brief:

1. All information in this survey is confidential.
2. No names are being used.
3. No one will be identified.
4. All surveys will be destroyed once the results have been collated.
5. No e-mail addresses or names are passed to any third party.

You will be advised of the survey results by e-mail. These will also be published at the web site http://members.westnet.com.au/gsmith/study. If you require further information, please contact me at gsmith@westnet.com.au.

Please read the instructions on each question carefully, as some of the pilot surveys were invalid due to questions not being completed correctly.

Finally, thank you for your interest and participation in this study, which, as far as I am aware, is the first of its type. It should form the basis of future research. Your involvement will contribute to knowledge about our industry.

Sincerely,

Greg Smith
INSTRUCTIONS

This survey should take no more than 20 minutes. Please answer all questions, marking boxes with an X. Please answer all questions, otherwise the survey is invalid.

1. Sex

M ■   F ■

2. Year of study

Year 2 ■   Year 3 ■

3. Course Major being studied

■ Public Relations

■ Journalism

■ Other (specify) _____

4. How do you see PR?

■ A Career   ■ A Job   ■ May lead to something else

5. What aspects of PR interest you most (**LIST 3 ONLY**, in order of interest):

_____ Goal-setting

_____ Integrated Marketing Communication

_____ Project management

_____ Budgets/cost control

_____ Production (print/web design)

_____ Writing

_____ Media relations

_____ Events management

_____ Investor relations

_____ Reputation management

_____ Research

_____ Community relations

6. What type of PR would you prefer to work in? (**MARK ONE**):

■ Consultancy

■ Government

■ Non-profit

■ Corporate (that is, in-house for one firm)

■ Anything I can get

■ Undecided

7. List in order (from 1–3) the areas of PR that interest you most.

__ Beauty/fashion

__ Travel/tourism

__ Non-profit

__ Entertainment

__ Health/medical/pharmaceutical

__ Food and beverage

__ International

__ IT

__ Financial

__ Industrial/manufacturing

__ Sports

8. Reasons for studying (and therefore presumably wanting to work in) PR vary. For the following, rate in order (1 to 9) what might motivate you to choose a PR career.

__ Desire to work with people

__ Money

__ Job satisfaction

__ Job security

__ Perceived benefits

__ Interest in current affairs

__ Career variety

__ Prestige

__ Creative aspects

9. What chance of success do you think you will have in obtaining work within PR:

◼ Less than 20 per cent

◼ 20–40 per cent

◼ 50–70 per cent

◼ 80–100 per cent

10. List the number of male and female tutors you have

Male _____

Female _____

11. Do you perceive any differences in the way your male and female tutors/lecturers teach?

Yes ■   No ■

If yes, what are they?

12. A census of the Perth PR industry and university courses this year showed that on average 74 per cent of students are female, with some courses up to 80 per cent female. Were you aware of that?

Yes ■   No ■

Why do you think that is?

13. Do you think men or women are more suited to a communications career?

Men ■   Women ■   Neither ■

Why?

14. Do you think a person's gender might influence his/her entry into PR?

Yes ■   No ■   Not really ■

Comment:

15. Do you think men or women would best be able to build rapport with clients?

Men ■   Women ■   Neither ■

If you answered male or female, why?

16. Number, from 1 to 3, the three qualities you believe make a good PR practitioner.

_____ Verbal skills

_____ Written skills

_____ Planning skills

_____ Organisational skills

_____ Knowledge of the media

_____ Strategic thinking

_____ Financial management

_____ Listening ability

17. Do you see any barriers that might hinder your career in PR?

18. Rate whether you disagree/agree with the following. Place X in the box.

	Strongly disagree	Mildly disagree	Mildly agree	Strongly agree
A. PR is an easy study option				
B. I am mildly interested in PR				
C. PR will suffice until other opportunities arise				
D. PR allows me to be inventive/creative				
E. PR offers good practical skills				

19. Are you aware that in PR, men are, on average, paid more than women?

(*PR Week* Opinion Survey, 2002)

Yes ■   No ■

What do you think of that?

20. In PR, do you think men or women are more likely to be hired for basic (technician) communication skills (that is, writing, editing, design, web/print)?

Men ■   Women ■   Both equally ■

The following information is confidential. It will be destroyed after the interviews and focus groups are completed.

Would you be available for a ■ focus group and/or ■ interview?

Your name:

E-mail address:

Phone number (optional):

1. Your gender   1 ■ Male   2 ■ Female

2. Your university   1 ■ Curtin   2 ■ ECU   2 ■ Notre Dame   4 ■
Murdoch

3. Which socio-economic (family) group do you come from? (ABS definitions).

1 ■ Low   ($6k-$21k)   2 ■ Average   ($22k-$58k)
3 ■ Above average ($59k-$70k)   4 ■ High   (above $70k)

4. Which of these traits best describes you? (Select one only).

1 ■ Positive   4 ■ Creative   7 ■ Quiet
2 ■ Personable   5 ■ Outgoing
3 ■ Decisive   6 ■ Organised

5. What was your favourite subject at school? (Select one only)

1 ■ Science   7 ■ Economics
2 ■ Geography   8 ■ Politics
3 ■ Maths   9 ■ Art
4 ■ English   10 ■ Drama
5 ■ Other language   11 ■ Other (list)
6 ■ History   _____

6. What influenced you most to study PR? (Select one only).

1 ■ Friend   5 ■ Influenced by media (TV)
2 ■ Knew someone in the industry 6 ■ Knew about it and made some enquiries
3 ■ Schools careers counsellor   7 ■ Always had an interest
4 ■ Switched to PR course   8 ■ Other _____

7. How do you think most people view PR? (Select one only)

1 ■ They have a positive impression
2 ■ They think it's about spin
3 ■ They're a little unsure about it
4 ■ They don't know
5 ■ Other (specify) ——————————

8. What type of work situation suits you best?

1▪ Prefer to produce my own ideas
2▪ Prefer to implement others' ideas
3▪ Prefer to weight up my ideas against others'

9. Rate how strongly you agree or disagree with the statement: "PR is 'fuzzy' in its logic".

1▪ Strongly agree   2▪ Mildly agree
3▪ Mildly disagree   4▪ Strongly disagree

10. Did you have any perception about PR before studying it?
1 ▪ Yes   2 ▪ No

11. Do you think students study PR because of their perceptions about it?
1▪ Yes   2 ▪ No

12. If "yes", what did you think about PR then? What do you think about PR now?

Q. 14. Do you think there is a balanced workforce in PR (as it relates to gender)?

1. Balance and performance is not gender-specific. (M)

2. Balance would better represent the needs of diverse clients. (F)

3. Like any industry, there should be gender balance. (F)

4. I can't see what advantage it would confer or difference it would make ultimately. If the job is done properly doesn't matter who does it, regardless of gender or age. (F)

5. There should be a balanced workforce in PR; just as there should be in other fields. (M)

6. It should be about hiring the best person for the job. (F)

7. A predominance of female PR and media practitioners leads to a bias toward women's issues and beliefs. Female beliefs should have an equal male counterweight in both the choice and analysis of issues. The genders might be equal but they still think differently on many issues. (M)

8. Those who best suit the job should get the job. (F)

9. It may bring a greater measure of external respect for the industry if more men were in it (sad but true). (F)

10. It's good for the industry, to provide aspects from both genders. (F)

11. Attempts to enforce arbitrary balances are futile. We should be attracting the best people for the job regardless of their gender, eye colour, race or shoe size. (M)

12. Balance is necessary to uphold principles of equity and diversity. (M)

13. It is always preferable to have a range of opinions, experience and views, so of course a workforce should be balanced rather than dominated by any one view. (M)

14. If PR is to be seen as a profession rather than a trade then gender imbalance should be addressed. It shouldn't be an issue. (M)

15. There should be a balanced workforce everywhere. (M)

16. Every workforce should be balanced. Employment should be about merit and what individuals, regardless of gender, can bring to the mix. (F)

17. I think like any function PR benefits from balance between creativity and a more business and structured approach to work. (F)

18. I believe there should be balanced workforce in every area that an equal amount of men and women are interested in pursuing - unhindered by stereotypes. (F)

19. A better gender balance would help ensure better client relations at all levels. If the industry is seen to be exclusive to women it is likely to not be able to fully understand or service the needs of all client groups. (M)

20. Balance can help, depending on who the client and stakeholders they are dealing with. Also, it appears that male and female approaches can be quite different. (There's a) need to be able to consider different angles. (M)

21. It should be a natural product of selecting the best people for the relevant jobs. (M)

22. We should simply get the best people. Do you think the engineering industry (or other male-dominated industries have suffered due to their gender balance? If we agree with the question, does that mean an 'imbalanced' workforce is good? (F)

23. I don't believe it makes any difference if there is a gender imbalance. (F)

24. Balance is not relevant. However, I think the upper echelons of PR should reflect the female dominance at lower levels. As the industry is so female dominated woman tend to primarily work with and around women. A male influence is needed to balance teams.(F)

25. In consultancies, particularly, you will usually have a client list which includes brands/services which target different audiences. It is helpful to have both a male and female (as well as younger/older for that matter) perspective on consumer insights. (F)

26. Teams work best when there is a balance of ideas, backgrounds and orientations - obviously gender plays a part in that. (F)

27. It can sometimes create a one-gender approach. (F)

28. I think the industry is best served by intelligent, articulate, strategic people, irrespective of gender. (F)

29. Some people may work better (or not) with (or without) men/women in the workplace. (F)

30. The high proportion of women in junior roles contributes to the image of the profession being tactical in nature – not corporate, strategic. The over-proportion of men in management positions contributes to the reality that the industry is a poor promoter of relationships in the workplace. There should be balance because half the people we communicate with are men. (M)

31. Yes, there should be balance. Yes, because men bring different skills and some corporations still simply prefer dealing with men - particularly in industries like engineering and mining. Men and women both have different qualities to offer and a mixed team creates a better dynamic. It's less effective marketing to men, lack of men's perspective. (F)

32. It creates diversity (F)

33. Balance in any industry is preferable but I'm not sure it will change the outcomes for the client. (F)

34. A balanced workforce can address the needs of all clientele at a particular time and deliver an even spread of creative thinking. (M)

35. It's not necessary to have men in this profession. (F)

36. Balance brings variety and different approaches to the work. But an office with too many women can be bitchy. I sure know that. (M)

37. There should be a balanced workforce in any industry. (F)

38. (Males and females) complement each other's skills, provide a gender balance in the office and help steer away from it being a traditionally female-dominated area. (F)

39. Does it matter? (F)

40. We need the right person for the right job, which can be any gender. (M)

41. Any workforce that contains a more equal balance of males and females is generally a happier and arguably more functional workplace (comment made from personal experience of almost 30 years in the workforce). (F)

42. All industry sectors should strive to have a balanced workforce. (F)

Q. 15. A census of the Perth PR industry and universities this year showed that on average that 74 per cent of the industry is female. Were you aware of this? If yes, why do you think it occurred?

1. PR has been promoted as an attractive career for women. (M)

2. Women are drawn to PR because of their confidence and their knowledge. (F)

3. A lot of girls study PR at uni I believe, as they think it's a fairly glamorous career, thinking it's lots of parties and schmoozing. Often they think of very consumer-oriented PR with lots of events. Most of PR is not really about that. It's more media relations. As you become more senior, issues management, corporate reputation. It's seen as a more female occupation due to the perception of events, schmoozing, very tactical work. PR is often perceived by men to be a glorified secretary's role. (F)

4. People think PR is glamorous so mostly women are attracted to this as a career path. (F)

5. Women have better natural skills for undertaking PR and are more interested in it. (M)

6. In the older age groups, I feel it could be due to secretaries and PA's having moved into the PR area or given 'PR' to do as part of their original role because they have secretarial skills. I suspect many small PR consultancies are run by women and if they're home-based then a woman is less likely to bring a man into that situation; people say the nature of women is better suited to PR and communications (that of course is debatable. (F)

7. Female high school students often have PR suggested because of basic psychometric assessment which identifies the creative/intuitive aspects of the profession as suitable for women. There has also been a strong promotion of PR as a celebrity profession through media, which seems attractive especially to young women. (M)

8. Senior government positions in particular are occupied by women and they simply recruit other women. It's quite scandalous. (M)

9. There's been a focus on softer/product marketing aspects of PR encourages PR houses to hire softer employees and housekeepers for event management. Women see it as a career in itself, particularly in sub-disciplines such as event management. (M)

10. Women are conditioned to believe PR is a right-brained industry and women are 'naturally' right brained. I've actually heard people say, 'you can talk, you get on with people, who don't you go into PR. (F)

11. I think PR has a perception of being a female industry a bit like nursing and thus men are not naturally drawn to it, unless they come in via journalism or publishing. (F)

12. It has traditionally been an area women have been seen to excel, so I imagine as a female student you would want to chose a career path that doesn't appear to have an overt glass ceiling. (F)

13. The industry generally has more opportunities today for females and, as women gain more senior PR roles they tend to engage more females. As the numbers of females grow in the industry they tend to influence others to pursue the profession. (M)

14. I think PR is a great profession for men and women but women have taken to it as an alternative to journalism with the opp. to work in with clients, flexible career paths, events, media, marketing etc and still write - without the issues of death knocks, chequebook journalism, male dominated media circles. (F)

15. PR shifted from being a career progression for ex-journalists (mainly men) to a more recognised professional option in its own right with university courses attracting more women. (F)

16. Young men tend to view communications as a career path for women. (F)

17. Women are better-suited because it is more natural for women to communicate. (F)

18. It is now perceived as 'female' sector. (F)

19. It was traditionally viewed as a female career path. (F)

20. More women entering previously male-dominated roles in media generally. (F)

21. Possibly women are drawn more to humanities. (F)

22. Males are actively discriminated against at [uni] course selection and at time of employment. (M)

23. PR is based strongly on communication skills, and women felt that it was an area they could specialise in. (F)

24. Women are more interested in communicating than men. PR is mainly about communicating. (F)

25. Representations in popular media portray PR as a 'cool' profession for women. I believe it is viewed as a 'chicks' field and therefore is not taken as seriously as it would if there were more men. (M)

26. The whole world of (white collar) work is becoming feminised, but PR is the most visible example of this phenomenon. PR work tends to work best as a group activity. Could this be another factor that tends to suit females more than typically solitary and competitive males. (M)

27. Maybe due to school/parental career choice (that is, what's encouraged or lack of understanding of what PR involves).

28. The PR industry perhaps is seen as a more a 'softer' alternative and perhaps men are more attracted to what are seen as more 'harder' hitting' industries such as journalism. Because there are more females in the industry, it naturally attracts more females. (F)

29. Because it's largely a communication discipline, which women are typically attracted to. (F)

30. Both can be suited but for reasons above women are attracted to the field. Men and women can be good at anything. Have worked with men and women who are brilliant and both who aren't. It's not a gender issue but a mindset. (F)

31. Females are more suited to PR because they are better communicators, possess stronger interpersonal skills, are more intelligent emotionally and enjoy being creative. (M)
32. It is an industry in which women can be just as successful/ possibly more successful than men and I was aware of this when I chose it as a career. Also, I believe women are sometimes more suited to the hands-on, creative, communicative requirements of PR. (F)

33. I think it's the creative aspect of the industry. Plus, I also think the PR industry allows women to progress to management positions, which traditionally has been difficult in other industries. (F)

34. I think it is not common for men to enter PR as it is traditionally seen as a job which involves a large amount of organising. Men are not typically known for being good organisers and are not really brought up in the household as being responsible for having to organise themselves much. The imbalance of responsibilities in the home may still contribute to this. I think men who get into journalism also see PR as a soft option and don't want the extras that come with it, such as events management. (F)

35. Perhaps because PR is increasingly seen as a job women are most suited to. Men may think they should be doing more 'blokey' professional jobs, like law or engineering. I also think the public perception of PR as a bit of a 'blow up balloons and make sure the coffee is nice' side of it doesn't appeal to men. (F)

36. Girls are still (surprisingly) encouraged to follow more creative paths. (F)

Q. 16. Do you think men/women/neither are better suited to a communications career? If men or women, why?

1. Suitability for PR is not gender specific. It comes down to ability, and either gender can succeed. It comes down to individuals and natural selection. Some PR tasks are better suited to men or women, but that is a generalisation. Some women perform better in the corporate PR world, if given the chance. Some men are brilliant organisers for events, which is traditionally a female area. Again it is the individual that counts. (M)

2. Women have better natural skills for undertaking PR and are more interested in it, this is because it involves large amounts of people skills, use of intuition and expression through writing. Women are naturally better at this. (F)

3. Some sectors of industry and commerce, such as design, cosmetics etc will benefit more from female input. similarly, men would be better suited to engineering or agricultural PR. (M)

4. Women are better-suited to PR because they are more level-headed. (F)

5. Women have greater empathic qualities, better listeners, able to multi-task, less reliant on relationships/contacts to succeed. I believe women feel more comfortable about entering the industry. Men rely on 'old boy" network and have more time to network/socialise outside of working hours. (F)

6. Both are equally – it's not a gender issue. (M)

7. A career in communications is all about building relationships. If you don't have the wherewithal to do that you will fail. (M)

8. Women are more likely to enter PR as a career in sub-disciplines, such as event management, so they may get more satisfaction out of that. Men often burnt out, in PR as the last option, tend to the cynical and the maladjusted. (M)

9. I unfortunately believe that being a physically unattractive, or poorly groomed person, and even possibly being a much older person, especially if you are female, would be a barrier to success in PR – as is probably true of most jobs. (F)

10. I think men, if they are interested in this kind of work, would be more attracted to advertising/marketing, business/commerce, rather than PR itself. (F)

11. Both have pros and cons. There is need for a balance. (M)

12. Perhaps they're (men are) taken more seriously. (M)

13. Everybody is different. I look for someone with integrity, honest and respect (and a degree). (F)

14. I think both men and women are equally suited to PR. (F)

15. Neither. Both are capable. (M)

16. Woman tend to score better in English/humanities subjects and tend to be better organisers than men, and PR is largely about organisation. (F)

17. Women are generally more intuitive; strong verbal and written skills; high emotional intelligence; detail oriented; can multi-task. (F)

18. Young men tend to view communications as a career path for women. (F)

19. Women are better-suited because it is more natural for women to communicate. Women are (also) more adaptable and able to make fast decisions. (F)

20. I think gender is irrelevant to ability to communicate and strategise. (F)

21. Women make better professional communicators. They can relate to a larger range of people. (F)

22. It suits both genders. (F)

23. Females are more suited to PR because they are better communicators, possess stronger interpersonal skills, are more intelligent emotionally and enjoy being creative. (M)

24. No media experience. (M)

25. Neither men or women are best suited. Both have varied and positive skills that they can bring to the industry. (M)

26. I don't think gender matters. (F)

27. I think both sexes can do a really good job at PR, though it tends to appeal more to women. (F)

28. The psychological make-up of females which affects their superior ability to balance several tasks at one time and that they are also recognised as possessing better fundamental communication skills. (F)

29. Depends on the specific person. You just need to be good at communicating with people: that's not gender specific. (F)

30. I don't think gender impacts on one's ability to excel in the PR industry. (F)

31. I believe this is true is some cases. There are men who I am sure are good communicators, but it is an intrinsic quality that most women possess. (F)

32. Women are naturally good communicators and organisers. (F)

33. It comes down to personal aptitude. Men can be equally good, perhaps even better than, some women in writing and client liaison, etc. I think neither are more suited than the other. It's a fairly flexible job. (F)

34. Everyone has different talents - gender doesn't necessarily determine this. Either you're good at PR-related activities or you're not. (F)

35. I think it is very dependent on the personality of individuals. Whilst my experience is that women dominate the industry and seem to have the personality fit for the job - this doesn't exclude males. (F)

36. I think women are more attracted to the field because men view it as 'fuzzy'. (M)

Q. 17. Do you think a person's gender influences his/her entry into PR? Yes/no. If yes, in what ways?

1. It depends on the individual rather than gender. (M)

2. Women are naturally more interested in the type of activities that are involved in PR, from event management to writing and client liaison. Young men (early 20s) find it harder because they are invariably less mature than their female counterparts, can't express themselves as well, and can't intuitively read group or individual dynamics so a lot of stuff just goes over their heads. (M)

3. Some sectors of industry and commerce, such as design, cosmetics etc will benefit more from female input. similarly, men would be better suited to engineering or agricultural PR. (M)

4. Yes, to some extent. I think as it is seen as a female dominant industry that it may be harder for men to get jobs in the industry over women. (F)

5. The gender imbalance makes it difficult to work within the mainstream media. (M)

6. In looking at gender differences, I suspect it is still the woman usually who has to drop work to attend a sick child, and this would impact on performance, although one would expect irregularly. (F)

7. Men become much more matey, joke a lot more with clients and don't take criticism as personally as women practitioners. (F)

8. The only impact of gender would be only in as far as women seem to be better communicators; there is no actual preference for men or women that I have experienced. (F)

9. Gender doesn't really have an influence, or an impact. It has an impact as much as any other characteristic, no more and no less. (M)

10. Men are more likely to see it as a career move after burning out in journalism or politics. Women see it as a career in itself, particularly in sub-disciplines such as event management. (M)

11. Gender is virtually irrelevant, as it is skill sets, personalities etc. that matter. (F)

12. I think the statistic of 74% of females entering PR proves gender influence and I would assume, as I have earlier, that female students have a perception that this is an area where they could pursue a successful career path. I imagine given the gender basis for females studying PR that maybe some men could feel it is not a 'manly' profession but I would only be guessing, as I have never heard any man say this. I would think this would come down to personality and interpersonal skill of the PR person. (F)

13. Yes, gender does influence, because it is now pretty well established as a female-dominated profession. (F)

14. As the numbers of females grow in the industry they tend to influence others to pursue the profession. (M)

15. Men tend to think PR is a 'woman's career'. (F)

16. I think gender is irrelevant to ability to communicate and strategise. Some corporates believe men are better at "tough" strategy, hence their number in senior mining and government PR. (F)

17. Both genders bring their own abilities and experience to the profession. (F)

18. Many men perceive PR as frivolous and touchy/feely. That's why more women pursue the career. (M)

19. Gender does influence entry. Males are actively discriminated against at [uni] course selection and at time of employment. (M)

20. I do not think gender matters. Both can be equally as suited. (F)

21. Assuming (as is the case) that senior positions still tend to be taken by men, then they may prefer to hire a woman onto their team. There need be nothing improper in this, simply a recognition that a mixed team may have greater overall strengths. To the extent that public relations is about relationships, gender may play a part. (M)

22. PR is one of the 'soft' careers that appeals to women. (F)

23. Both have skills that are gender-based. The old adage: women are better communicators than men, is often bandied about but quite simply untrue. (M)

24. If it is male-dominated, then I feel creativity is stifled. (M)

25. I think only now that men may be influenced or put off by the imbalance of gender; that is, not many men are doing it, so why would I? (F)

26. Similar answer to question 16. Girls are still (surprisingly) encouraged to follow more creative path. (F)

Q. 18. Do you think men/women (or neither) are best able to build rapport with clients? If men or women, why?

1. It depends on the client. Serious clients would generally go for men, wankers for women. (M)

2. It depends upon the gender of the client. Men and women relate differently to the opposite sex in all walks of life and this is also true in PR. However, diversity is the spice of life and I see no particular problem with the different ways that female PR practitioners relate to their clients. (M)

3. I could be either, depending on the client and the consultant. (F)

4. It depends on clients. We do a lot of mining/infrastructure/primary industry work and they still prefer to deal strategically with a male (not that it makes any difference to the level of work done). Some other industry sectors seem to prefer women ... horses for courses. (M)

5. Neither men or women are best at building rapport. It depends on the client. I don't think its gender, rather personality, that drives this. (F)

6. Women are more focused upon not verbal signs and obtaining consensus. (F)

7. Clients are usually men and they relate better to other men on a professional level. That said, women have advantages, too, such as mentioned above: they're better at getting along with all types of people. Male clients often won't take women seriously and will get on better with men. (M)

8. I think this depends entirely on the personality and interpersonal skills of the person, not the gender. (F)

9. Clients (decision makers) generally tend to be men, networking opportunities better established by men – golf days, drinks, etc the BOYS club really does still exist. (F)

10. Do not agree either gender has an advantage, but better gender balance would help ensure better client relations at all levels. (M)

11. It depends on person. I work with men and women and it comes down to their individuality. Both can bring experience and strength to client relationships - not cut and dried. (F)

12. Business is still very much a 'boys club'. (F)

13. I have seen good and poor operators of both genders. (F)

14. Building rapport has nothing to do with gender. (M)

15. Neither are better at this. It depends on the individual's personal attributes unrelated to gender. (F)

16. Most of the 'big-end' clients tend to be represented by men and men like to deal with men. (M)

17. I find this a very hard one to answer definitively; but have favoured women again on the grounds that most clients (in certain sectors) are male. Sometimes they prefer the male bonding potential of having a male PR consultant, but mostly I suspect they might prefer an attentive female client (I recognise that this answer, and some others, could easily be misinterpreted). There is of course a difference in how individuals work with different clients. I (male) was always formal and businesslike with my clients (some later became good friends, but only once they were no longer clients). Some of my female colleagues found it much easier to strike up an easy rapport with these same clients; yet other female colleagues were even more formal than me. (M)

18. Neither would be my answer. Both are equally able. Rapport is about personality not gender. (M)

19. I think it depends on the specific person. Women may be seen as the friendly nurturers, but sometimes in the business world women aren't taken as seriously as men, particularly by senior execs. (F)

20. As a young woman in the PR industry, it can be difficult building rapport and earning respect from senior male clients. However, this could be more of an age issue, than gender. (F)

21. If the consultant is an effective communicator I believe they will be able to build a strong relationship with their clients, regardless of gender. (F)

22. It depends on the individual. Some people can easily built rapport, others can't. While it can certainly be a learnt skill, some will still have an advantage because they can sell ice to the Eskimos (that is, are skilled and persuasive communicators) anyway. (F)

Q. 19. Are there any barriers that you believe could hinder a person's career in PR? Yes/no.

1. Employers may feel a job is more 'suited' to a female, and would not hire a man. (M)

2. As in some other industries, aspects relating to personal presentation, grooming, speech, etc – all things that generally can be modified or improved on by the individual if necessary. And of course skills/abilities. (F)

3. As in all careers, it is difficult to balance a family's needs with a full-on career. (F)

4. Government and corporates are still (in the main) uncomfortable working with female dominated professionals on equal footing (consider nursing etc) a 'Female' PR profession will take longer to gain acceptance. (M)

5. Personal ethics: harder to get on if you're honest. You need to be able to sink into the dark side comfortably. (M)

6. In government political interference can impede a person's PR career. (F)

7. Lack of communication skills, tact, definitely need to be a good communicator. (F)

8. Ability and lack of common sense. (F)

9. Gender does influence entry. Males are actively discriminated against at course selection and at time of employment. The main barrier to PR entry is that the education system discriminates against males entering the world of PR, through course selection process. Males are not encouraged to think of it as a choice and when they do it is made more difficult for them to be selected despite results and aptitude. (M)

10. I have heard of many young females (with uni degrees) who entered the industry with consultancies and were expected to work long hours doing all of the office's general work (little of which is genuine PR work but menial tasks such as taking the boss' dry cleaning in or getting coffees.) They were treated rudely by supervisors and more experienced colleagues. They decided to leave PR. This treatment is not at the hands of males but other females. Others have received this treatment but hang in there and move on within the industry. (F)

11. I see many students competing for junior roles, and have anecdotal evidence that women are favoured in the interview process because they often appear more assured, whereas young men can still appear gauche. They are barriers of skills and commitment. Not everyone has the stomach for a full-time PR role (and perhaps we are guilty in higher education of not fully preparing students for the pressures of real work.) (F)

12. PR tends to be full of good-looking, well-groomed people, so someone who doesn't fit that mould may find it difficult to get ahead (F)

13. Lack of understanding of the political environment in which the practitioner works - needs to understand the culture and the 'small p' politics. (M)

14. Age, gender and looks. (F)

15. If the person is not confident, a good communicator and able to adapt to suit different clients I think PR would be difficult. (F)

16. A lack of ability/aptitude for writing. Writing is such a large part of PR, if you don't have the skills, it will be very hard to succeed. (F)

17. The 'old school' PR people who have been working in the industry for years and have become set in their ways and aren't necessarily open to younger, fresher creativity. Also, the recent tendency for government to become more

policy driven, which puts a number of impediments in place that can staunch the feeling that creativity and autonomy are encouraged in PR. (F)

Q. 20. Do you think there should be a balanced workforce in PR? Yes/no/doesn't matter. Why?

1. I can't see what advantage it would confer, or difference it would make ultimately. If the job is done properly doesn't matter who does it, regardless of gender or age. (M)

2. Yes. To match the balanced audience. A predominance of female PR and media practitioners leads to a bias toward women's issues and beliefs. Female beliefs should have an equal male counterweight in both the choice and analysis of issues. The genders might be equal but they still think differently on many issues. (M)

3. Those who best suit the job should get the job. (F0

4. Having a better balance may bring a greater measure of external respect for the industry if more men were in it (sad but true). (F)

5. Attempts to enforce arbitrary balances are futile. We should be attracting the best people for the job regardless of their gender, eye colour, race or shoe size. (M)

6. I think there should be a balanced workforce everywhere. (M)

7. I think like any function PR benefits from balance between creativity and a more business and structured approach to work. (F)

8. I believe there should be balanced workforce in every area that an equal amount of men and women are interested in pursuing - unhindered by stereotypes. (F)

9. The industry is so clicky that I think everybody generally works within their own networks and establishes themselves with the people they need to know in order to fulfill what they need to do - regardless of gender ... it's more individual. Generally PR people work in teams, which would include men as part of the creative development / concept team. (F)

10. The industry generally has more opportunities today for females and, as women gain more senior PR roles they tend to engage more females. A better gender balance would help ensure better client relations at all levels. If the industry is seen to be exclusive to women it is likely to not be able to fully understand or service the needs of all client groups. (M)

11. We should simply get the best people. Do you think the engineering industry (or other male dominated industries have suffered due their gender balance? (F)

12. Gender segregation is dangerous. As the industry is so female dominated woman tend to primarily work with and around women. A male influence is needed to balance teams. (F)

13. I think the industry is best served by intelligent, articulate, strategic people, irrespective of gender. (F)

14. Some people may work better (or not) with (or without) men/women in the workplace. (F)

15. There should be balance, because half the people we communicate with are men. (M)

16. Men and women both have different qualities to offer and a mixed team creates a better dynamic. Having less men in the industry could mean less effective marketing to men, lack of men's perspective. (F)

17. Balance in any industry is preferable but I'm not sure it will change the outcomes for the client. (F)

18. Balance brings variety and different approaches to the work. (M)

19. Does balance really matter? (F)

20. Diversity is a strength. PR should represent the diversity of our society. (M)

21. We need the right person for the right job which can be any gender. (M)

22. I can't see what advantage it (balance) would confer or difference it would make ultimately. If the job is done properly doesn't matter who does it, regardless of gender or age. (M)

23. In consultancies, there is an imbalance favouring women. In corporate work there's more of a balance between the genders, but a preference for males in the senior roles. When I arrived at (Company), two years ago had 25 employees - one of them male. One of the first thing I did was look for more gender balance and we now have four male members of staff: nowhere near the balance I'd like, but there is a clear dearth of male candidates available. Where they appear to exist is the corporate finance areas. (F)

24. Personally for me it doesn't matter. I like working in a predominantly female workforce but it does have its disadvantages, too. (F)

25. Doesn't matter. (F)

26. It doesn't matter. I think as long as the people working in PR want to be working in PR and love their job it doesn't matter if it is all men or all women. (F)

27. I would like to see some more men around the office, but also I think men have a lot to offer and a slightly different perspective on things. In PR the perspectives the better. (F)

28. It would be ideal, but it doesn't matter - ultimately the most competent and confident people should be working in PR, regardless of gender. (F)

29. Men and women have different perspectives, and can offer a broader range of ideas and opportunities than only one gender or a gender biased group of PR professionals could. (F)

30. In an ideal work, it should always be the best person for the job. (F)

Q. 21. Do you think gender impacts on individual performance in PR? Yes or no. If yes, then how and why?

1. It depends upon the environment. For example as a woman I have been more effective in male-dominated work environments and less successful in women-orientated organisations and I think this is about complementing each other strengths and abilities. (F)

2. Again, it comes down to individuals not their sex. (F)

3. Different skill sets based on how people are nurtured and encouraged through their development and schooling. Different 'drives' according to how genders are nurtured (e.g. aggressive macho male stereotype versus the calmer more creative female stereotype). (F)

Q. 22. Do you think a workforce gender imbalance might have any effects/s on the PR industry? Yes or no. If yes, what effects might they be?

1. *(This response is more from a media perspective, even though the respondent works in PR)*. (Imbalance) is already reflected in the greater emphasis on lifestyle issues within mainstream news and current affairs, although this is as much a result of the similarly disproportionate female employment levels in the mainstream media. There has been an increasing emphasis on women's lifestyle editorial rather than complex investigative issues. The emphasis on appearance and marketing appeal suggests that such skills (serious journalism, aka PR) are not an important criteria for employment. Market forces are presumably causing the glut of women in PR but it is interesting to observe the subtle impact on society caused by this fundamental shift in values within the public relations industry and its associated political/media clients. (M)

2. Focus on softer/product marketing aspects of PR encourages PR houses to hire softer employees and housekeepers for event management. (M)

3. I think that the PR industry is in trouble. Serious management of organisational reputation or bottom line financial issues does not usually fall

into PR but into areas like strategic business or marketing or advertising. PR is a process and is seen as promotions and events and therefore not serious elements of core business. Further marketing and advertising and multimedia are also eating into traditional PR areas so the profession is becoming fragmented. (F)

4. If the industry is seen to be exclusive to women it is likely to not be able to fully understand or service the needs of all client groups. (M)

5. Effects caused by people being concerned that it might be an issue. Is this about equality in the workplace or perception of the industry as a whole? The PR industry is already suffering a crisis of confidence – where is our place, what is our role? Whether male or female we live or die by the performance and ethics of individuals. (F)

6. Industries that are perceived as 'female', for example, nursing, are generally given less prestige and remuneration. (F)

7. The high proportion of women in junior roles contributes to the image of the profession being tactical in nature – not corporate or strategic. The over-proportion of men in management positions contributes to the reality that the industry is a poor promoter of relationships in the workplace. (M)

8. Less effective marketing to men, lack of men's perspective. (F)

9. There is positive discrimination (against males) at entry level and ongoing feminisation of the industry. (M)

10. The whole world of (white collar) work is becoming feminised, but PR is the most visible example of this phenomenon. (M)

11. Low entry wages, compared to other sectors, is also a factor for males ignoring the industry and favouring marketing disciplines. Also, if more females graduate, it makes sense that more females will get jobs. Industries trying to equalise their gender balance in male-oriented industries will tend to prefer female PR professionals, which may discriminate against male applicants. This systematic preference over time will lead to industry-wide deficiencies, as I think we are now seeing. (M)

12. The feminisation of the industry is something I worry about. Look at the two most heavily feminised industries – teaching and nursing. Look at the pay rates, the conditions and the prospects in the 'caring' professions. I fear the public relations industry, particularly in the marketing communications space is becoming heavily feminised to the detriment of the credibility of the industry as a whole. When you only represent 50% of the population how can the intellectual property you provide be accurate, representative and the best informed. (F)

13. If the industry is seen to be exclusive to women it is likely to not be able to fully understand or service the needs of all client groups. (M)

14. Gender imbalance could affect PR. The industry is excluding males and becoming female-only and restrictive and long term there will be no room for any males, their thoughts and opinions. Diversity gives an industry strength. (M)

15. Some male clients may feel intimidated about so many women in the industry, though they shouldn't. (F)

16. If the industry continues to be dominated by females, then the industry needs to come to terms with issues such as maternity leave, work/life balance and flexibility (portability of skills when following the career path of a partner interstate and overseas). (F)

17. If the imbalance continues, men will continue to steer clear of the industry. (M)

Q. 23 Do you think there is a difference in the way males and females work with clients? Yes or no. If so, how?

1. Men and women have expertise in different areas and can relate to clients differently. Men may be reluctant to pursue a PR career, which would result in a loss of creative talent. Women are often not able to market products/services to men effectively. (M)

2. Females are more intuitive and can usually find out or work out much better what a client actually wants. Men just tend to do what they think a client wants and keep barging on until they are told otherwise or client leaves. (M)

3. Men rely on 'old boy' network and have more time to network/socialise outside of working hours. Men become much more matey/joke a lot more with clients/ and don' take criticism as personally as women practitioners. (F)

4. Women are better communicators, and more likely to work to a goal rather than to achieve notoriety (ego trip) than men. That is, they don't care as much who gets the credit, so long as the goal is achieved. Thus, they make better advisors and strategists. I think it would be good discipline for men to learn to work in an environment where the outcome is the priority, rather than focusing on the micro stuff (that is, winning the war, rather than the battle). (F)

5. In all industry men and women work differently but I don't think that alters the outcomes for the client. (F)

6. A mixed team is likely to have a wider range of experience of different audiences to draw on (this statement applies equally to age and ethnicity as well as gender). But how many old PR consultants do you meet (that aren't the chairman)? (M)

7. Unsure of specific effects but believe there will be some. (F)

8. I think it is important to have at least a few men working within a female-dominant PR agency to give their perspective and opinions on certain topics. It could hamper a client whose product is aimed at middle-aged men, if there were 20-year-old girls working on the account. (F)

9. It may mean that we never see men influencing corporate bodies on communications issues. If women got to do things their way all the time it would be no fun and not a challenge at all. It's kind of like having a lack of male teachers in classrooms – the boys don't have role models. If there are no men in PR then this trend is likely to keep continuing, as they won't be around to mentor other men. (F)

10. I think men massage people's egos more and women like to be honest and up front, not so much ego boosting, just common sense and a need to get things done at the end of the day. Women are slightly better at relationship-building, too. (F)

11. I think PR people are expected to always have the answers, or are often simply told how things should turn out and are then expected to make that outcome happen. A lot of corporate heads don't heed PR people's expert advice or even ask for it. It is a matter of making them understand how the media works and there are always people who think they know better ... Hello! The media just doesn't work like that. Many people like to tell us how to do our job. (F)

12. When women compete with women in the workforce it can become a dangerous place to be! Gender balance (and by this I mean equality in management also!) may help to address this issue. (F)

13. Women tend to try to seek the underlying agenda or heart of a matter. Men perhaps have a more black and white view, which may give them a more straightforward perspective on a situation. Women and men also communicate differently – and this can work as both an advantage and disadvantage, depending on the client. (F)

14. I find women are more thorough, and men are more laid back. (M)

Q. 24. Are there any aspects of working in this industry that affect your ability to work with clients, other industry professionals, media, target audiences? Yes or no. What are they?

1. Being female and a young age is still an issue with old stalwarts in any area you go into, which is part of a lack of understanding and therefore not valuing the role of PR in the workplace. (F)

2. Age. (F)

3. I can't bear, sometimes, to do the rubbish that this industry requires. (M)

4. One thing not mentioned so far is the individual's tolerance of disappointment. In-house PR consultants can become demoralised by receiving a steady stream of negative calls from the media; consultants can be depressed by receiving negative responses to their (outbound) media calls. Yet it's much worse when you work for yourself: there may be no one to share the frustrations with or to share your temporary triumphs. To this extent, PR work tends to work best as a group activity. Could this be another factor that tends to suit females more than typically solitary and competitive males. (M)

5. A lack of confidence can hinder professional relationships. (F)

6. Gender bias where male management treats a female PR professional as 'the girl who does that media/PR stuff'. PR is not taken seriously, few have any idea about what our role really entails (including ridiculous hours and backbreaking effort) and essentially, we become a necessary nuisance! (F)

Q. 26. Are there any ethical issues that affect your work within the industry? Yes or no. What are they?

1. We chose not to work for industries or clients that we feel morally disinclined to do so. Aggressive, overbearing clients who show a continued lack of understanding is another aspect that affects ability to work with them. (F)

2. Occasionally you may be faced with a conflict of interest – especially if you develop a specialty in a specific field. Also, you may hear that a client is not happy but has not yet dropped its consultancy – do you approach the client and 'poach' them, or wait until someone else does? If you find out a client has another consultancy, so you still try to woo then or leave them alone. (F)

3. Being paid to market a product/service which you do not have faith in. (M)

4. Personal ethics: harder to get on if you're honest. You need to be able to sink into the dark side comfortably. Honestly, I'm too honest for this industry. Spilling from the honesty issue, there's a matter of personal pride. I sometimes have difficulty living with myself at some of the lines I have to spin. (M)

5. Politicisation of the PR process ensures that within government communications is about reinforcing government agendas and not necessarily with highlighting the disadvantages of public domain decision making. I think PR suffers the same problems that most industries in a pluralistic and most modern economy suffer and that is defining what is the message that best pertains to the public good. How is the truth or the most comprehensive vision of a decision developed so people have the knowledge they need to make the best civic decision. (F)

6. Spin doctoring that amounts to fabrication of the truth is of great ethical concern to me. PR that aims to keep the public in the dark in the light of knowledge that could save lives, protect the environment, bring down corrupt Governments, uncover health dangers is unethical and in many cases criminal. (F)

7. Ethical issues are conducting research on children, protecting their rights. (F)

8. Need to look at PRIA code of ethics and stick to them and more importantly, individual ethical and moral framework. (F)

9. Ethics are fundamental. They affect every aspect of my work. (F)

10. Whether the work we are doing for a client is ethical, do they want us to 'spin' a story, should I work for a client even if I believe that the work they are doing is not ethical. (F)

11. The fact that the PRIA does not 'hang out to dry' anyone who lowers the reputation of the industry by operating outside the Code of Ethics. (M)

12. Should I work for / represent company X (they may pay me well, but do I approve of their product or their labour practices?)
   a. Is my primary objective to provide good advice to my client, or to make money out of them? (The two may be incompatible)
   b. Should I lie, or be evasive, to protect my client or employer? If so, what will this do to my reputation as a professional.
   c. Should I tell the emperor he has no clothes, or will the honest truth affect my career advancement? (M)

13. The need to protect an organisation will always create ethical dilemmas for practitioners. (M)

14. Privacy/confidentiality. (F)

15. Big business trying to stamp out the little guy through nefarious and underhanded tactics - sometimes the PR professional doesn't know that there is another agenda! (F)

16. My personal integrity and credibility is never for sale to an employer. While I always endeavour to show my employer in the best possible light in any situation, I would resign rather than compromise my integrity. As far as I'm concerned, any employer that expected that is not the sort of company with which I want to be associated. (F)

ADDITONAL ANALYSIS

This section contains additional analysis of material which was not canvassed as part of the formal survey, but resulted from answers provided by practitioners. Basically, these are key concepts which appeared in answers.

1. Female skills/traits

Critical to the Study is the ability to try to determine what 'makes' a PR practitioner. It was important to learn what practitioners think; for they are the ones who are the industry. Their views and the way they work shape the way the industry operates and is perceived by others – their publics. The most important aspects are the basic building blocks (skills and traits) of practitioners. From my initial attempt at trying to determine an industry profile, these are what (presumably) makes practitioners practice.

Analysis of any answer is open to the reader's interpretation. In fact one (female) participant wrote the following (after reading the summary): "I was imagining a not-too-professionally appealing headline: *Study suggests women 'fluff' better than me*, or some such horror forever locking women into the perceived 'soft' end of PR. So much of this is just so 'wrong'. The terms self-serving, stereotypical, dangerous, unfounded, appalling, outdated come to mind. Not to mention infuriatingly ignorant!" I wonder if she could have been more to-the-point?

I liken my comments to those of a newspaper leader writer; made after consideration of the facts and as unbiased as possible. This is purely a sociological analysis. I would hope that any future studies could incorporate more aspects of the psychological profile of practitioners – something I am not equipped to undertake.

For the purpose of this Study, skills are defined as those abilities (physical or mental) which are learned throughout, and contribute to, a person's career. Traits are considered (either scientifically or generally) to be inherent in a person, male or female. In some instances, I had to make a value judgement whether what was being referred to was a skill or trait.

1. FEMALES SKILLS/TRAITS

SKILLS	TRAITS
Women seem to be more professional. (F)	Women have better natural skills for undertaking PR and are more interested in it, this is because it involves large amounts of people skills, use of intuition and expression through writing. Women are naturally better at this. (M)
I think women are more focused upon engaging clients to develop shared concepts. (F)	Greater empathic qualities, better listeners, able to multi-task, less reliant on relationships/contacts to succeed. (F)
I have had some very poor communicators as communication director roles who were female. (F)	Women are aware of the issues involved and are dedicated to working through them. (F)
Women tend to score better in English/ Humanities subjects and tend to be better organisers than men. (F)	I think women are more sensitive to the issues, perhaps more subtle in their way of dealing with things. (F)
Women tend to listen and find a solution that will appeal to the client and sell the idea with a smile. (F)	Females are more intuitive and can usually find out or work out much better what a client actually wants. (M)
Women have shown a greater aptitude for the new wave of PR. (F)	Women (in general) tend to bullshit their way through client interviews. (M) *Note: difficult to categorise*
PR involves a lot of detail work, computer skills. It's been my experience that women are a little better suited to these things. (F)	Compared to men, a greater proportion of females are disinterested in non-lifestyle news and current affairs. This is reflected in their choice and presentation of PR issues, angles or viewpoints. (M)

Women are better communicators, and more likely to work to a goal rather than to achieve notoriety (ego trip) than men. That is, they don't care as much who gets the credit, so long as the goal is achieved. Thus, they make better advisors and strategists. We think longer term and will work to build a relationship rather than tell clients what to do. I think this is why advertising attracts more males (they are expected to tell the client what to do, whereas in PR we work with the client. Women also tend to rely on their ability to service the client more than men. (F)	Female high school students often have PR suggested because of basic psychometric assessment which identifies the creative/intuitive aspects of the profession as suitable for women. There has also been a strong promotion of PR as a 'celebrity' profession through the media, which seems attractive, especially to young women. (M)

Women are more focused upon non-verbal signs and obtaining consensus. (F)	People say the nature of women is better suited to PR and communications. (F)
Women may find it much easier to relate to female clients, and in some case charm or get on very well with male clients. (F)	They're more adaptable in getting on with people, and more sensitive to clients' needs. (M)
Women are colleagues; men are 'mates'. (F)	I think that the essentially conciliatory, creative, coordinating, people-orientated nature of PR means that women have the natural skills for the traditional PR service roles.
Women tend to be better at listening and responding to client needs. (F)	Women may be better suited to a communications career in a majority of cases, because I believe research has shown women to be better at empathising with others and listening well, both critical to communications. However, this it not true in all cases. (F)
Tend to be more clever when choosing the way to communicate. (M)	Relate better to other women and are more likely to want to hire women; can relate to a larger range of people. (F)

Have some tactical advantages: for example in dealing with journalists who in certain sectors (eg IT, automotive) remain predominantly male. (M)	Have better innate communications skills than men. (M)
Tend to be better at multi-tasking and are also very people-focused. (F)	Are more creative, which is an essential aspect of the industry. Women are more trusting. (M)
Women ask more personal questions and remember the smaller things, which mean more to the client than we think. (F)	More adaptable in getting on with people. (M)
They are better at multi-tasking, creative	Women are conditioned to believe PR is

	a right-brained industry and women are 'naturally' right-brained. I've actually heard people say, 'you can talk, you get on with people, who don't you go into PR. I've found women are actually better communicators. (F)
	Women are more interested in communicating than men, and PR is mainly about communicating. (F)
	Females are better communicators, possess stronger interpersonal skills, are more intelligent emotionally and enjoy being creative. (M)

First row left cell: concepts, client empathy, etc. (M)

2. MALE SKILLS/TRAITS

SKILLS	TRAITS
Better at networking. (M)	Tend to do what they think a client wants and keep barging on until they are told otherwise or client leaves. (M)
Better at translating PR processes into business language and repacking for reputation management and sales and marketing. (F)	Will tend to try to develop 'mateship' more. (F)
Tend to be more instructive and thus engender confidence with their knowledge. (F)	Male clients often won't take women seriously and will get on better with men. (M)
Some corporates believe men are better at 'tough' strategy, hence their number in senior mining and government PR. (F)	There's a perception of PR as a 'soft' alternative in comparison to journalism. Women are aware of the issues involved and are dedicated to working through them. Many men tend to only complete 90% of the job, leaving detail to others. (F)
Tend to be better at the tactical level. (F)	Tend to be more direct with their clients and typically a more commercial mind. (F)
Far more technical expertise and generally more factual (rather than vacuous) and accurate in writing. (M)	Men in PR would be more likely to access the camaraderie angle with male executives than women would, who may have to work quite hard at convincing these same executive of their professional value. (F)
	Clients (decision makers) generally tend to be men, networking opportunities better established by men - golf days, drinks, etc the BOYS club really does still exist. They also seems to establish

	friendships. (F)
	Men are mates; women are colleagues. (F)
	Can be more aggressive/assertive in pushing their ideas. (F)

QUALITIES

- If the client is a woman, she is likely to be more trusting of a female rather than a male PR consultant. (M)

- Women are more adaptable in getting on with people. And that is necessary. (M)

- Everybody is different - I look for someone with integrity, honest and respect (and a degree). (F)

AGE

- In the older age groups, I feel it could be due to secretaries and PA's having moved into the PR area or given 'PR' to do as part of their original role because they have secretarial skills. (F)

- Most PR consultants and many in-house practitioners are young (20 to early 30s). Few make it into their 40s for a whole range of reasons (for women it might be work-life balance if they decide to have children. Because of biological factors, more women than men are likely to leave at this crucial stage, leaving the PR industry short of experience and talent (and leaving the plodders in charge of the show). (M)

- In my experience in Australia and internationally, males dominate the industry, especially in senior strategic positions. (M)

- Women have been winning most full-time and casual jobs for the past 10–20 years. Before women's equality in the workplace, attractive women in particular were more likely to marry and be housebound. They are now highly employable and most choose a career rather than be married at a young age. Their workplace domination is probably more noticeable in the PR industry simply because of the nature of the PR/media industry itself. (M)

- I have been rejected a number of times at interviews, as I'd rather work part time, yet I could achieve results in half the time someone more junior than me can, even if they work the extra three hours a day. (F)

- I would speculate that men in PR mostly run their own businesses or hold very senior positions which leaves the service and lower-paid positions to the women in the workforce. I also think that men in PR have re-positioned themselves as strategists or policy makers or marketing which are more mainstream and move away from perceptions of events or promotions. (F)

- It's still an industry where experience is measured by how old you are.

- Age affects my ability to work with clients. (F)
- Throw in some older more experienced women, and it (age) shouldn't make any difference. (F)

3. DRAWBACKS IN PR

- Family responsibilities. PR has some odd hours, which make it hard for mothers. (M)

- I suspect it is still the woman usually who has to drop work to attend a sick child, and this would impact on performance (although one would expect irregularly). (F)

- One thing not mentioned so far is the individual's tolerance of disappointment. In-house PR consultants can become demoralised by receiving a steady stream of negative calls from the media; consultants can be depressed by receiving negative responses to their (outbound) media calls. Yet it's much worse when you work for yourself: there may be no one to share the frustrations with or to share your temporary triumphs. (M)

- Being female and a young age. This is still an issue with old stalwarts in any area you go into, which is part of a lack of understanding and therefore not valuing the role of PR in the workplace. (F)

- As in all careers, it is difficult to balance a family's needs with a full-on career. (F)

- Age. (F)

- Sometimes the image of this profession as being spin/publicity orientated can affect how seriously you are taken when making an introduction, because most people don't 'get it'. (M)

HISTORICAL ASPECTS

- In a State of male-dominated industries (mining and agriculture) PR has been one department that females have been encouraged to populate. (F)

- The preponderance of males in very senior positions is as much an artefact of the 'old school' PR, when journalists made the move to the dark side (and most journalists were male). This seniority imbalance will progressively shift as these old 'crusties' (self included) drop off the professional twig. Government and corporates are still (in the main) uncomfortable working with female-dominated professionals on equal footing (consider nursing etc) a 'female' PR profession will take longer to gain acceptance. (M)

- It has traditionally been an area women have been seen to excel. (F)

- It's been the case for more than 10 years throughout Australia. Same percentage when I studied at RMIT in the early 1990s. (F)

- PR has been increasingly being perceived as 'female' sector. (F)

- PR shifted from being a career progression for ex-journalists (mainly men) to a more recognised professional option in its own right with university courses attracting more women. (F)

- The whole world of (white collar) work is becoming feminised, but PR is the most visible example of this phenomenon. (M)

IMAGE and PERCEPTION OF PR

- How many old PR consultants do you meet (that aren't the chairMAN)? (M)

- PR tends to be full of good-looking, well-groomed people, so someone who doesn't fit that mould may find it difficult to get ahead. (F)

- There's been a dumbing-down of the profession. These days a pretty face counts for more than knowledge. (M)

- Women are likely to be employed in a profession that favours appearance. (M)

- People think PR is glamorous, so mostly women are attracted to this as a career path. There is also a possible employment bias within PR firms operated by women, that being their preference to work with other women rather than men who may be sexually threatening and who don't have marketing appeal based upon appearance. The emphasis in all communication is nowadays visual rather than written, and females are more attractive presenters with greater marketing appeal. People are more likely to get a job if they're an attractive woman rather than a male or an unattractive woman. Again, however, this is true in all professions. (M)

- PR is seen as 'fluff' while journalism is seen as 'tough'. (F)

- I unfortunately believe that being a physically unattractive, or poorly groomed person, and even possibly being a much older person, especially if you are female, would be a barrier to success in PR, as is probably true of most jobs. However, it's particularly important in many PR roles that are taking about reputation management and promotion of positive image there would be a reluctance to hand over your company's reputation and image management to someone who did not take care in their own appearance. The stereotype would be that good-looking women would do better in PR. A charismatic, energetic young guy would often sit more comfortably with executives than a similar young woman. (F)

- I believe it is viewed as a 'chicks' field and therefore is not taken as seriously as it would if there were more men. (M)

- I think it is seen as a 'fluffy' role and equated more to something women would do. (F)

- The industry is so clicky that I think everybody generally works within their own networks and establishes themselves with the people they need to know in order to fulfil what they need to do, regardless of gender . . . it's more individual. (F)

GENERAL CONCERNS

Though there was room for practitioners to express concerns about gender, some deviated from the topic to express general concerns about the industry. Their comments have been recorded here as a matter of record.

- My only concern is the amount of tripe generated by some practitioners. (M)

- An increasing emphasis on women's lifestyle editorial rather than complex investigative issues. (M)

- There are too few good professionals and the PRIA has no real quality assurance program in place - nothing as rigorous as the law or accounting professions. Until we take ourselves seriously, other won't. (M)

- I think the gender imbalance of females, especially the 40-something generation that heads up the PRIA or the 20-something set that heads up the Young Guns, has a negative impact of the professional reputation of the PR industry in WA as there is a perpetuation of the stereotyped 'big-boobs, big-hair', or 'young buns' 'click' of the same women - that do not encourage the business marketplace to see PR as a strategic professional skill. (F)

- I have heard of many young females (with uni degrees) who entered the industry with consultancies and were expected to work long hours doing all of the office's general work (little of which is genuine PR work but menial tasks such as taking the boss' dry cleaning in or getting coffees.) They were treated rudely by supervisors and more experienced colleagues. They decided to leave PR. This treatment is not at the hands of males but other females. Others have received this treatment but hang in there and move on within the industry. (F)

Perceived tutoring differences

1. Men are more relaxed and expect less standards from students. Women tend to expect more. (F)

2. The females tutors are more interactive. They try to get opinions from you, compared to the males, who tend to stick mostly to the facts. (M)

3. Females are more approachable and you do not need to be buddies with them. (F)

4. Probably due to stereotypes and perceived ideas from society. Women are known as being good communicators. (F)

5. The males are boring in PR lectures/tutorials (the ones I've seen). Females have conviction and passion for the industry, and it shows. (F).

6. Their approaches are always different. Males are more straight to the point, and less theoretical. (F)

7. Women include students more in the class. (F)

8. Women tend to be more creative, organised and focused on finer details – all aspects needed for success in the industry. Also, women tend to be more nurturing, which assists with developing and maintaining relationships. (F)

9. Female lecturers/tutors seem to be more interactive and participative whereas the male seem to tend to stick more to facts and figures. (M)

10. Females communicate more easily (that is, their ideas are conveyed and understood more clearly). (F)

11. I find most of the time male tutors will be very objective in handling a class (they stick to class plans better and define the key themes better). Females tutors will generally proceed with the class as a 'community' activity. (M)

12. Males are more easy-going. Women have more standards (that is, attendance at tutorials). (F)

13. Males are more direct and factual. Females integrate stories and real-life experiences. (F)

14. Males are more creative and "live" teaching. Females tend not to stop talking. (F)

15. Males tend to be straight to the point, and humorous at times. They are also more patient. Females tend to be more strict and attentive to detail, well prepared and organised with material. Although they can be moody at times. (M)

16. Males are more direct in teaching approach. (F)

17. Women are more personal and in-depth. Men concentrate more on facts. (M)

18. Females tend to be more strict in the way they teach. They follow rules and schedules. Men go on tangents, allow group discussions and have a loose schedule. (F)

19. Males tend to be more supportive and flexible. (M)

20. Females are more open, take a personals interest and tend not to teach by the book. (F)

21. Some males concentrate on getting the work done and done well. Some females have been 'fluffy' and bad. They tended to get sidetracked. (M)

22. Female tutors have more of a willingness to elaborate on discussion topics and engage in further in-depth coverage. (M)

23. Women are more personal and nurturing. Men love their statistics. (F)

24. Female teachers seems to be more concerned and interested in the students.

   (F)

25. Women have more structured tutes and set goals to achieve by the end. (F)

26. Men seems more laid-back, easy-going. Women sometimes act as 'teachers' and don't treat us as equals. (F)

27. Males tend to be more direct, whereas females seems to spend more time discussing issues. (F)

28. Women are more in-depth. (F)

29. (Generally) males are more casual about the way things are done. Females are more strict and organised. But this doesn't apply to all. (F)

30. Males more understanding and mark fairer. (F).

31. Some female tutors tend to be really moody and its affects the way they teach in class; whereas male lecturers are usually neutral. (F)

32. Female tutors are generally more dedicated than males. They are also more understanding and approachable. (M)

33. Females are more polite, less arrogant and friendlier. (F)

34. There are differences in the way they present material, and their approachability. (F)

35. Male tutors tend to be more entertaining and attention-grabbing. (F)
36. Female tutors are more caring and still always show concern about students' progress, whereas males are more strict with students. (F)

Reasons for female predominance

1. Women find it easier to get into PR because most people in the industry are female. (F)

2. Women can be more sensitive. (F)

3. Women dominate because PR requires creativity and intuition. Not many guys have that, where it is second nature to females. (F)

4. Females are better listeners and communicators, whereas males prefer to be in management roles. (F)

5. Communication skills, empathy, attention to detail – all traits that women master. (F)

6. Women are more thorough and can communicate more openly. (F)

7. Women are more perceptive of other people and generally better listeners and in some cases more articulate. (F)

8. It's more of a female job because the PR industry don't do the same things. And I feel that males prefer a set job and don't like overdoing stuff, like we have to do in PR. (F)

9. Women are better at dealing with people and give greater attention to detail. (F)

10. The glamorous work-life image that is perceived through the media. For example, Eddie on Absolutely Fabulous, or something from Sex in The City. (F)

11. Certain stigmas that have been associated with the PR industry that have indicated that it is a 'woman's job'. (F)

12. I think it's more of the perception of the industry being more female oriented and that it's a lot easier for a female to get in. In addition to that, I feel that generally females tend to be more creative than males and female in general tend to have better interpersonal skills with people they have just met as compared to males in general. (M)

13. PR has a feminine connotation to it. It stops men from entering because they and women perceive it to be a world of entertainment, beauty, cocktail parties etc. (F)

14. Females are more aware or pay attention to details and have a better ability to deal with major and minor tasks. (F)

15. Marketing and PR are seen as 'girly' units as they are about communication, which is believed to be an area that females understand or are better at than men. (F)

16. I think it's a perception, especially when people think about PR they think 'events', and it comes across to people that girls tend to be able to get more cooperation from organizations because of their looks. Bluntly put, it could be that belief that more males are the 'bigger names' in the organisational ladder, and they are more susceptible to a woman's charm. (M)

17. People have a false perception of what PR is. Males just think it's a female course. (F)

18. It seems fashionable to younger women, and the job is about multi-tasking, which I feel is more applicable to females. (F)

19. It is perceived as a feminine industry/career. Males and female interests vary naturally. Women are more confident in communications. (F)

20. PR is more creative than factual and number-crunching, which tends to attract males more. (F)

21. A large part of PR is about communicating and networking. Traditionally this has been a role taken by females. (M)

22. I believe that PR requires a certain level of attention to detail, and women also seem more adept at that. Women are more inclined to understand how/what the company's image should be. (F)

23. Neither are better suited. There are many different areas in communications. I believe men would be better in some areas, and women in others. (F)

24. The industry is female-dominant because of public perception. Females (have) added credibility and ease of communication. (F)

25. Women are perceived as communication specialists. While that may be preconceived, it therefore means less men enter the industry. (F)

26. PR has a 'glamorous' connotation to it (that is, cocktail parties and events) therefore women are attracted to it and men find the idea off-putting. (F)

27. Women are better at communicating. (F)

28. Males are more interested in other industries. (F)

29. Males are typically interested in and excel in numbers-based occupations, and females are typically more creative. (F)

30. Women dominate because they are better at communicating than men. (F)

31. There's a perception that the career is 'feminine', as opposed to civil and mechanical engineering, which is (seen as) 'masculine'. (M)

32. Perhaps journalism is more competitive and prestigious, and men prefer this environment. Women enjoy communication and 'behind-the-scenes' work, therefore PR is their preferred option. And it is more flexible. (F)

33. Women have more of a desire to work with people, are more chatty and work well with groups of people. (F)

34. Because men prefer to do commerce and science courses. (F)

35. Women are more social, mature and better communicators. (F)

36. Possibly because it's generally perceived as a god job for females – lots of working with people, etc. (F)

37. Maybe women are perceived to be better communicators – more humanistic. (F)

38. Maybe they're just more suitable. (F)

39. Women are better communicators. (F)

40. In general, females enjoy interacting with people more than men. (F)

41. Women are looking for gender equality in society. (F)

42. PR is seen as 'girly'. There's a stereotype of 'PR bitch' that perpetuates. Women want to be in this industry. (M)

43. Guys go to other institutes like TAFE, where they are able to concentrate on logical and mechanical stuff. (F)

44. Females are natural communicators and it is a modern industry in fields of interest to women (that is, creative). (F)

45. Women seem to be people-orientated and not so much inclined towards maths/science, whereas I believe men leaving school are more interested in those subjects – maybe to be seen as 'manly'. (F)

46. Women are more communications-oriented than men. (F)

47. Females are more interactive and sociable than males. (F)

48. Females have better communication/writing skills than guys in general. (F)the industry is traditionally thought of as female. Stereotypes still exist, where males should be interested more in science, etc. (F)

49. Females tend to be better at accepting challenges, and being more serious than males. PR could be considered a very challenging career. (F)

50. Females are easier to communicate with. (F)

51. Females are easier to talk with. (F)

52. Females tend to be more active socially, and therefore love communicating. PR is a communication industry. (F)

53. The dominance of women is perhaps because PR is concerned with communication, which may mean it is a more attractive career and study option for women than men. (F)

54. There might be more females simply because of genetics – girls have longer attention spans, meaning they find studying easier/more desirable? I'm not sure, and this is not based on any factual/statistical knowledge. (F)

55. Women tend to be more willing to 'upgrade' themselves. They also tend to look at the bigger picture. (M)

56. Women like being creative. (M)

57. Being a career dominated by organization and communication I feel it is a role that women have often been relegated to. (F)

58. Females are more gentle and critical toward issues. The can make friends and create good rapport with people more easily. This is not to say that males can not do so, but males' masculinity always makes it harder for others to approach and accept them. (F)

59. Women are still said to be more communicative and able to build relationships than men . . . and diplomatic. Probably we believe it. (F)

60. Women are better communicators. (F)

61. It appears women are increasingly seeking professional careers in creative fields. (M)

62. The profession is more appealing to women. Organising and event management come more naturally to women. Men do not perceive the industry and profession highly. (F)

63. Generally females are more comfortable with communicating than males. (F)

64. The trend in PR currently focuses on women's success in fashion/entertainment fields. (F)

65. It appears to be an attractive job, with diversity and creativity. There's appeal that it could take you around the world. (F)

66. PR involves many aspects that historically women have always done (organising, communications). I think this trend continues as we see more women in the workforce and drawn to PR. (F)

67. Some people still think of PR as it is portrayed in shows like 'Ab Fab'. (F)

68. It probably just reflects the fact that more women are studying than men generally, particularly at Notre Dame. (F)

69. Even on work experience this is evident. The field appeals to females more because it is creative and fun and includes creative writing, which I always thought females excelled at, compared to males. I think men tend to follow more powerful careers and positions than females. (F)

70. I think there is some gender-role confusion. Young males do not know what they are supposed to be and do not have the emotional support women have. We are currently raised to believe that women are superior to males and do not know what to do to gain acceptance and respect. (M)

71. Most males (at least that I know) choose to enter a trade after high school. (M)

72. PR is just perceived as a female industry. (F)

73. Traditionally men in Perth work in labour-related, or more male-dominant (traditional) roles. For that reason, Perth may have a perception/tradition that PR is done better by women. (M)

74. I don't think guys have as much patience and show attention to detail (suited to PR) as girls. (F)

75. Males tend to do commerce in general, and girls are more interested in the creative side, for example, PR. (F)

76. Females perceive PR to be a 'glamour' industry. (F)

77. Women are more interested in building relationships and communication, which are integral parts of PR. (F)

Suitability for PR

1. PR is probably more suited to females because of the creative or communication aspects, which women tend to be better at. (F)

2. Neither would be better. It depends on what area they go into. Some fields would be more appropriate for women. (F)

3. Both are suited. It depends on the person's character and personality, not gender. (F)

4. Women are best suited because they are understanding, patient, empathise. (F)

5. Women are more intuitive. (F)

6. Women are better suited because they are more understanding than men. (F)

7. It depends on the type of PR career. Media planning and event management may be more suited to women. (F)

8. Both would be suited. Men get to the point quickly and provide a direct, fast source of information. Women get to the point in a more roundabout way, therefore they are good for relationship-building. (F)

9. It comes down to the individual and their personality. There are certainly some women who could not do PR well. (M)

10. It depends on suitability and personal traits. (F)

11. PR is multi-disciplinary, and different people are good at different things. Gender might play a small part in determining what one person excels at but does not limit an individual's capability. (F)

12. I think women are still biologically 'programmed' to have that communication ability, whereas many men would have trouble in that area. (M)

13. It's more a case of willingness to succeed and continue in the field that's important. (F)

14. They're both capable of communicating effectively. A communications career just sounds like it's more suited to women that's why men choose not to do it. (F)

15. Women are better suited as they are easier to approach. They have a better understanding of mindsets and feelings/thoughts, and are clearer than males. (F)

16. Depending on how you look at the questions, the answers are different. In the sense of choosing to go into the industry, once again it's not the gender but the personality and interest of the individual that matters. In terms of getting a start in the industry, I think it's a lot easier for females because somehow they tend to portray a more friendly image straight from the start. (M)

17. Women are more suited because they are better at communicating. (F)

18. Women tend to exhibit more confidence in public affairs. (F)

19. Both sexes are equally suitable, as they as they have good communication skills. (F)

20. Neither is more suited. It depends on the individual. (F)

21. I think women are better suited, as they communicate better than men (where does gossip come from?) Women are more attentive to detail. (M)

22. Individual personalities are the determining factor. (F)

23. Women because they are approachable, emphatic, nurturing and chatty. (F)

24. Neither, as there are advantages and disadvantages between masculine and feminine traits. (F)

25. It depends more on an individual's personality rather than gender. (F)

26. Women usually are better at communicating. (F)

27. Women are better-suited as they are more creative, persuasive and dedicated to their career. (F)

28. Most females give a better first impression, more presentable, great smile and are warm and loving. The give out a better vibe. (F)

29. Depends on the type of person. (F)

30. Women are naturally better communicators. (F)

31. Women are better suited because they are more effective communicators. (F)

32. Depends on personality and character. (F)

33. Neither are better-suited. It's an individual things. (M)

34. Both are equally capable. It depends on the individual. (F)

35. Women are more patient, more tough and think more about the future. (F)

36. It is better to have men and women in this career. (F)

37. Females tend to be more active socially, and therefore love communicating. PR is a communication industry. (F)

38. I think suitability is based on personality, not gender. (F)

39. Both are equally capable. (M)

40. The business world is male-dominated. Mates take other mates more seriously. (M)

41. As it can be a learned practice (better communication) I feel either gender can do it well. (F)

42. Females' way of thinking is different from males'. They (women) will think of a lot of pros and cons before making decisions, whereas males are usually not as careful. (F)

43. Women generally tend to (and like) talking more. (F)

44. It depends on the personality, not on gender. (F)

45. People just have a hard time taking women seriously. (F)

46. Women in our society tend to be taught to be organised and to think of all of the small things and they seem to be able to empathise with people more whereas men aren't taught to think beyond themselves and empathy (Which perhaps gets confused with sympathy) isn't encouraged in young boys. (F)

47. Neither are better-suited. I feel it's mindset, not sex, that determines suitability. (M)

48. Although men in our traditional society are respected more than women. Neither would be better-suited because you need to be a good communicator and writer to be effective in a communications career, which applies to both genders. (F)

49. They both have attributes that would contribute positively and negatively to PR. (F)

50. Women are proven better communicators. (F)

51. Audiences are both male and female and in order to appeal you need representation from both genders. (F)

52. Women are more relationship-focused. They would more often understand others' points of view. (M)

53. Women seems to be more emotive and display higher communication skills than males. (M)

54. Women are better communicators, although ultimately it comes down to the individual. (F)

55. Women are natural talkers/communicators. (F)

56. Individuals communicate differently due to personalities, and the role for communications differs. It also depends on the message/topic that is being communicated, and to whom. (M)

57. Women are more creative, better at multi-tasking and communicating. (F)

58. Both have different skills of equal values to offer. (F)

59. Workplaces would be more effective with both genders, but not necessarily 50/50. (F)

60. Men would be suited because they don't get emotionally involved/attached to the issues at hand. (F)

61. Women are better communicators and can build stronger relationships. (F)

62. Neither are better suited. It depends on the individual. They shouldn't be stereotyped. (F)

Influence of gender

1. No. It depends on personal choice. (F)

2. Although the industry is female, it is now being shown that the entry of men is rising. (F)

3. To be honest, I think gender does have an influence. It also depends on the organization. (M)

4. Gender would be a factor if men know the field is dominated by women then they may feel reluctant to enter it. (M)

5. Gender does influence entry into PR because males think PR is women's work. (F)

6. Gender in society is a major focus and people are taught how to act and think depending on their gender. (F)

7. Gender not really a factor. But it depends on the individual and what qualities and attributes they may bring to a company. Females and males are equal in that sense. (F)

8. Depends on the person. (F)

9. Both sexes are capable of excelling. (F)

10. Gender isn't a factor, as communication skills is the critical thing. (F)

11. It may be hard for males to study PR because of the number of females. They may feel alone or isolated. (F)

12. Unfortunately, perceptions of gender and a person's ability/skills are entwined. People need to recognise that skill and ability is more important than gender. In some industries it is still strictly a boys' club, and females are only good as receptionists and personal assistants. (F)

13. It depends on how they work and interact with people/publics. (F)

14. It varies. But for some jobs a male would be better suited (for example, WESTRAC or CAT) and for others a female would be better (Coles-Myer). (F)

15. You generally need a proportional representation to balance the industry. (F)

16. If you are good at what you do, and have passions, gender will not be an issue, unless it is in a field like sports or fashion. (F)

17. I don't think gender is a factor, as PR is used by both large and small companies, so it's not as competitive, and PR isn't always used at top-level management level (perceived to be a male domain to some). F

18. Most careers can be said to have gender bias. (M)

19. I think there's a gender influence, but relates to looks. Most of the time pretty women or a handsome guy will have the first opportunity for a PR job. (F)

20. There may be a stigma on males entering the industry. But this may change as male/female roles in society change. (F)

21. Gender could be a factor; particularly because of the way many people are brought up with stereotype behaviour. (F)

22. Regrettably, I think women are used more often as 'something to look at' (for example, a team of female news presenters) and this makes them more desirable in PR. (F)

23. It's all a matter of personal taste and preference. (M)

24. I think it comes down to individual aspects (for example, personality, credentials). (M)

25. I hope gender may not be a factor in influencing someone to enter PR. (F)

26. Employers are led by personal preferences. However, this does not only relate to gender but to age, and probably even haircut. (F)

27. This would depend on who is hiring the staff. A classic 'old-school' employer of a company may only trust men. I wouldn't go for a job where a man's work would be more valued over mine (regardless of education and experience) and the dominant coalition doesn't trust my competence because of my sex. (F)

28. I might get told off for it but I believe equal opportunity legislation currently favours women. (M)

29. It seems gender may be tied in with they type of PR, that is, females have easier entry to fashion and males easier entry to corporate PR. (F)

30. I now think there will be a higher demand for males in PR. Females will still obtain jobs but I think it will be easier for males. (F)

31. Because it's obvious that women are dominant, there must be bias in employer views. However, if men are good enough, they should make it. (F)

32. Gender could be an influence on someone as to which firm they enter. If it's a male or female firm. (F)

33. I would hope gender wouldn't influence this. It would come into play if a form needed more men or women. (F)

34. The fact the PR industry is dominated by women may discourage the hiring of more women, or it may create a perception that women are better at it, prejudicing males. (M)

35. Because there are few males in PR, they may get preference. (F)

36. Women can work at an all-female company and believe they are empowering the sex and may find a job this way. However, men don't have the opportunity on not competing against women in a male-only company. (F)

37. Whoever is best for the job will generally get it, regardless of gender. (F)

38. Some organizations prefer men or women. Some PR may be better-suited to a certain gender. (F)

39. It is an influence in that sometimes it depends on appearance. (F)

40. It wouldn't have an influence unless he or she was unbelievably good looking. (F)

41. Females are more likely to be employed if they are the point of contact for the business, or employed to be in the public eye, or dealing with high-profile people. (F)

Rapport

1. Both would equally build rapport. It depends on the communication skills of the person. (F)

2. Because women have a more nurturing side to them and empathise with people. They remember dates, i.e. sending gift baskets to clients for an occasion. (F)

3. For PR issues, often women are more understanding and sensitive to the issues. F)

4. One sex would not be better than the other. Everyone has their own way of expressing rapport. It comes down to personality. (F)

5. Women would be better as they have usually larger social circles than males, as they are better at maintaining friendships through contact, etc., whereas males are not as inclined to do so. Women are more sensitive to relationships. (F)

6. Women would be better due to public perception on different views on different professions. (F)

7. Men are more protective towards client confidentiality and have better success at networking. (M)

8. To a large extent this would depend on the interaction between a client and a PR person. It's an individual thing. (M)

9. Neither would be better at it. Men have charm and charisma, too. (F)

10. Females have a tendency to notice superficial details that fuel conversation; hence build better rapport. (F)

11. Men would be better as they are less shy. (F)

12. Females are good at forming friendships and talking general 'chit-chat'. (F)

13. I think men may be better, only because in the corporate world men tend to be looked up to. They are seen as the more confident and in charge. (F)

14. Both are equally capable. (M)

15. Men probably would be better suited as they can more easily relate to other men in a male-dominated society. (M)

16. Men might be best at building rapport, as they can be less intimidating. (F)

17. Women can sometimes adapt better than men in a situation, however on face value men are accepted quickly and perceived to be better at managing and communicating (no emotion involved). (F)

18. Women are more personal, can relate more easily to people of any gender and age. (F)

19. This may depend on the industry they are working in. For example in fashion PR women would probably be better, while in sport men would be better. (M)

20. Women are good at building relationships. It's in out nature. (F)

21. Men would probably most able to build rapport with male clients, and women with female clients. (F)

22. Females are better because they are natural talkers. (F)

23. Men would be better because they can separate their emotions from business. (F)

24. Women would be better because of their communication skills and ability to develop an emotional connection. (F)

25. A well-presented person, male or female, will get on well. (M)

Barriers

1. An unwillingness to create something different may hinder your career. (F)

2. Lack of awareness of a changing media environment. (F)

3. Prior experience is always vital, but graduates without this advantage may find it hard to establish themselves, or may take long(er). (F)

4. Lack of experience, skills, confidence and knowledge. (F)

5. In Perth there's not a nig enough market for PR practitioners. (F)

6. The small market in Perth means less opportunities. (F)

7. Lack of jobs and competitiveness of industry. (F)

8. Limited amount of jobs make it hard to gain experience. (F)

9. The limited amount of job available in the industry. (F)

10. Perth doesn't have as many options for employment in PR as there are in the eastern States. (F)

11. Number of job places may affect my career, making it difficult to find a job. (F)

12. Amount of people seeking a job in PR with the same qualification. (F)

13. Too many (PR) people, not enough jobs. (M)

14. Barriers are the huge amounts of people graduating and wanting the same jobs. (F)

15. Too many females. (F)

16. Although there are lots of women in the industry, their numbers in management are few. (F)

17. A barrier could be my age and my foreign background. (F)

18. My age. (F)

19. Age. (F)

20. Age might be against me at 41. (M)

21. Lack of experience, small and competitive industry in Perth. (F)

22. Limited experience. Lack of networking. (F)

23. Working with so many women usually leads to a 'bitchy' work environment. (F)

24. The competitiveness of the industry and the fact that many jobs are available only through a network of contacts. (F)

25. The rising interest in PR may make it difficult to get a job. (F)

26. Female employers. Not enough high-profile positions. (F)

27. There are too many people studying this Degree, and not enough jobs. (F)

28. Women do not have the 'balls' to stand up and work hard for the high-profile positions. (F)

29. Competition. (F)

30. Competition (F)

31. Competition. There are so many graduates all competing in a small area (Perth). (F)

32. The limitation for PR in Perth is the small population. This can only be overcome by moving to a more populated city or specialising in a certain aspect of PR. (M)

33. There's only a small number of jobs in Perth, compared to the eastern States. (M)

34. The large number of enrolments in universities will lead to an 'over-supply' in the industry. (M)

Wage difference

1. Ironic, considering women dominant. (F)

2. It sucks. What a crock. (F)

3. Great for me, but should be an even playing field. (M)

4. Because there's so few men in the industry, they have become a 'commodity'. (F)

5. There are less men in PR so this may make them more highly-valued. (M)

6. I believe men are paid more because they currently have higher positions within organisations. That is more to do with 'length of service' rather than having to do with their sex. This should invert within a decade as the women who are entering the field recently match them for time in the profession. (M)

7. This (imbalance) will continue to be the case, until the next generation of managers who do not think so traditionally come into play. Men usually have less inhibition and are able to promote themselves on a regular basis, whereas women tend to promote the team as opposed to individual work. Women are, generally-speaking, more emotive. (F)

8. Maybe men tend to assume higher positions and are therefore paid more. (F)

9. Not surprising. Men usually get paid more than women in other occupations. (M)

10. Men probably fill more management positions. (F)

11. Earnings should be based on an individual's performance. (F)

12. It's ridiculous that gender affects pay rates when the same job is being done. (F)

13. A patriarchal society base is to blame. (F)

14. If they have the same qualifications, they should be paid the same. (F)

15. We (still) live in a patriarchal society. It needs to change. (F)

16. Males may be in higher-paying positions (management). There's a general tendency for men to be paid more in all industries. (F)

17. This is so unfair. But PR isn't the only industry where this is a problem. (F)

18. I think it is still typical of most professions for women to be paid less than men on average. And it's ridiculous. (F)

19. It's the same old story. It's a boys' club. Older generations of men don't respect women or their work. It's getting better with my generation, I think. (F)

20. The wage differential is surprising. (M)

21. Salary discrimination is bad, but I expected it to be so. (M)

22. I'm hoping I might be able to change the imbalance. (F)

23. Males have the power in society. (F)

24. It's not fair and I can't believe it's still the case these days. (F)

25. It is unfair. (F)

26. It's shitty. (F)

27. That should be revised. (F)

28. I should change courses. (F)

Technician role

1. Women would be hired as these things are (stereotypical) duties. (M)

2. I feel this is more to do with women dominating the lower, cadet style, positions within the industry, rather than having to do with their sex. (F)

Perception/thoughts on PR, then and now (from second survey)

1. PR to me was initially all about the glitz and glamour of meeting people and to 'get' around. Also, the interpersonal relations skills that will be strengthened during the course of studies. (M)

2. I imagined a significant amount of creative (possibly manipulative) writing. PR seems to be more solidified in its approaches. (M)

3. I first thought it was about drinks and parties. Now I know it's about communication. (M)

4. I first thought it's about your relation with the publics. Now I think it's all about writing. (M)

5. My thoughts of PR has always been the same. Just that now my interest within PR is more defined. (M)

6. I didn't know much about it when I started. Now I love it – it's creative and exciting. (F)

7. I thought it was glamorous work, mostly events management; like Samantha Jones' character from the TV show Sex in the City. Now I think it's less glamorous, with a focus on media relations and creating perceptions. (F)

8. I thought PR was about liaising with the media and other companies, and managing events. Now I realize there's a lot more to it. (F)

9. I think a lot of students think it is a lot of events management and glamorous, rather than ethically-driven. (F)

10. I originally thought PR was about selling companies/organizations through 'wheeling and dealing', with different sources to create networks. I now seems to believe that it is more about image, branding and perception. (F)

11. I used to think of PR as a lot of interpersonal skills, as you meet al. l kinds of people, and there would be a lot of social functions. After studying PR, there is a lot of thinking and writing. (F)

12. At first my view was PR was a fast-paced industry, requiring a lot of networking. Now I see it involves a lot of writing and networking. You must be organized. (F)

13. I thought it was lots of communication with people from all walks of life, and now I think you really only deal with the same people (for example, business-minded). (F)

14. I think PR is a lot more writing than I thought, and perhaps more difficult. (F)

15. PR means you have to be detailed [sic] and organised. (F)

16. I didn't know too much about PT. I just looked into it and it sounded fun. Now I know it's fun, but there's much more writing involved than I initially thought. (F)

17. There is more publicity/promotion/events management focus, rather than strategies/theory. And it's hard work. (F)

18. PR is about communication of the business to the outside world, and support to the firm's marketing department. (M)

19. I thought PR would be about going to parties, getting dressed up, working with good-looking people, like on the TV. But it's much more detailed, logical and hard work. Nothing like the perception whatever. (F)

20. I thought of Absolutely Fabulous initially. Now I know it's not as glamorous, and much more professional. (F)

21. My perception was that in PR I would have to be interested in the world in general, especially in people. Now I realize it's much more in-depth than I expected. But the same, in general. (F)

22. PR is a very people-oriented field and is all about providing and image of something to the public. I still feel this way. However, PR is more strategic and theory than I thought it would be. (F)

23. PR is about managing a company's reputation, smartly and positively. It provides a link from the company to its various publics to present (the) profession in a socially-responsible manner. (F)

24. I thought I was more about spin-doctoring, and it was purely to control the image of a company: nothing more than that. But now I think there's a lot more to it than that. (F)

25. I always thought PR would be an interesting field, with constantly-challenging and stimulating situations. And I still see the industry as being like that. (M)

26. I thought PR was about providing ideas and information at a senior corporate level, as well as playing a lot of golf. I now know it's a bloody hard-working industry. (M)

27. Initially I thought it was based around spin-doctoring, public speaking and selling and image. Now I tend to think it's more about selling an image to the public. (M)

28. Most of what I thought about PR came from television and film, showing that it was glamorous. Now I see it's so much more than that, and less glamorous: sometimes never. (F)

29. I thought PR as about parties and events planning. I didn't really know about the technical and research components (F).

30. I thought it would be creative. Now it's boring and repetitive. (F)

31. Used to think it was all about events, parties and organizing people. Now it's more liaising with clients, organizing problems with corporations/media. (F)

32. Most students would think it's about being social and glamorous. I've realised that PR is about your ability to coordinate the communication channels for your organisation in order to create and sustain a positive image in public. (F)

33. I thought PR as an industry that promoted events, or publicise a company. Nothing has changed. (F)

34. I thought PR was about organizing the company's functions and pubic speaking. PR is about communicating to the public about the goodwill of the company. (F)

35. I thought PR was more flexible and about spin, whereas now I realize how structured it is. (F)

36. It's not just cocktail parties. It's work. (M)

37. It's not like *Sex in The City*. It's real work. (F)

38. I believe that students begin to study PR because of their perceptions, but once in the course they find these ideas change. (F)

39. I always view PR as an influential medium, an industry capable of making a difference. After studying PR I now know this to be true. However, I also know the importance of ethical behaviour in making sure this is true, and that PR can make a difference in the wrong way. (F)

40. I thought PR was for a 'people person'. There are more aspects to PR than I thought. (F)

41. I thought it was about spin, publicity, propaganda, marketing, events management. Now I see there's ethical communication and persuasion, mutual objectives, humanizing corporate organizations through aligning organization goals with public expectations. (F)

42. I knew it was a job that involves the media and big companies. Now I am aware all companies can have a PR officer, and that all forms of PR are thought-invoking. (M)

43. I thought PR was about relating to 'publics'. Now I think it is much more sinister and complex (propaganda, etc). (M)

44. A creative job but still about spin. No I know there is a strong focus on ethics, but I am still unsure as to how true this is in the real work environment. (M)

45. I thought it was glamorous. But I am much more informed now and much more interested. (M)

46. It's more technical than just organising events. I didn't realise the level of PR for crises, etc. (F)

47. I thought PR was about spin and cover-ups. Now I think it's about communication and is an essential part of most organizations. (F)

48. Many people I know have gone in with misconceptions that PR is similar to practical media studies, or that the course will involve more practical work (writing, etc). (F)

49. I used to think PR was about portraying the image/the face of a company. Also for self-gratification of looking good. Now, PR has an important role to play in an organization, and it's logic isn't fuzzy. (F)

50. I thought it seemed a little glamorous, based on instincts, not books. Now it's more based on theory than I realized. (F)

51. I thought PR was when you represent an organization and help them organize their management. Now I think it's something where it is spin, and includes marketing, reports, advertising, cleaning up any mess that is created, and also building the image of the organization. (F)

52. Then: all about spin, and my perceptions formed the assumptions of PR. Now: from the positive perspective PR is the base to relationships between organisations and the public, and they are sometimes stereotyped by people. (F)

53. I thought it would be very simple: about spokespeople. But now I think it's broad. (M)

54. I've always thought PR is about building image only. I now think of PR not just about building image, but also to manage and anticipate future issues and conflicts. (F)

This industry focus group took place in the boardroom of Scarboro Surf Life Saving Club on Monday 5 December, from 5.30pm top 6.45pm. Participants were informed that the session would be videotaped and voice-recorded. Identities would be anonymous. Originally six practitioners indicated they would attend. However, one had to withdraw for family reasons, and the other (a male) got the days mixed up (does this say something about women being better organisers?). There were four mostly senior female practitioners present. HF is currently undertaking a PhD, lectures at ECU and has managed the communications department of large WA Government Departments; RW is a media relations specialist for a government agency; HL has worked for several government departments and was working in an international promotions role at the time; HM has several years' PR experience and is working for a quasi-government research/charitable organisation with a staff of 300. (A copy of the session, movie and MP3 are included on CD).

HF: Is it being linked to a particular timeframe (chronological order). There are links to the development of PR as a tertiary sector subject. I suppose my first question: is there imbalance? PR is still very unclear. There's PR and advertising, PR and marketing, communications PR, social reform PR. There's so many elements that there still is a lack of clarity as to what constitutes pure PR. I observe that with the corporates their PR teams are mostly men and can come from law or engineering and they look as though they communicate well, you know the business well and they move across into PR without having any of those skills we would consider PR skills. In government it's different. Here's an overwhelming predominance of women. But there's other factors that favour women in government. They have family-friendly policies, and the hours are more flexible. In small business I see men who will start there and go move across into marketing. I see in the literature one of the fundamental issues is that they're still justifying what PR is. It's almost a defence why PR should be legitimate source of power.

HL: People out there find us (PR) a bit confusing. One of those disciplines people don't understand, and that's why we always battle. People want it to do more marketing. Yes, there are more men in the corporates. Consultancies are more dominated by women.

HF: If the consultancies are ostensibly women, what does that say about selling communications services into the large companies and how much value they place on it. If they are actually putting PR in an operational model, and not strategic. We say be strategic, manage relationships, yet our core output is about being operational (this media release, this brochure, this event). It goes back to people not understanding that they want something that's about forward planning but their ability to understand what PR does is based on this 'thing' newspaper, or this coverage. It just about being on TV or in the newspaper. Another observation is that it's very much about politics. You can say I want PR to be strategic, and I want you to manage my reputation in the future, yet you have ministers that are completely reactive because they are going to take a hit politically. You be strategic, and then one hit and the whole thing goes to hell. I think that genuine politicisation of government tends to filter down to PR in particular because it's about reputation. It poses some real challenges about how strategic we can be. With the large corporates you can actually plan, because it's tied to a business outcome, rather than a political outcome.

RW: For me (I entered it because) it was about writing. I guess I fell into it accidentally.

HF: I was a journalist and we moved back to Perth, so I had to find something related, and PR uses writing. I really enjoy writing and crafting things. I like planning things and working on future projections.

HM: I was working as a waitress at the Hilton. The PR team used to come in, and it all used to look very glamourous. I used to listen to their conversations and it sounded interesting. But I was attracted to the glamour, and it was quite glamorous in those days. But of course the culture has changed now. From there I did my TEE and later a PR degree, which I didn't really know a lot about. But in terms of my skills, I was good at English and the non-scientific, mathematical, things. In terms of my skills I thought I'd be good at that (PR). It was all new then. My class was one of the first to go through ECU. Even at that time it was very female-dominated. It never occurred to me that it would be a female-dominated industry. If you were to compare it to advertising and marketing, I would think the skills involved and needed are more female in PR, for me in terms of the hard sell that's involved in marketing and advertising, compared to the softer sell that's possibly involved in PR. In terms of the people I've worked with, the guys tend to go more into marketing and management, whereas the girls go into writing and media roles.

HF: All my students (at ECU) think it's about glamour and parties. But that's all you want to do when you're 20. One of them wanted to be a Paris Hilton. It's a maturation things though. As you mature and you realise what is involved, your view quickly change.

HL: The fact that people go into it because of that (glamour), is not something that bothers me, but it's a fact and that's the perception, and I find that is a hindrance when you want to build a serious career. But getting back to women in PR, I think they certainly tend be better multi-communicators and better at the subtleties of observation within communication. I think it's one element. I wouldn't say they're more nurturing, although do those things even fit with PR. I do believe that in that communication and listening area, and being able to pick up the subtleties of interpersonal communication and the dynamics, which goes wider to the political dynamics of what's going on, there's probably an edge there. But I don't know whether that would be a motivator for men not to go into PR.

HF: I've met some really hard-arsed female PR practitioners. There's no nurturing going on there. I think it comes back to a construct of power. Maybe it's a chicken-and-egg thing. If you think of an organisation that you require women to build relationships to influence and manage media, you need a particular skills set that may be exclusive to the hard-arsed approach that you need. The more senior you are the more hard-arsed you have to be, because you have to change other senior people who have been doing things a certain way for so long; so you become a change agent. You have to be quite forceful. So your skill set changes from a mid-level PR practitioner, which is about relationships and doing all the nice things, and you're everybody's mate at the mid-level. But once you step up to a more leadership role you've actually got to be clear on what you're delivering on. And that becomes about power, which depends on how much power your CEO is prepared to give you. And that changes it again. I actually see quite masculine traits in really senior female PR practitioners. It's a power issue, rather than a gender issue.

HL: Whether you would look at other women in senior management and how much of those types of qualities they've needed to get there. But there's a perception of you holding parties, but (in effect) you are really in a corporate policing role. We were talking about more women in consultancies. Many women have started them, or gone to work for them, mainly because they are more flexible, and cater more for a family lifestyle. There would be a heavier need (reason) for women there.

HM: I appreciate your point about the senior women being hard-nosed. But in terms of the essential core of what PR is, I'm not sure if they fit in to that. They're moved away from that. Their staff would have it. As their role has progressed into a leadership they would develop masculine or leadership qualities.

HF: We actually have to define PR. People run around saying strategic PR, which is a different skill set to operational PR. But operational PR is what I have observed that most people think is PR.

HL: The whole thing about being strategic is another 'crap line' that needs great investigation.

HM: Being strategic would be ideal. When you're in your normal routine, you don't have time to do strategic things. In NFP we don't have the budget for outsourcing, so your dealing with the available resources.

RW: It's a matter of perception. Where I work, I'm in the media room and there's three men and one woman (me), while in PR and that's all women with one men. So we're viewed as the hard-arsed people because we say 'no'. PR does the magazine and does the corporate parties. That perception is encouraged there, too. I see no evidence of where it's not discouraged

HL: I find that disconcerting not from the fact that people won't be motivated to get into it, but that there's a negative stereotype being perpetuated. If people think all you do is parties it makes it hard to be perceived as serious. Things like the Young Guns foster the perception of 'young buns'. The promotion they did had shots of them with girls with champagne in one hand and mobiles in the other. That's really negative and a hurdle the rest of us have to get over. Maybe it's funny if you're coming through the ranks.

HF: I think there's a danger of viewing it just through gender. One of my assumptions about masculine behaviour is that men are more expedient than women. Women will work at things and try to make it work. And they will labour and work over things to produce a more optimal outcome, while guys will just come in and say, 'nah, it's not working, gone'. So by being really expedient, and PR is fraught with this endless relationship-building, often for a momentary win that become nothing as you move on to the next (political) goal. Blokes get their gratification from their power hits and from having obvious wins. They will move forward, and if you're in a fluffy field, where you fluff around, where it changes on the basis of personality, where your boundaries are not consistent they will bail. And they're not even going to be attracted to it in the first place. Guys like expediency, they like boundaries and they like power. That's what motivates them.

RW: That's why they're attracted to the media room. They're got no conscience.

HF: Don't talk to me about building relationships. And the political environment can change. I mean, they think 'what a waste'?

RW: It also might have a lot to do with the product you're promoting. BHP for example is a more masculine industry, whereas at DCD they're hardly any men at all.

HF: That's positioning. You've got to look at it what is the role of PR. In government it's about telling people what you're doing. It's often an unpalatable message across government and that is intrinsically an unhappy message and you never win with it. Do men want to do that?

HL: You (could) think how often have you had a male partner, and they tell you about an incident at work or family or friend where they've given some news to someone and they're taken it really badly. And you ask him: 'well, what did you say?' They tell you 'oh, you're sacked'. It's like whether you pick a mother or father to deliver bad news to a child. In most cases, compassion and empathy is where females definitely have more skills. Possibly it's the reason why so many women have risen in these positions. There's the age-old thought that women can do more things at once. I don't know whether those sort of multi-skilling roles are attractive to men.

HM: I also think it's interesting in the way PR is perceived in television. For example, in Ab Fab. There have been other sitcoms. They've all been females in these roles. I'd like to see where that sits.

HL: Where I am now, we have run Rally Australia, but there has been this plethora of blondes. It's great experience to come in and work at this event. But I wonder if once you've done all those operational promotional roles, writing, brochures and launches and, and you want to go higher do you suddenly want to give it away when you realise it's like that.

HF: Once you've passed a certain level, your job satisfaction reduces because the very thing that draws you to it is no longer part of your core business.

HL: It's common in a lot of businesses that people start out doing something they love. You start out doing something you love, the business grows and you end up doing accounting and management.

HM: I've now got myself into a management position, but moving away from what I originally did, but in a bid to make my role more interesting and challenging.

HF: It's a classic organisational misunderstanding of PR is seen as a process, separate and apart from whatever it is your selling. An organisation can say they want you to be strategic and do all these things, but you are actually a process: sit down and write that media release, sit down and develop that event, produce that web-site. Of course it's a collaborative process with the person that's got the content. So you can't actually be a content-free PR person, and yet because of the systemisation of PR that's what you're forced into. So you have PR process separate from your core content, your business content, and I think if you just stay in your PR process without engaging with your content and trying to get greater depth with that it does become boring.

HM: PR is such a formula. After I had been doing it for 10 years, it just becomes basic, like using the 10-point plan. Here's your template, just fill in the blanks. Or someone else can just complete it and send it off. It become such an easy job.

RW: It (PR) just becomes mainstream and not special, and not rewardable with promotion, which discourages men from going for it. I think a of women in their 30s they think I'm going to have kids anyway, so they don't strive to go into another career. Men think: 'well, I've got another 20 or 30 years of working, I should transfer my sills into something else. Women may think it's all too bloody hard and I'll have kids.

HM: That's a good point. I admit that there's been a few times I've thought if I get pregnant, I'll work from home. So it really does suit that female thought process in that regard.

HL: It's not the easy way out, but it does enable you to work say two days a week, and fit in kids. A lot of (government) PR units are set up, depending on the resources, the structure is that the career path is set out with the skill sets not being very flexible. You usually have to go through the media role, then progress. The career paths tend to make you go sideways.

HF: And why isn't there more blokes in government? I think it flows from the degree of complexity. If my supposition about masculine behaviour is true . . . men think: 'I've got to handle the minister, the DG, executive directors, staff and I've got multiple issues. Who would do that?' Women are more inclined to do that sort of thing successfully. A bloke would get impatient with that.

HM: I think men are more attracted to the corporate and consultancies. I thought in consultancies it was even, and most of the bosses have been men.

HL: I've been struck by the propensity of government to outsource. I think it might be connected to males in the industry. You'd go to PRIA functions and it would be all the old boys. I'm wondering if the men who has those senior PR roles before, like a CEO or advisor, and who had all the corporate knowledge, whether now it's not valued as much because we can outsource the expertise. And now you have women who are managers who are far more operational and hands-on. I can remember working with chaps who had a more advisory role, which is something I do not see those female managers doing now.

HF: And if you do that type of role; people question what you are doing. It's not like you're doing something visible. The climate of the government is that you have to produce something, like a magazine.

HM: I've worked in organisation where you do the day-to-day things, and suddenly the organisation is in the news, so they call in the men to handle the crisis. They don't view it as a PR role because the PR team didn't do it.

RW: I wonder if that resulted from when these men who were in senior roles and they got PR confused with promotion and they hired all these dolly birds for motor shows. Maybe that's where it started. They thought promotion and PR were the same.

HM: I can remember you had to be careful when you were applying for jobs, because you could end up with a topless bar job because it was regarded as public relations. Again, there's a perception problem.

HL: I think there's still a problem with the way the industry promotes itself. There are some negatives which have come out of women being involved with the PRIA. There's that female mafia perception. [All commented briefly on the low membership].

HF: Their (PRIA's) biggest problem appears to be the struggle between national and state and payment of fees, and what goes where. The profession's changing and the PRIA is not keeping up. Other associations become more professionalised. They have mandated education standards. So it's difficult (for the PRIA) to establish legitimacy. Professional codes are so strict in other professions. It was critical for your career to attend. There's nothing compelling PR practitioners to attend these things.

HM: When I attend PRIA functions, I saw it as just an opportunity to exchange business cards with fellow members.

HL: It gets quite repetitive sometimes.

H: There's been a shift in the last seven years in terms of PR in WA. For a long time they decided they needed corporate communicators, or generalists who could do a bit of everything. But with this government there's been such an emphasis on handling the media. That's because the main local paper (and we're a one-paper town) has such an inordinate amount of power. Because of that it shifts the power of how you construct a PR team. In the east there's a variety of ways you can segment yourself. But in WA if you get a bad rap in the West you're done. People run around and they're saying 'it's terrible'. You've got to completely respond and you try to tell them it will blow over by tomorrow. Because of that incredible micro-focus on one newspaper it means PR teams all over the State have to adjust. And there's been this increasing and obvious focus on people with issues management skills and people who have strong media contacts, or can build them quickly. You can be a great writer or strategist, or whatever. But it comes down to 'is the West going to do us over today?'

RW: I used to work in an office and there was one guy who we used to say because he had a dick he would get ahead.

HF: Reverse discrimination, where you have one bloke among a bunch of women.

HL: Women are often other women's worst enemy. If you're shafted at work, very often it's by a woman. There's a lot of female management stresses. I know someone who points to arguing with men and calling each other names and it's forgotten the next day. But women will not forgot that. It can be quite toxic.

HF: I think in this regards it needs a look at culturalisation of men and women.

HL: It would be interesting to see what similarities there are in the UK and the US.

HF: In my five years in the US, I found PR very much a profession, and that's related to the number of schools teaching it. It's taken very seriously. It's anchored to anthropology and sociology. In the US the approach is more pragmatic. Mass Comms includes PR, advertising and journalism. But here we separate things. Marketing says it's the over-arching discipline. And they sit in different schools.

HM: Maybe we should look at the way the universities sell the subject and structure it.

EDITH COWAN UNIVERSITY

The student focus group at Edith Cowan University was held in a lecture theatre, from 7.45 pm to 8.30pm. It consisted of 10 fourth-year PR students (eight female and two male) and was observed by tutor, Mr Vince Hughes, MBA. There was a mix of students, with two from Norway (1M, 1F), one from India (M), two from China (F) and one (F) from Hong Kong. For responses, students are identified by number (from left to right, and by gender (M or F). The format was to put forward results of earlier surveys and to ask students to respond to the results. All students were informed their identities would remain anonymous and that participation was voluntary.

Importance of balance in PR

- I think it's good (to have balance). You get more points of view and different angles. It makes opinions more diverse and makes people look at things differently. (F4)

- It depends on the individual. (F8)

- Family circumstances. Most of the time women work part time, quit their jobs. (F4)

Reasons for doing PR

- Women are more likely to stop work to have children. There's a gap when you might start your profession, then you have five or 10 years to raise your children, then you have to start at a lower level to restart your career. Whereas men have had career continuity, so the women have to play catch-up. (F8)

Creativity

- Is it that boys don't choose PR because they just think it's a woman's job? (F4)

- When I was thinking of doing PR I was thinking of business, and I thought 'be sensible and do business'. And then I looked at the units and said 'no, you'll fail miserably, those units are not interesting to me'. So (and this may be sexist) men they want to get into management the business/financial side might interest them more than women, who want to have that slight creative ability so they're getting into PR. (F9)

- I agree with that. I was thinking that maybe men work better in a hierarchical structure (like business). Because PR is more creative and you need to be flexible, I think women can be more flexible and creative. (F8)

- The structure thing of the financial side. Men seem to like that structure, so it appeals to them more to do business. (F9)

- I agree with all that. But by the same token, marketing and advertising have a lot of men in it and that's creative. I don't know if the creativity argument is strong here. (F10)

- I think it's the image of PR. If I were a guy I would probably choose something more manly, not 'serious', because I take PR very seriously. I think the reputation of PR is pretty feminine. For a guy maybe it doesn't sound too cool. (F4)

- I think it depends on the industry as well. If I am a company and have to hire a PR person because women are better-looking and it is better for a company when a woman talks, because society sees women as more persuasive and gentle. I think women are better at talking. They are talking all the time. You can't stop them. (M5).

- The way women persuade: maybe they can read things better. Many people read things as black and white, and it's fair to say that most men see things as black and white. A woman's way of persuasion might be a little more subtle than a man who will stand there and just say 'you will believe what I am saying'. A woman, on the other hand, will say 'well, I really understand but here's another suggestion'. Maybe it's just a subtle communication difference that helps in PR. (F9)

- Maybe it's about multi-skilling. We've heard that men are apparently only able to do one thing at a time. Probably in PR because we have to do some many things, that's why women are suited. (F7)

- I think it's more about cultures and location sometime. In Asian culture you find men in the industry because men dominate over there. (M1)

- In Hong Kong and China women do most of the PR work. I think most of the PR workers are less energetic than men. Men are stronger so it's better for women do an in-house [read office] job. (W5)

- Women are more interested in people. (W2)

Society

- What about the aspect, that its about the way society has brought us up. A child is 15, 16 and looking at their future. Maybe girls look at their careers a little less seriously than boys at that stage, and maybe that's why boys would want to go into the business/management aspect because they know they can get higher. We learn it's hard in PR for women to get into top-level management. Maybe it's the way we're raised. Boys think 'I've got to raise my family for the next 45 years and I have to get a good job', so they opt for the better-paying path. (W9)

Teaching of PR

- Two schools of thought about the way PR is taught. One in the business stream, the other in the creative stream. I've had strong interest in that and I still haven't come to a conclusion on how to handle it. (Hughes).

- Marketing is creative, and that's in the business school. (F4)

- HR resource management has an element of PR to it, yet it's in business schools. Especially with corporate communication. But a lot more men will go into HR rather than PR. (W10)

Gender imbalance

- Okay for us, if we're the majority. (F10)

- Maybe sometimes it's what societies want. The men in management maybe just want girls in the PR department. (M1)

[Student F4 was concerned there was a problem with the industry because this subject was being studied. It was pointed out that I didn't think there was a problem with the industry; rather just that I wanted to now why this phenomenon is occurring. It was pointed out that some scholars perceive there to be a problem in that too many women can lead to a "ghettoisation" of PR].

Ethics

- With women being in PR I thought about men and their attitude in other industries; like corruption. It seems to be more men involved in that (way). Would men perhaps not act as professional or ethically as women in PR? (F8)

- Sounds awful saying it but maybe women are more likely to be sympathetic to other peoples' points of views. (F9)

Gender roles in PR

- I've been doing some work in a consultancy and I've noticed about 80 per cent of women, and all the men do the work for the mining companies, or energy (where the money is). But all the women do the launches and events and that kind of thing. And they're not getting paid more. (F10)

- Notice Condoleeza Rice in a PR role. Are females sometimes used in these front-lines roles to soften the hard news? (Hughes)

- I know a lot of guys that can be just as persuasive as women; so maybe is it just a certain type of person that is attracted to PR. (F4)

Traits

- I was thinking that you could go to that notion that females the idea of women and sex; that females can be more persuasive through using their charm. (F9)

- Some jury studies say good-looking men who have been charged with an offence have a better chance of getting off than if you're ugly. If you read that into PR, so maybe if you're good looking are you more persuasive. (Hughes)

- It's like in Amsterdam; people feel more compassion for pretty whores than ugly looking whores. (F4)

- Maybe it's about our society and culture. (F8)

INTERVIEW 1, PH, 21 NOVEMBER

PH is one of Perth's leading PR professionals, and is general manager of one of the three largest companies. He has worked in media and PR for 20 years, first as a newspaper journalist for 13 years. The company employs eight men and 27 women.

Over the years I've seen the direction of PR very much slanted by the media's perception of what PR is. The media projects PR as being about events, celebrities, the glamour of the industry. They are just aspects of PR.

The girls in PR are all coming from university, that's undoubtedly why there are so many now working in the industry. I look at one of our young ladies, here. She got into PR through radio, where she was doing behind-the scenes stuff, music section, doing promotions in the cars. In the end she said 'no, I don't want to do that; I want to do something more substantial'.

Our company used to be more evenly balanced. Back in 96-97 there were about the same numbers of each sex. Then from 1998 to 2000 it very much picked up and ran with female employees. There were more females coming out of uni, but blokes were wanting much higher salary packages.
"We've always had two guys at the top of the company, as MD and GM, with the exception of recently when we have appointed a woman GM. If you look at the top 15 companies in the Business List, there are a number of companies with females at the top. (However, those companies were all started by women).

[There were some pertinent comments made on women taking breaks from employment when having families. From 17-20 mins].

Women are very good communicators (in general), they have an ability to articulate information in a manner that is often easily understood and coherent. As such they actually have the starting point for being a PR practitioner. Journalism, I find, is a very hard and factual industry, in most instances. In general news you've just got to write the facts. You might get into feature or health writing. I think women just get fed up with writing the hard nuts and bolts. A lot of the women we have had find PR a panacea. I like writing, I like dealing with publics, I like handling sort out issues and handling accounts. So, what can provide me with that type of ongoing career? They see PR, they look at it (and we have several former female journalists). And why? Because they are excellent communicators; they are good at telling a story, they are good at writing, they actually enjoy writing. And writing is the critical aspect, whether male or female, which takes people down a potential career in PR.

Then they get into what should I do. Should I be a copywriter, a brochure-writer? But they don't go down that path because it's about the sell, or has too much fluff. PR offers them a halfway point, in that it can be halfway there.

In general, when it comes to strategy, I wouldn't be going to my senior women over my senior men. Sorry. Tactically, of my top five or six, only two are women. In some cases it just gets downs to experience. In a general PR sense, the two women would be part of the senior team, but if we had a rally major crisis, say with an oil company (for whom we have a female account manager). Why? Because our backgrounds in government and issues just mean that the men here can provide the best solutions.

The reality is that the human body clock for women kicks in between 30 and 40. If they are in a stable relationship, the women are more than likely to go off and have a family. But we are now encouraging these women to come back. We want to make it easier for them to resume their careers.

There are some instances where clients (mostly in the corporate sector, particularly in mining and resources) prefer to work with men. It's just that those industries are traditionally male-dominated. Their culture is just that way. Some meetings I've walked into a mining-related client meeting with a female colleague, and the comment has been that I've brought along my personal assistant. Would you be able to make us a coffee? And it's been made in a demeaning sense. They only talk to me and have eye contact with me. They just don't want to know her. And there are other anecdotal stories where clients have said 'you don't need to bring her next time; she wouldn't understand our business'.

I don't bemoan the fact that the industry is predominantly women. I think it would be good if we could attract more men in to the industry. I believe that in the WA market there is a lack of good corporate-orientated young male practitioners. The majority of those that come though are female, and if someone could answer me why is it more difficult for females to pick up the 'corporate' reins of an account, I'd love to hear it. I could actually develop an education package that could be slotted into the universities. It just seems to me that the young guys have a better understanding of business. That's probably a slight on female practitioners, but it's not meant to be. It's just that when they come through, it is a significant effort to get them thinking about corporate reins, particularly investor relations. Things like profit, triple bottom line and such, mean nothing to them.

I could walk into a university and ask who wants to work in entertainment or tourism and the hands would shoot up. And I could ask who wants to work in investor relations, and no hands would go up. Then I'd ask who wants to earn $100K in eight to 10 years? The hands would go up. Of those, who would want to work in investor relations, and the hands would drop. So I'd walk out and say none of you are going to earn much.

INTERVIEW 2, IW, 22 NOVEMBER

IW is a male practitioner with 30 years experience in communications (12 in Perth). He has a BBus (Communications) and Grad Dip Marketing. He heads a semi-government organisation which has one of the State's largest PR budgets. The organisation turns over more than $200m a year. He also works closely with external PR consultancies.

(About 10-12 years ago) PR might have been seen as a soft and attractive profession. PR didn't have a lot of the hard-nosed stuff, such as issues management. There was a lot of events management. If you encountered a female PR operative in those days (and they may have come out of journalism) they probably had a reasonable understanding of the media. But these days everyone is a reporter. Everyone's got a camera on their phone. I think having that capacity: to want to part of a pleasant profession with career opportunities, but allowing women to develop their profession.

I think there are things around the edge around PR that leads them to think it's a pleasant profession.

I think PR about 15 years ago was media relations; getting the company story across, putting corporate views out. PR has grown in line with the growth of the media.

Up until 15 months ago, I dealt with for more than three years a company that had never had a male practitioner. In some respects I felt that was objectionable. You had to have no penis and be blonde and you'd get on in the industry (and an e-mail from a friend of mine who runs a consultancy interstate tackles this point). He calls some of these females in the industry "grimbos". I thought that was an interesting observation.

There's a whole lot of blondes out there in black dresses who are very good at functions, but when they come to write press releases create 'lobsters' (with a whole lot of shit at the head). They just can't nail it in the first three paragraphs.

Really, I don't have a simple answer as to why there are more women in this industry. As far as our account is concerned (and apparently this is the biggest). There are some places that if you didn't have a penis you'd never get a job there.

Sometimes you have to look how education works. That's probably where the answer lies.

I think physiologically and mentally (left-brain, right-brain) there are differences in the way males and females work, and their approach to things. But some of the planning women do are better than men; particularly event management. They have that attention to detail (such as colour) and I don't mean that to be sexist. But things like that can add value to an event. I think in the area of community relations they're good at that, because sometimes it's better to put a women in front of "CAVES" (Citizens Against Everything). They have a softer negotiation skill and can find the middle ground.

Dare I say it, but in the public sector there is strong evidence that certain women can evolve and develop power bases, and will have amazing pulling power with a CEO, where a bloke mightn't have; given that there's an 80 per cent chance the CEO will be male.

It's a bit like human resources, where there's a very similar trend, where HR specialists tend to be female.

INTERVIEW 3, AH, 30 NOVEMBER 2005

AH part-owns of one of Perth's top three PR firms, employing 21 people, including nine in PR (eight women and one male – him). Originally a TV journalist, he has been in PR for 13 years, including a stint for the British Government. He has worked in Perth for the past seven years, ever since he started his current business.

The PR profession is a very loose profession. Unlike engineering you don't have to be part of a national body. Therefore it's going to be harder for it to make any conscious decision, if people think there's a problem, to address the imbalance.

I think it does matter if there are a lack of men coming through. I think that any industry that gets unbalanced is doing itself a disservice, like in engineering, because you need all types of viewpoints. And men and women do communicate differently. Women are naturally better communicators, but sometimes you need a male communications approach to communicating, writing or speaking, because their approach often more robust. So I think it (imbalance) is actually an issue. The trouble is whether you can see it as an issue. It's not in our firm. But for the profession as a whole I think it is an issue.

There's no doubt guys are naturally attracted to technical subjects. That's the case in our company, where it's evident that we have more women applying for the PR and design jobs, yet for the web side of things, which is mostly technical, we attract males, which are the predominant group. The guys have vacated the design space and left it to women, and the women occupy the PR space. The other big problem, which you can already see in universities, is that most of the kids are foreign students and don't have the capacity to work in our industry. If the unis go down this track they will just produce people that are only of use to their own countries.

I think women are certainly generally more empathetic than males, and that certainly helps in PR. One of the other areas that women excel in is that they are better organisers. Most of them when they try tell us why they want to be in PR they name event management as the reason. Either they have an interest in organising things, or they have an interest in parties. That's fine. Either interest is valid, but they're in it for their organisational ability. It's one of the reasons women thrive. They are good documenters and they are thorough. Because in a consultancy people need to be thorough. I take their organisational skills as being high on the list on why they want to be in the profession.

It's easier to train a guy on how the business, or a client's businesses operate. On the other hand, it's much easier to train a women to build a relationship with clients. At the end of the day, which is more important? As I'm the guy who has to understand how the business runs, then I place an emphasis on relationship-building. Also, if they don't understand something, women will ask a question, and males generally don't do that. I guess it is similar to guys taking up engineering skills.

As for characteristics of PR people, there can be very aggressive females and some males who are at the opposite end of the spectrum. The people who are good at PR are usually somewhere in the centre. The good males have some of the feminine characteristics: the ability to build relationships, have empathy, communicate clearly The very good women also have some of the necessary robustness to be tough and use in negotiations, and some of the slight aggression you need to have to work with the media. It's a hybrid type of person.

I have think women enter PR because they probably have an inkling of what PR is about when they apply (that's PR is a spin-off of marketing, for example). If they've heard of it's because it's been connected to fashion, or parties. That doesn't matter, but at least something has led them into the profession. Guys don't get that because they're not interested in that type of stuff. They don't think "oh, good, it's about organising things: I'll go into that'. So they don't have anything nudging them towards the profession. I also think the organising aspect is important. Women are good organisers and they know it. Even in their teenage years, women are organising things, whether it's the school ball, or their friend's party, sister's wedding. Therefore they're very attracted by the notion of event management. I just don't have any theories on why men are attracted; just that they're not.

If you wanted to draw males into the profession, you would have to study what other professions do. They start in the schools. By the time you get to uni, the decision has been made. You have to start off in the schools, explaining what it is and enticing the right sort of guy into the profession. Guys will quickly sort out if they're interested. But there's probably a raft of guys out there who could potentially do quite well, but are foundering around with no knowledge of PR. Oddly enough, in WA we are better placed than anywhere else to demonstrate we have a role for males. Unlike Sydney and Melbourne, which has the 'fluffy' stuff PR like fashion and entertainment, the reality is most Perth PR is business. I think that's one of the hardest things for women when they leave university here, because in order to do PR they see they have to go into 'serious' business, not fluff, so they have to understand mining companies and so on. At the end of the day, you have to find out what might appeal to guys. Whether it's saying, 'look, I spend a lot of my time on mine sites and dealing with heavy industry'. Something has to be said to them.

INTERVIEW 4 KS, 6 DECEMBER 2005

KS is one of Perth's most senior and respected practitioners and academics. Only recently retired, he is now an Adjunct Professor in PR. Originally from a radio and newspaper journalism background (eight years), he has 44 years' PR experience, for consultancies, multi-nationals and governments (in Australia and Indonesia).

PR was born out of journalism. Back in 1962 the face of PR was all male. Journalists were very anti-women. To be a woman journalist, there was true glass ceiling. They never rose above a B-grade. Their highest aspiration was to be women's editor. There was an 'old school', sort of Victorian-Edwardian hangover that maintained this anti-female culture. Senior women journalists were becrying [sic] the fact they couldn't get the same opportunities as men.

PR has always been about information 'in' as much as information 'out'. It was often the information you gathered that was most important. And the best collectors of information were journalists. So the PR companies recruited the best journalists, but only male. You wouldn't have head-hunted a woman. The ABC was a bit of an exception, and did not discriminate.

I was managing Eric White and Associates in Perth when I came back from Jakarta in 1981 and I employed a woman to run one of our major accounts. Jim Griffin, who had been the manager, and was now a director, said 'I don't know about that client accepting a woman'. But she was a great success.

Among the first women were Jan Barry and Marie-Louise Sinclair.

Jan Barry also became the State manager. Theoretically there were no barriers, but it didn't happen because of the culture. We respected our colleagues and they were getting the same pay, at a time when many women were not getting equal pay. But at the same time their perception was they couldn't get the top jobs, except in 'women's writing', which is what we'd now call lifestyle stuff. And the lifestyle stuff is still mainly the women's preserve. This, of course makes them valuable in PR, because that's where the modern marketing style of PR find its outlet. I believe the type of PR has changed. We were employed much more strategically. As I said, in obtaining information. I can remember at one stage having not written a release in two years. I just finding out information. It was more what we'd now call public affairs.

As to why women are entering PR, it's really a mystery to me. I would say PR is perceived as a glamour industry. This, I think, does have implications as to why women enter it.

I made a transition from public affairs to marketing PR by way of advertising in 1968. I joined Ogilvy and Mather who had just arrived in Australia. They had senior women in advertising running major accounts and it worked. They were mainly food and service-type accounts. But they all had PR aspects to them. It was what we now call IMC. To me that is the major part of PR today and that's where women are fitting in. It's the lifestyle aspects of PR that is emphasised. The exception is government, which appears to employ a lot of women.

Education has certainly helped women break the glass ceiling, simply because the men didn't think they had to.

If we start to generalise, we can have a problem. I think the male desire to be in control is stronger than the women's desire to be in control. It's about power. I think that in PR, power is what drives the men, I'm pretty sure, but it's not apparent in the lower echelons. These days men don't get attracted to PR because it's not as certain as other things they can now do. PR's power (in government) never has been 'fully there' when it comes to exerting influence. There was time when the PRIA looked down at government PR people because they considered them more journalistically-oriented. They wouldn't admit them as members.

INTERVIEW 5, DAN EDELMAN, 8 FEBRUARY 2006

Dan Edelman could well be regarded as one of the world's pre-eminent practitioners. His New York-based practice has offices in several countries, including Australia. He was interviewed by phone.

Almost every service industry now has a high proportion of women. They've come into the workforce in numbers unseen. It's a remarkable development and is particularly obvious in occupations such as legal, accounting and communications..

PR certainly has disproportionate numbers. It's sometimes said there are not enough women in leadership roles. But that's not always true, particularly when it comes to PR. We have company presidents in five countries, including Italy, Brazil, Spain and Australia, plus in many capital city offices. Women's salaries are also much higher now, so it's inaccurate to say they do not get the same opportunities in PR.

Women can handle anything. They're not limited in what they can tackle; certainly not from their perspective. However, they tend to be more numerous in health and consumer product industry PR. The crisis and financial management side of things still seems to be the men's domain.

Maybe men have more choices. There are now a lot of women doctors.

With regard to having more men in PR, I don't think it's something you can force, because then you wouldn't have enough staff. It does come down to the best person for the job.

As far as the numbers go, I think it's as high as we can go (with women).

PR is more appealing to people now, and women certainly can compete equally.

INTERVIEW 6, MR, 22 MARCH 2006

MR is a male practitioner with a degree in journalism. He worked for six months in journalism (country paper) and then switched to PR. He has two years' experience and is working for a WA Government Department.

Maybe blokes see PR as being a bit airy-fairy. Maybe men are a bit more forthright, and because PR is a bit fuzzy they shy away from it. It's probably a male thing.

You've definitely got to be confident; to be able to pick up the phone and talk to people. You're out there.

Because I'm working alongside an industry that's traditionally male-dominant, I see that a lot of older men don't like being told by women (particularly younger ones) how they should do things (from a PR aspect).

In journalism it isn't really good money, so that could be a reason why some men will do PR. I thought I would just keep doing journalism as a freelancer, on the side.

There's certainly more job security in PR than journalism, and more room to move up and quicker than in journalism.

I can't see blokes doing events. It's too much about keeping everyone on side. Too much crap. Probably women have more patience and are able to deal with unhappy clients, and they are probably more thorough.

INTERVIEW 7: JW, 22 MARCH 2006

JW majored in PR and has been working in the industry for 10 years. He currently works for a Perth consultancy.

The trend of more women has certainly been noticeable. Even when I studied there could be 20 in the class, and only three men. It was a common joke that there were so few men doing it. However, there was never any stigma about the males doing it.

I think it's good to have a better balance in the industry, and of course, at university.

But it's hard to say why this (imbalance) has happened. Women might be more aware of attention to detail and also with the design of various communication materials. They take more pride in presentation and appearance, and I don't think most males think that way. Those things are important in PR.

Women can probably handle more than two or three things at once. I think there's been a bit written about that.

There could be a perception that PR is soft and fluffy. But there's all sort of PR, from issues to promotions in bikinis. There seems to be confusion out there. Maybe it's a female thing that they just grasp the many facets and can adapt to them.

PR is a job that is flexible, and you can work at it for two or three days a week. That would suit women better. Men, I think, would prefer to work fulltime. Maybe that's a traditional thing. Certainly if women have children, PR would suit them in that regard.

You have to have a strong personality in PR. You have to be able to pick up the phone and talk to anybody, and deal with all sorts of people in many industries.

Maybe PR is not seen as serious. It's hard to know. It's often portrayed as spin. A lot of journalists see PR people as 'spin doctors'. Maybe, women can handle challenges from journalists [better than men].

Maybe there's just not enough substance for men in PR.

INTERVIEW 9: MB, 28 July 2006

MB is a (male) senior lecturer in communication theory at the University of Technology, Sydney. The interview took place by phone. It was prompted late in the study by a colleague who mentioned that MB had asked about the study and had some 'theories'.

I have only just recently been exposed to this (increasing number of women in PR). At a recent course I conducted for the PRIA there were only 12 women. So I asked them why there were no men, and they replied that they "were much cheaper than men". They went on to explain that at the top end of town, in financial PR, however, most, if not all the practitioners were men. But I don't know if that was just "gender-talk". I have no evidence to back it up.

The rest is really just my thought process which flowed from that. In New South Wales we have an extremely high UAI (Universities Admissions Index) score to enter communications courses – PR and journalism. It's 96 per cent, and we attract the top four per cent of the State's students, who happen to be women. So you look at the HSC (Higher School certificate) there is a female dominance at the top.

I think that also PR has changed in recent years from being not so much about persuasion, but now it's more project management. We don't so much have to try to convince organisations to run material, because 60 per cent of the news is PR-driven anyway.

Like I said, I've only just encountered the issue and haven't given it much thought.

INTERVIEW 1: LS, 24 NOVEMBER 2005

Lisa is a 27-year-old third-year student, who has also worked for several years in other areas, and briefly on PR internships. She was completing a double major in PR and marketing, and is considering doing honours.

I found the male students to be quite determined. Their work is quite good and they really apply themselves. Maybe they're more determined because they feel they have to prove themselves among the women. The majority of the guys I know get good marks, so they must work hard.

Males in PR seem to be a little bit more sensitive than other male students in other disciplines. They are more organised and methodical. The majority of them, I guess, seem to have more feminine characteristics. You can talk to them more easily than some of the other male students. They possibly don't fit in with what might be termed the general male culture.

They're very creative, with innovative ideas and very helpful, when I've done group work with them. I haven't had to ask for their work. They're quite organised. But they're not quite as helpful as females.

I started many years ago doing secretarial and PA work, which involved a lot of organisational tasks. And there was a lot of interaction with the marketing department. I also did a few units of PR at TAFE and realised what I had been doing was PR. I went travelling and when I was away I realised this is what I wanted to do.

PR is an easy subject if you just want to pass. You'll never fail. But there's quite a lot work in getting a high distinction.

The stereotypical PR person needs to be organised, methodical, a very good communicator and network easily. That implies an outgoing person, which men are more likely to be, as they don't have the inhibitions that women have, and they don't think too far whether they're hurting someone else, or saying something they shouldn't be. So they're not that sensitive, in general. But it depends on the person. I just think those qualities are needed for a PR person to be successful, and women generally have them more than men.

Listening is important. A PR person ends up running their little department and they have to listen to the other external departments, so if you're not listening you're not going to be sending out the right message. [*Do you think the male or female students have better listening skills. Perhaps?*]

Event organising seems to be quite popular at uni. It comes up every time in what students are interested in.

The men I know are doing very well. They are in consultancies and government. I would think men have the edge in (obtaining work) PR. Because there are so few of them and they are a lot more fun to have in a department. I imagine, though, that the level of how serious person is determined by the culture of the organisation.

INTERVIEW 2: JB, 3 December 2005

JB is a 19-year-old second-year male student majoring in PR and multi-media. He will study in the US in the first semester 2006, before competing his degree.

I was the only male in my tute of 25 this semester. In lectures it's dominated "majorly" by females. You look around and you might see 10 guys among 50 or 60 females. So I did think at some stage why there were so many females. You kind of keep a bit more quiet when there's 24 females. When there's so many you don't want to get on the wrong side of them. I've only worked with females this year, so it's difficult for me to measure other males.

I don't think they treat you differently. In group work you can still put your point across. But I guess like it's like any group; there's good and bad. But I could always get my point across. Maybe you feel a little intimidated sometimes because of the overwhelming number of females. So I tend to just sit back and watch them. I don't think any of the other guys have any problems with being among so many females. We all tend to get along well with people. I know my mate can talk to someone and in 30 seconds he has them laughing.

I don't think you could go far in PR if you were shy. As for common traits, we get along with people well, make friends easily. I think also we weren't really sure what we wanted to do when we left school. PR is something where you get to interact with people, which I wanted to do. I also didn't like the fact that I might be stuck in front of a computer screen doing multi-media for the rest of my working life, so that's why I took a PR option as well and I can see which one I prefer. I didn't choose advertising because there are a lot of guys in it, so I thought that if I chose PR I would have a better chance because there weren't many guys in it. With advertising I always pictured it as sitting at a desk and trying to think of ideas. With PR I thought it would be more interactive and I could get out of the office a bit more.

I think being creative is important in PR. Maybe the fact that I do multi media and that my mate plays an instrument indicates we are creative. I think the kind of males we are is a real mix. One of my mates can be a bit feminine, but the other guy is laid back, a surfer and smokes a bit. I guess I'm in the middle. The females are also a mix, some are assertive, some are chatty, others quiet. I think the ones that makes their voice heard are the ones that will do well in PR.

To be honest, one of the things that has turned me off PR is that it seems ambiguous compared to marketing and advertising. It's hard to measure PR, and you don't know if the work you are doing is working or not. If you're doing marketing and advertising you have a better gauge. Sometimes you feel as though you've been studying for two years and don't know if you've done anything. I think this is one of the big issues we come across. Everyone likes to measure things at the end of the day to see how they're going. Males like that sense of competition and they try to beat other individuals, so they like to be measured. That's where it's frustrating because PR is hard to measure. We have sat down and talked about it. And it just seems you never know where you're at with it.

When I was the only guy in a group I was constantly trying to get them to do things my way. I found a lot of their writing was a lot more flowery. I guess if you're trying to make things positive for the client they could do it. But I found myself better at organising or managing things in the group situation. Maybe they were better at the creativity, and I was better at managing. Maybe that comes back to the view that men lean towards more business-related subjects. I found many of their ideas didn't have much value in that they would only fix one part of the jigsaw, when they should have been looking at fixing the whole problem.

I found generally the girls were more comfortable with me. They tended to get on each others' nerves. Maybe it was just the novelty of having a male in the group. In places I've worked, where there were males and females, the atmosphere is better than when it's all males. It tended to get boring sometimes, because you tend to talk about the same things all the time.

INTERVIEW 3: EP, 7 DECEMBER 2005

EP is a mature-age female student who completed three years of a teaching degree. She is now in the final year of a Communication Degree at Murdoch University.

I think because of the lack of prestige given to the profession it's sort of seen as women's work. It's difficult to define. I thought I'd like to do PR after having my children and I'd met some people who had done events (which is not just what PR is). Before I started doing PR, people would say 'what does it mean you do?' And I just couldn't verbalise what a PR person did. I remember that most of the males that asked me, they would say it's like 'party-planning' or advertising. They seemed to think it was a really pathetic thing to do. Maybe that's why men aren't drawn to it. It's not a stigma, but really just the idea of what PR is. I think they think it's standing on the corner doing surveys, like in marketing.

At the end of PR campaign, you don't really come out with figures, hard-and-fast results. It's just what worked and what didn't. A lot of it is feedback. I sort of think it's a social thing: that society regards it as a female profession. Talking to a lot of students, most of the ones I worked with are using it (PR) as a component for other things. They use it as an elective, or part of another degree, say in journalism or marketing. I think that social idea of PR really affects what people think.

I think movies like *Wag The Dog*, show how manipulative it can be influences how PR is seen, although that's from an American perspective. But they make it sound ugly, with people manipulating things. I think that's what people think PR is (manipulating things). Even I get sceptical. We had a lecture from someone who works for the Premier's Department. And they coordinate things like what colour of tie the Premier is wearing: even if he shouldn't wear a tie. There are things like they pick and choose who will and who won't be interviewed. So that's all manipulation.

I would never have looked for media releases on a web-site before I started doing PR. I guess I didn't grow up with that, unlike the younger students. This makes me wonder if the public actually look up things like that.

Many of the male students at Murdoch in the Communications course aren't doing PR; they are doing journalism. The males did have a different approach. They tended to come from a marketing or political perspective. I always feel that men do marketing and women do PR for some reason. It is just my perception. I think I like the whole communication aspect of PR. I'm 'big' [sic] in trying to find ways of trying to communicate well. It's important that when we send out messages, we get the right one across and that we're not manipulating things.

I like writing because it gives you the time to create a good coherent message.

There's a mix of people doing PR. There are the outgoing ones, but there are also the quiet achievers. They tend to get quite passionate about some of the work we had to present.

I think writing is the most important component of doing PR. Presentation is also important because people "read" things visually. By that I mean that we take in images more quickly than just reading words. Then I think organisational ability is important. I would probably be happy just writing media releases, because I enjoy writing.

A lot of the men in PR are ex-journalists, and they're not viewed as a PR person. They're given a title that eliminates the fact they are doing PR. Generally, men that do PR often give it a title so it doesn't look like they're doing PR. I've always thought of it as a profession that women do, like nursing. I wouldn't think of women becoming marketers. I don't think they do it consciously. It's just that they have this ideas that there are certain roles men do, and some that women do. It's like when they enrol, at uni someone says: 'what are you doing?' And they get the reply that 'oh, that's for girls'.

I guess people do not really know much about PR. When you go to a high school careers night, every boy wants to be a pilot or girls want to be dressmakers or nurses. We are making choices at earlier ages, and really no one really knows about PR. So how will they make an informed choice?

Because there's this whole idea of women having to look after the children, simply because women "have" them. It like there's this debate about male and female roles, which might never disappear. We've gone through three waves of feminism, but we're back to where we started. There's the idea of men being linear thinkers, and women being better at multi-skilling. We stereotype PR. It's similar to thinking all men that do party-planning are gay. But are they?

I have young girls in my unit, and we were talking about feminism and what rights they have. They didn't realise that in many occupations women still get paid less than men. They just thought all that [EEO] was in place.

INTERVIEW 4: SW, 16 DECEMBER 2005

SW is a recently-graduated female with a PR Degree and working in events management. She is about to commence a Masters Degree in media studies.

The women PR people I deal with through events I think feel that they more marketing-aligned. The men are more serious and aligned with business-development. I wouldn't say the men are overtly masculine, but neither are they 'wimpy' or 'girly'.

I think probably PR people need a quite 'forward' trait, of being able to step up and take on a leadership role or make decisions. Maybe you need to be able to have an element of risk-taking. Just being very definite about what you're doing. And yes, I'd agree with all those general things that you need to be a people-person, and I would agree with that, because you do need to have a way with people, of making them comfortable.

I hate going to a function and having to network. It feels very false, I suppose you just 'schmooze' people. I guess I'm not someone who can make small talk. I suppose that's a character trait.

I'd say that probably the nature of PR being "behind-the-scenes" industry probably means that when practitioners are recognised it is probably projected as fluff and bubble, and not actually what they do behind the scenes. It just comes out at functions. That's where I think the fluff and bubble impression comes from.

I wonder if people choose PR without knowing what it is? For me I thought I would do something in management and work in hospitality. But I quite like writing, so I could be good at journalism. I did one unit of journalism, and thought it's okay. But I don't want to do this as a living. No one could give men an answer of what PR was. They sort of said it was like marketing, but more strategic. So I did the unit, enjoyed it and kept going.

For me I was trying to find a match in the area I was working in, and that's probably different to a lot of uni students. I know a lot of students say they choose a subject because they want to be a journalism, or a film-maker. You don't actually do PR to do PR. You get a skill base and then you go and apply it. It's not like a lawyer or doctor: once you finish you are a doctor or a lawyer.

When I started uni a lot of people were doing a bachelor of arts. You don't really get anything at the end of it. To a certain degree I think communications has replaced the BA. The skills are more relevant, but don't set you in any one direction, and I think that appeals to a lot of students.

INTERVIEW 5: ZM, 11 JANUARY 2006

ZM is a male second-year student who is disillusioned with PR and is switching to marketing/advertising.

I also have a class with first-year students, and there's two out of 20 students being male. My classmate has noticed a difference as well. For the most part we are ignored in class. It's almost as though we're shoved in the corner. He is very placid, and quiet. Unusually, he's not really that outgoing, which is definitely a trait of the girls. They are very out there, very loud.

There's a definite issue with it (being ignored). I've experienced not being taken seriously by teachers. It's the same with my mate. Mostly female teachers. Maybe that's got something to do with it.

I think PR is perceived as a con industry. Speaking to people who don't know much about it, they think it's about telling people what they don't want to hear. I went to PRIA night (student challenge). If there were journalists there. It was just a "bitchy" night. They would talk to one person, then criticise them when they walk away. I think the whole point of the industry is to be honest, and these people are not doing that, and that's among their own.

The internship proved to me what I had started to think about the industry. I'd say that it true that the industry isn't very black and white. When I was doing my internship, I'd be there and ask them: 'exactly what do you do? What's involved?' They were connecting A to B, jumping up in the air and saying they were brilliant. It's very grey. And that's why I'm switching to advertising/marketing, because PR is not very definite. You don't exactly know what your role is.

The teaching is different. I was taught PR is part of marketing, and some places teach the opposite: that marketing is part of PR. I think it's taught differently everywhere. They need a consistent standard across the country, at least in the way of what it's supposed to be.

I think females would have a different method of teaching from males, though I can't tell because I don't have any male teachers. But I'd say most of them have been very wishy-washy. It was like they were unsure of what they were teaching.

I think that anyone that hasn't done PR would see it a female-dominated industry. And that's a turn-off for guys, I think.

One of the differences between advertising and PR is that they both put a positive spin, and leave out the negative. But you pay for advertising.

I still think PR is a new industry. People say it's been around for ages, but it's only trying to take on a modern approach now. It seems PR has taken over a lot of marketing and advertising roles, branding, events management and journalism. They stick themselves in the middle and say 'we can do everything'. In my internship the company said it was doing advertising and marketing. What gives PR the right to do marketing things? No one in marketing does PR things.

I think one of the main skill to have in PR is to be able to be able to say something without saying anything, and I think women are pretty good at that. That does make it [PR] fuzzy. I think that's a motherly instinct (every woman has a chance to be a mother) and it's ingrained in females. Of course guys can have that ability, but it's more apparent in females.

Sometimes people are more comfortable talking to a [PR] women if there's an issue to deal with. It could come down to that nature thing, in that woman is caring and sensitive.

I think there's also an aspect of how the media portrays PR. I've often mentioned that I'm doing PR and people refer to Eddie in *Absolutely Fabulous*.

It's a very pretentious industry. When you go to a [PR] function, it's all put on. People just have their hand in each other's pockets. Even one of my teachers said she same thing.

It's [PR] not here or there. That whole schmoozing up to people, and buttering them up, I think that's a load of shit. Maybe it doesn't equate to what I've been taught: that you have to be honest. So I dislike the industry immensely.

A big issue is when you try to find out what PR is. They don't tell you much. Maybe if they tell you more at the start it might correct the problem of so few guys doing it. Then again, it might work the other way. But I wouldn't have been able to say what it was when I started. But then, I can't tell you what it is after two years.

INTERVIEW 6: FM, 16 DECEMBER 2005

FM is a female and former primary-school teacher now doing a Grad. Dip. She has some work experience in PR.

I'm sure none of the younger students wouldn't want to work in NFP. They all like fashion, and music. But then again, they're young and that's just natural.

My main opinion about PR is that when you go through school nobody knows about PR. I imagine most people think of it being advertising. I suppose it's also that conditional perspective that a lot of people have that men need to go out and get a job with a career that pays well, but women can be a bit more 'airy fairy' about their careers. I can just get a job I like, have kids when I like, then go back and work part-time. Maybe males are looking for higher paid jobs, but PR teds to be more middle management. Maybe it's a money thing and males just do a business degree which will get them further.

Maybe it is the traditional ways that men and women think. I thought that the units in PR were more interesting than business units. With units like accountancy, I just think I would have failed. I just feel the need to communicate, and that's what PR is.

Women are very much into pleasing the boss, as opposed to breaking 'out of the mould' a bit. Maybe men breaking out of the mould is more acceptable. A guy may be able to present a radical idea better, simply because he's male.

I think that a lot of women are more interested in talking through situations. With job satisfaction, men like to prove with figures they have succeeded, whereas women like to know the internal and external environments are working well. They just may have different approaches.

The higher people go up in pay, the more hours they are expected to do. Maybe women know that predominantly they will be the main child carer, so they gravitate towards PR, which you are not always expected to work long hours.

Looking at the males at uni, they are quite fit and attractive (not that I'm interested). Maybe they consider it a similar line to advertising, which may be a little more cutthroat than PR, and they may think 'I might have a more glamorous life'.

If you want to get into TV you have to have certain look, be a certain age. There was one young guy and he was good looking with a deep voice. The journalism tutor was mesmerised by his voice; so he was 'in there', as far as the tutor thought. Who cares about his skills? I made a judgment about someone. She was really scruffy, and it turned out she was doing journalism, and PR was just a side unit. But I had made a judgement based on appearance. It's not that you have to be the best-looking person, but you have to look professional.

Maybe females feel more capable of getting a personal relationships going quickly, whereas males may feel on guard or not wanting to look like a sleaze. A man, especially being friendly to a woman, may come across as bad, whereas a female being friendly to a man is somehow more professional-looking. So maybe it's safe to have females in that [PR] position.

When you're trying to put forward an idea to senior management. Maybe men can be a little more aggressive, but in fact [because they are in PR] are not accepted readily by management. Females may be a bit more submissive and can take a different tack, whereas the men would get fed up more easily knowing their idea will not be accepted, so they'll just give up. Maybe if there were men in the industry it's going to promote the whole industry. Management will be including PR in the mix more often. On the other hand, there also needs to be more women in the top end of business.

I am such a typical 'girl'. I was more inclined towards social sciences and English. But I have a sister who is so scientifically-minded.

One good thing for PR was with Tom Baddley [ABC TV newsreader] going to PR. That's good for the public to see someone move from serious news to the Western Force [WA-based Super 14 rugby union team]. Maybe that's a good rap for PR. I didn't know PR existed when I was younger; so how do people find out about it [PR]?

I know in Year Nine I started to learn about advertising. You know that it's a job, but PR wasn't. It's portrayed as airy-fairy, I suppose.

One thing I have discovered is that I enjoy writing, whether it's media releases or brochures. Not that I would want to do journalism. I don't actually think if I knew PR existed when I was 17 I would have done it, though.

INTERVIEW 7: SD, 6 FEBRUARY 2006

SD is a third-year male PR student, who worked in a junior role for a WA government department, before being told to go to university. The interview was conducted by phone.

At one stage there were just two guys in one [PR] class, so, yes, I've noticed there is a situation with the low numbers of males.

A PR degree always seems to have had a female-type work tag attached to it. In Perth the PR industry is small and a lot of the males really don't seem to get a look-in..

It's not a 'hard-core' career. It's so broad, and it means so many things. It's not specific. It's not like being a doctor or an engineer. I like the idea of having a specialised titles, but with PR you just don't get that. I guess that PR is not a career on its own: it tends to be consumed by other aspects of a business, such as marketing.

I think males can equally have what is generally regarded to be female characteristics, such as nurturing and ability to organise and listen. But females also have the ability to be up-front. Some of them are extremely up-front. But it's no good to be a freight train.

I've heard the UN had asked the Australian Government to help push more women into management positions; so maybe there's a push to have females in PR management, and that might be coming at the cost of males. I think whoever is the best person for the job should get it.

Maybe females are just more attracted to PR than males. Perhaps there's a social stigma for men if they don't do the traditional male subjects and occupations. I come from a family that always been tradesmen, and most people from my home town worked in trades. But I always liked music and art. There was the whole entertainment thing of being vibrant has something with me doing PR, I imagine.

I've heard some people talking that there's a perception in PR that you are always only a spokesperson for whoever you work for, and that you never really get involved with driving the business. So that could be a disincentive for males not doing PR. I guess it gets back to me thinking that it's an inadequate subject.

The sheer number of people doing this course is huge, but the imbalance is bound to have some effects. I guess that may or may not work in my favour. On one hand, it might mean that because there are so many females, employers might not look favourably on a male. But it also might make males more valuable. The saturation of female might mean that males are seen as less capable among so many females.

But any saturated industry is not healthy. Diversity is something which is bad, and is sorely lacking at university. I hope someone goes on to point out the pitfalls.

INTERVIEW 8: LEIGH, 15 APRIL 2006

Leigh is a 20-year-old male third year PR student.

I'm just as keen on PR now as when I started. I haven't particularly been deterred by the number of females, although it was evident they are the majority.

I never noticed any talk about it being unusual that I was doing PR. There may have been some comments but nothing dramatic. Such comments would have been made in reference to the large number of female students, as opposed to singling out me as an individual. Among students we mostly joked about it. There was no serious discussion. Of course there were comments from people outside uni, mostly along the lines of PR about being a bullshit artist.

I don't think the number of women in PR will work against males. It may work to their benefit in that it could make their work more evident, and give them a greater reputation, as men will be more easily identified, being a minority. I think that being a male might actually help. There may be benefits as firms seek greater gender balance.

As regards the type of skills PR people need, obviously good communication skills and creativity for some jobs. I like to think I have those skills, and that I have a friendly nature and I'm easy to talk with.

The males in my classes certainly aren't stereotyped, based on the males studying PR in my classes.

As to why more women study PR, I think verbal communication is seen as a 'woman's domain': that there's a general feeling women are better communicators.

JOURNAL ARTICLES

'A few good men', *PRism* (journal published by Massey and Bond Universities) June 2005.

'Public relations dominated by women', *PRprobe* (Bond University PR journal) April 2005, http://www.hss.bond.edu.au/probe.

INDUSTRY MAGAZINE AND ON-LINE ARTICLES

'PR gender study', May 2005. *Inside PR* (PRIA Qld magazine, p. 10).

'Girls, girls, girls', October 2005, *Behind The Spin* (UK). Vol. 10.

THIRD-PERSON ARTICLES

'PR-fect match', *Sydney Morning Herald*, 23 March 2005.

'Women over populating PR', 15 March 2005, national PRIA newsletter and website. Also appeared in WA *Newsbrief* (April 05).

'Where have all the good men gone? (lack of male public relations executives)', December 2006, *B&T Weekly*, http://findarticles.com/p/articles/mi_hb4931/is_200612/ai_n18074590

LaVergne, TN USA
19 December 2010
209377LV00003B/118/P